The Working Class in American History

A list of books in the series appears at the end of this book.

The Making of Western Labor Radicalism

The
Making
of Western
Labor Radicalism:

Denver's Organized Workers, 1878–1905

David Brundage

University of Illinois Press
Urbana and Chicago

Library of Congress Cataloging-in-Publication Data

Brundage, David Thomas, 1951–
    The making of Western labor radicalism : Denver's organized workers,
    1878–1905 / David Brundage.
        p.   cm. — (The Working class in American history)
    Includes bibliographical references (p.   ) and index.
    ISBN 0-252-02075-8 (acid-free paper)
    1. Trade-unions—Colorado—Denver—History.   I. Title.   II. Series.
HD8085.D4B78   1994
322'.3'0978883—dc20
                                                                    93-34180
                                                                    CIP

For Susan and Jonah

Contents

Acknowledgments

It is a pleasure to acknowledge the debts I have incurred in the writing of this book. Able librarians and archivists have helped me at every turn. I am especially grateful to Cassandra Volpe and the late John Brennan of the Western Historical Collections at Norlin Library, University of Colorado, Boulder, and to the staff of McHenry Library, University of California, Santa Cruz. I would also like to thank the staffs of the Western History Department at the Denver Public Library, the Colorado Historical Society, the Colorado State Archives, the University of Denver library, Harvard University's Baker Library, the Bancroft Library at the University of California, Berkeley, and the Idaho State Historical Society.

Research for the book was made possible by a Travel to Collections Grant and a summer stipend from the National Endowment for the Humanities and by a Regents' Junior Faculty Fellowship and several Academic Senate Research grants from the University of California, Santa Cruz. Donald Gann and Nicholas Gould provided able research assistance and the staff of the Social Sciences Division of the University of California, Santa Cruz, helped on a variety of matters. The Burger, Fairchild, and Martinez families offered welcome hospitality on my extended stays in Denver.

Many people have contributed to my understanding of this topic. I would especially like to thank John Laslett, who directed the dissertation from which this book grew, and Gary Nash and William Roy who made up my fine dissertation committee. Lyle Dorsett, Matthew Downey, James Giese, Joyce Goodfriend, Stephen Leonard, Thomas Noel, Lee Scamehorn, and Joseph Velikonja made helpful suggestions for research or guided me to important sources. Carl Abbott, Jennifer Amis, David Anthony, Constance Coiner, Dana Frank, Takashi Fujitani, Jonathan Garlock, Jaclyn Greenberg, Lisbeth Haas, Dirk Hoerder, Reginald LeMay, Kerby Miller, Grey Osterud, James Prickett, Steven Ross, Alexander Saxton, Deborah Schopp, Cynthia Shelton, Frank Stricker, David Sweet, Devra Weber, and Paul Worthman read all or parts of the manuscript at various stages and offered many valuable criticisms.

The late Herbert Gutman gave the manuscript a thorough critical reading, pressed me for more discussion of Denver's second-generation immigrant workers, and provided, through his own work, the most important inspiration for my own. At a somewhat later stage, David Montgomery provided a characteristically incisive reading of the manuscript. The book's final shape owes a great deal to him.

At the University of Illinois Press, Richard Wentworth and Lisa Warne-Magro were consistently helpful, and Rita Darlene Disroe provided expert copyediting. Thanks also go to the editors of *Labor History* and Northern Illinois University Press for allowing me to include material here that appeared in earlier publications.

My father and mother, Albert and Kathryn Brundage, gave me their love and support of every kind. It causes me great sadness that my mother did not live to see this book in print. My wife, Susan Stuart, and our son, Jonah, have sustained me with their love and patience. The book is dedicated to them.

Introduction

In 1907, thirty-two-year-old Emma Langdon paid a visit to seventy-five-year-old Charles Semper at his ranch nine miles outside of Denver. Hailed by industrial unionists as "Colorado's Joan of Arc," Langdon was one of Denver's most prominent labor radicals. She was born in Tennessee in 1875 and moved to the Colorado mining district of Cripple Creek in 1903, where she and her husband worked as printers for the *Victor Daily Record*, local organ of the Western Federation of Miners. During Colorado's bloody labor wars of 1903–4, when the state militia tried to halt publication of the paper, arresting its editor and most of its staff, Langdon defied martial law by setting type and getting the paper out alone. Deported from Cripple Creek by the militia, Langdon moved to Denver in 1904, where she began a long career as an organizer and publicist for the WFM and its successor, the International Union of Mine, Mill and Smelter Workers. She was also an organizer for Colorado's Socialist party, and in 1905 she was one of the founders of the Industrial Workers of the World.

These last two organizations, the Socialist party and the IWW, formed the core of a labor radicalism that was a major force during the first two decades of the twentieth century. By 1912, the SP could boast of 118,000 members, forty-two state organizations, three hundred newspapers and periodicals, twelve hundred elected public officials, and a charismatic leader, Eugene V. Debs, who polled nearly nine hundred thousand votes in his run for president that year. The IWW was a different kind of organization. Though it claimed more than 100,000 members in 1917, it never grew as large as its founders had hoped, and it experienced constant turnover in its membership. Yet the Wobblies were a dramatic presence in these years, capturing the imagination of immigrant workers and left wing intellectuals alike with their practice of what David Brody has called a "trade unionism of the dispossessed." Labor radicalism was a phenomenon of tremendous importance in Progressive America.[1]

If Emma Langdon personified this vibrant labor radicalism of the early twentieth century, Charlie Semper seemed to epitomize the cautious craft unionism of the nineteenth. Although he too was a printer by trade, Semper's resemblance to Langdon ended at this point. A pioneer resident of Colorado, he had been a founder of the Denver Typographical Union in 1860. A lifetime of high wages and sound investments made Semper a man of fairly substantial means by 1907, though he continued to take an active part in the affairs of his union. In his craft union commitments and his high standard of living, Semper appeared to be an almost archetypal labor aristocrat, the kind despised by working-class radicals of Langdon's generation.

The ideological gulf between these two should have been immense. Yet when she wrote a survey of labor issues in 1908, Langdon devoted a full five pages to her meeting with Semper and to his life history. "The pleasure of the visit was not to be forgotten," she wrote. "How my heart filled with reverence for this couple [Semper and his wife] who are among the few surviving pioneers of the labor movement and the man a charter member of the first labor organization of the Centennial state!" Far from despising Semper, Langdon seemed to feel that she was standing on his shoulders.[2]

Langdon's proclaimed "reverence" for Semper suggests a continuity between the nineteenth-century labor movement and early twentieth-century radicalism that historians have not yet explored. Most historians have focused attention on what appears to be a steep divide between the two centuries. On one side of the divide lies a rich world of proud skilled craftsmen, labor republicanism, and social reform, embodied especially in the Order of the Knights of Labor. On the other side of the divide, apparently, lies a much more constricted world of constantly warring business unionists, socialists, and a small band of revolutionary unionists in the Industrial Workers of the World. The IWW has hardly lacked historians. But the organization has usually been seen as marking a sharp break with the past, owing more to the violence associated with frontier conditions or to the rapid emergence of an exploitative corporate capitalism in the mining West than to traditions embedded in the world of nineteenth-century craft unionism and labor reform. The distinctive "moral universality" of the earlier movement had been shattered.[3]

In this book, I offer a different interpretation. By focusing on organized workers in Denver, Colorado, from the late 1870s to the founding of the IWW in 1905, I illuminate the essential continuity between late nineteenth-century trade unionism and labor reform and early twentieth-century labor radicalism. Denver provides a good setting for such a study.

This rapidly growing city possessed a vital labor reform movement revolving around the Knights of Labor in the 1880s, a strong working-class Populist movement in the 1890s, and a powerful radical industrial union movement at the turn of the century. To be sure, radicals never dominated Denver's labor movement in these years, but they did play a crucial role within it. At the IWW's founding convention, Langdon was joined by no fewer than six other Denver residents, among them William D. Haywood, who would come to be regarded by many Americans as the very personification of the Wobblies. Denver was not a "typical" city, of course; no city is. But if continuities exist between these eras of American labor history, they should be visible in Denver.

There is no doubting that the IWW's ideology and practice were distinctive. Wobblies departed from the craft unionism of the American Federation of Labor by advocating an industrial form of organization that would embrace workers across lines of skill. They also rejected what Samuel Gompers, president of the AFL, called "pure-and-simple unionism," the view that the labor movement should confine itself to fighting over wages and working conditions and avoid entanglements with those seeking more fundamental social change. For the IWW, the labor movement's final goal was nothing short of the destruction of capitalism and the creation in its place of "an industrial democracy, wherein there shall be no wage slavery, but where the workers will own the tools which they operate, and the product of which they alone will enjoy."[4]

This position gave the IWW a great deal in common with the Socialist party. But the IWW's ideology differed from that of the Socialists in one crucial respect. While the SP placed its hopes for socialism in the political mobilization of working people and the creation of a socialist state apparatus, the IWW's vision bore considerable resemblance to what was known in the European working-class movement as syndicalism. Without totally rejecting political action, Wobblies nonetheless believed that even the most massive electoral support for socialism was meaningless as long as capitalists exerted dominant control over the industrial economy. As a result, they saw the revolutionary union, not the political party, as the main tool for the construction of socialism and they also held the union to be the embryo of the future socialist society. This was a syndicalist point of view, though the IWW's insistence on an industrial unionism that embraced the emerging factory proletariat as well as skilled craftsmen (the type of workers who often dominated European syndicalist organizations) led its spokespersons to label their position "revolutionary industrial unionism" or "industrialism," rather than syndicalism.[5]

The IWW has also been remembered for its efforts to organize workers across lines of race and nationality. It was staunchly egalitarian on the question of race and put forward a vision of working-class internationism far more sweeping than that of the Socialist party and in dramatic contrast to the restrictive practices of the AFL. Not only did it welcome African Americans, Chicanos, and eastern and southern European immigrants to its ranks but it also opened its doors to Asian and Asian American workers, breaking with a long and often violent anti-Asian tradition in the American labor movement.

Finally, the organization was famous for its cultural activities. "Wherever, in the West, there is an IWW local, you will find an intellectual center," observed the radical journalist John Reed in 1918, "a place where men read philosophy, economics, the latest plays, novels; where art and poetry are discussed, and international politics." Such activities provided Wobblies with a crucial arena for sociability and recreation while simultaneously countering the powerful conservative ideological influences at work in American society. In their songs, writings, meetings, and cultural events, the IWW tried to build what Lawrence Goodwyn, in a different context, has called a "movement culture": a set of cultural institutions that would continuously develop and strengthen solidarity and class consciousness among working people.[6]

In this book, I demonstrate that far from marking a radical break with the past, these central aspects of the IWW's ideology and practice had deep and continuous roots in the ideas and experience of the Denver labor movement. In chapter one, I provide a context for the study by examining Denver's economic development over the course of the later nineteenth century. Although in this chapter I focus attention on the emergence of structured class inequality in the city, I must stress that labor radicalism did not emerge as some kind of automatic response to class inequality or to harsh conditions. Rather, it emerged gradually as one thread within a broader social and cultural world of organized workers. Nor was this larger world itself in any way "determined"; it was rather built by Denver's working men and women as they built the city's labor movement.[7]

In the next four chapters, which proceed chronologically, I examine the roots of the ideological and organizational currents that came together in the IWW. In chapter two, I discuss the history of working-class organizations in Denver before the mid-1880s rise of the Knights of Labor, focusing especially on the Denver branch of the Irish Land League. In the early 1880s, the Land League cultivated mass struggle, secularism, and interdenominational collaboration and championed the public involvement of women. Although these ideas emerged under the leadership of middle-class Irish Americans who were hostile to trade unionism and close to Colorado's antilabor Republican party, they served as the key intellectual building blocks with which the Denver Knights constructed their ideology.

In chapter three, I examine the Knights of Labor, focusing not only on their strikes, demonstrations, and political initiatives, but also on their efforts to build a movement culture within which working people could fulfill their needs for enjoyment, sociability, recreation, and education. As part and parcel of these cultural efforts, some leaders of the Knights launched a political attack on the saloon, a key institution in urban working-class life during the late nineteenth century. In this chapter, I dissect the internal tensions in the labor movement that resulted from this development.

In chapter four, I focus on the nascent form of syndicalism that ran through Denver's workplace struggles of the late 1880s and early 1890s and took an increasingly organized form in the trade union upsurge from 1887 to 1892. This protosyndicalism was never more than a minority strain within the labor movement, and its emergence led to further internal conflict. But Denver's radicals were not isolated from the labor movement here, as radicals were in some cities. On the contrary, Denver's radicals were deeply involved in the larger movement and typically offered variations on accepted trade union wisdom regarding workers control and the relationship of workers to politics.

The emphasis on industrial unionism that would be fundamental to the IWW emerged during the depression of the mid-1890s. As is well known, the Western Federation of Miners played a critical role in advancing the cause of industrial unionism in Colorado and throughout the West. But the growing militancy of immigrant laborers and industrial workers in urban centers like Denver played an equally important role. This militancy was partly a response to deteriorating economic conditions and partly a result of workers' politicization by the radical wing of Colorado's Populist party.

Thus key strands of the IWW's outlook gradually took shape within the city's labor movement over the course of the late nineteenth century, especially in the years after 1886. As I demonstrate in chapter six, these strands came together to form a coherent labor radicalism within the American Labor Union in Denver on the eve of the bloody labor wars of 1903–4. The timing is important. As in other cities, violence frequently marked Denver's labor disputes. But violence was not the cause of labor radicalism. Rather, it emerged at this time as a response to larger changes around the turn of the century, particularly the growing unity of employers and the increasingly divisive practices of the AFL.

Radicalism, of course, was not the only working-class response to these events. A wide variety of political viewpoints could be found within the Denver labor movement throughout these years, as communitarians, single-taxers, Christian Socialists, and followers of Edward Bellamy all competed for workers' support. More important were the AFL-oriented trade unionists, who generally exercised leadership in the Denver labor movement and who won a series of decisive victories in the early twentieth century. Their vision of trade unionism was far narrower than that of the radicals, and they increasingly focused on political alliances with friendly politicians (mainly Democrats), to the detriment of both third-party and syndicalist programs. These unionists, just as much as Emma Langdon, staked a claim to the mantle of union pioneers like Charlie Semper.

Yet while it remained a minority trend, early twentieth-century labor radicalism in Denver was extremely significant. It had a powerful impact on the local working-class movement, and its key ideas and practices would soon be taken up by the Industrial Workers of the World. As this book shows, Denver's labor radicalism was not the product of frontier conditions or of jarring social dislocations. Rather, it gradually evolved from twenty-five years of working-class history.

1 Denver in the Later Nineteenth Century

"The most marvellous growth of modern times," wrote William M. Thayer in 1890, "is the city of Denver, Colorado. . . . In 1858 there were only a few tents and huts on the spot where the city now stands. Less than fifty people were there through the winter of 1858–59, drawn thither by the discovery of gold. A barren waste was all that met the vision in every direction. . . . What do we see now where these pioneers pitched their tents or reared their humble cabins? The largest, richest, and most beautiful city of its age on earth,—a sparkling costly jewel on the bosom of the 'desert.' "[1]

Like many other middle-class visitors to Denver in the last decades of the nineteenth century, Thayer was struck by its similarities to eastern cities. Larimer Street seemed but a smaller version of Broadway. The five-story Tabor Block, the Windsor Hotel, and the new state capitol building together produced an approximation of the skyline of New York, or at least Philadelphia. And Denver boasted a thriving commerce. "There is a dash and animation to the place," another traveler observed, "that suggest prosperity, wealth, and Eastern stability."[2]

Other commentators also stressed Denver's similarities to eastern cities, but from a very different perspective. For a working man who signed himself "Vindicator" in the mid-1880s, what boosters liked to call the "Queen City of the Plains" resembled eastern urban centers mainly in its "fetid atmosphere," inadequate housing, and its degradation of "the honest workman." Denver was becoming "a seat of iniquity," he proclaimed, but it was far from unique. Rather, it exemplified "the demoralizing state of people who live in cities."[3]

There was truth in both perspectives. From its founding through the turn of the century, Denver's population, commerce, and industry all climbed dramatically. Its growth fell into two distinct phases. From 1858 through the mid-1870s, Denver grew slowly from a rough frontier town to a city of about 15,000. Though small-scale manufacturing emerged in these years, trade dominated Denver's economy. Commerce remained important in the second phase of Denver's development, which began in the late 1870s. But in the last two decades of the nineteenth century, the city witnessed substantial industrialization as well. Denver's population climbed rapidly, reaching over 100,000 by 1890 and over 140,000 by 1900. When Thayer penned his description, among western cities Denver trailed only San Francisco and Omaha in size and was the twenty-fifth largest urban center in the country.

As "Vindicator" argued, however, urban-industrial growth brought with it exploitation, poverty, and misery for many of Denver's citizens. Underlying these developments was the emergence of structured class inequality in the city. Although the tents and huts of pioneer Denver may have contained a rough social equality—among white males at any rate—distinct social classes began to emerge as early as the mid-1860s. The gulf between the working class on the one hand and the middle and upper classes on the other widened tremendously with the onset of industrialization in the years after the late 1870s. The fact that, by the late nineteenth century, most of Denver's workers were immigrants or the children of immigrants did much to accentuate the division between social classes.

Patterns of class formation varied widely from city to city in the late nineteenth century. No "typical" industrial city existed, yet research in urban and labor history allows us to conceptualize three broad categories of industrial cities in these years. The first category consists of the handful of very large cities. These had invariably started as important centers of trade and finance but had undergone diversification, becoming great manufacturing cities as well. By 1890, New York, Chicago, and Philadelphia were not only the largest cities in the country, but the largest manufacturing centers as well, turning out a variety of products from textiles and clothing to meat and steel. Working-class formation in such cities was a complex process. A wide array of immigrant groups competed for jobs and housing, while great differences in wages and work experiences and a sharp geographic demarcation between workplace and neighborhood made the building of strong citywide labor movements extremely difficult. Though such cities were often centers of radical labor thought, working-class support for political radicals usually paled beside that for powerful ward-based political machines.[4]

The second category consists of those small industrial cities that specialized in the manufacture of a single product. Concentrated mainly in the Northeast and Midwest, these cities either processed regional specialties or utilized local skilled and unskilled labor pools to serve the growing market for capital or consumer goods. Labor movements were not always strong in such places. Although iron workers turned Troy, New York, into one of the strongest union towns in America, cotton workers in nearby Cohoes remained disorganized and weak. Nonetheless, the structural dimensions of class formation in such cities were broadly similar. These were relatively homogeneous places, where a single immigrant group often dominated the work force. Local industrialists were highly visible (and sometimes highly vulnerable) and home, work, ethnicity, and politics were frequently linked.[5]

Denver lay between these two poles, falling within a third category of urban places. Cities like Minneapolis, Kansas City, Indianapolis, Omaha, Seattle, Portland, and Denver typically added a variety of manufacturing specialties to their traditional regional commercial activities and grew rapidly without ever becoming major industrial centers. By the late nineteenth century this type of city was more likely than not to be found in western regions of the country. If the industrial towns and the giant cities of the East and Midwest together constituted the urban-industrial core of late nineteenth-century economy, cities in this third category were the economic nodes of its periphery. Thus, an understanding of Denver's economic development, urban growth and patterns of class formation provides a necessary context for an understanding of its labor movement.[6]

Economic Development and Urban Growth

Denver was founded during the Colorado gold rush of 1858–60, which, along with earlier mining rushes to California and Australia, helped spark the rapid global expansion of capitalism in the middle decades of the nineteenth century. Drawn by the discovery of gold near the confluence of the South Platte River and Cherry Creek on the high plains east of the Rockies, hundreds of men made their way to the area in the fall of 1858. Rival town companies quickly laid out speculative town sites, Auraria on the west bank of Cherry Creek and Denver City on the east.[7]

Though the initial discoveries never panned out, dramatic strikes in a densely wooded ravine called Gregory Gulch, thirty-five miles to the west, quickly made that area what Horace Greeley called the "chief hope of gold-mining in the Rocky Mountains." Spurred on in part by Greeley's enthusiastic reports, prospectors poured into the mining towns of Central City and Black Hawk in 1859 and 1860. Meanwhile the less glamorous little settlements on Cherry Creek, consolidated as "Denver" in the spring of 1860, rapidly became the "commercial emporium" of the region, providing a wide array of goods and services to miners on their way to the diggings. By the opening of 1860, Denver boasted twelve wholesale houses, twenty-seven retailers, two dozen doctors and lawyers, and thirty-five saloons. The town's population, approximately twenty-one hundred at the end of 1859, grew to nearly five thousand within a year.[8]

Nonetheless, Denver's future was far from assured. After the boom years of the early 1860s, Colorado mining underwent its first economic slump. The inexperience of many miners and the primitive level of ore refining led to a wave of business failures and a subsequent drying up of capital. As the regional economy slid into depression, Denver stagnated as well, its difficulties compounded by the disruptive effects of the Civil War and disastrous fires and floods in 1863 and 1864. The most serious problem, though, was Denver's lack of rail connections. The surprising 1866 decision of Union Pacific Railroad executives to bypass Denver in favor of a northern transcontinental route through Wyoming appeared to seal the town's fate as a permanent backwater. "Denver is too dead to bury," the UP's vice president, Thomas Durant, was reported to have said. In 1866 the town's population fell to thirty-five hundred.[9]

But the 1860s also witnessed the emergence of a group of merchants, bankers, and investors determined to reverse the town's declining fortunes. William M. Byers, publisher of Denver's first newspaper, the *Rocky Mountain News*, former territorial governor John Evans, and a number of other local commercial leaders joined forces in an effort to make Denver the dominant town of the region. They won a key battle when the Colorado Assembly transferred the territorial capital from Golden to Denver in 1868, a distinction the latter retained with statehood in 1876. But the most important task Denver's business community faced was that of linking the town into the rapidly emerging national railroad network.

Here, concerted action proved the key to success. In November 1867, Evans, Byers, David Moffat, and Bela Hughes organized the Denver Board of Trade—modeled after those in Chicago, St. Louis, and Kansas City—to work for a line connecting Denver with the Union Pacific at Cheyenne. At a public meeting on 14 November Hughes told Denver residents that if they wanted their town to survive, they would have to rally behind the Board of Trade's effort to build the railroad, soon to be incorporated as the Denver Pacific. Over the next few months, Evans directed the financing of the new corporation. He persuaded investors to purchase stock, workers to donate their labor, the county to pass a $500,000 bond issue, and Congress to grant nine hundred thousand acres of land. The remarkable cohesion among Denver's capitalists and the influence that they were able to wield in the larger community set a pattern for years to come. At the same time, the character of the struggle indicates the extent to which the town's fate lay in the hands of large corporations outside of its control.[10]

The completion of the Denver Pacific and the Kansas Pacific railroads in 1870, connecting Denver with Cheyenne and Kansas City, laid the foundation for the town's emergence as the leading commercial and political center of the Mountain West. Between 1867 and 1872, the volume of mercantile business nearly tripled, climbing from under $6 million to approximately $17.5 million. From January 1871 to December 1873, over two thousand new buildings were constructed in the town, with brick structures replacing the log dwellings of earlier years. Newcomers began pouring into the town, giving it an official population of 14,197 by the time a census was taken in January 1874. The British traveler Isabella Bird found Denver "a busy place" by this date. It was, she observed, the "distributing point for an immense district, with good shops, some factories, fair hotels, and the usual deformities and refinements of civilization."[11]

Despite the national depression of 1873–78 and a grasshopper plague that struck Colorado's farms in 1875, Denver continued to grow, claiming a population of twenty thousand by the time of statehood in 1876. No Denver banks closed in the wake of the financial panic of 1873. The flow of eastern capital into the region, the volume of local business, and the value of local real estate all declined between 1875 and 1877. As a result, unemployment rose substantially, especially in the winter of 1876–77. But, overall, the years from 1867 to 1877 were marked by Denver's gradual recovery from the much leaner years of the middle 1860s.[12]

Developments in nearby mining districts during this period provided the main spur to Denver's growth. Technological improvements in gold mining and smelting and the growth of silver mining at Clear Creek gave a breath of life to Colorado's mining economy as a whole, and the territory gradually emerged as a dynamic center of innovation in the science and technology of mining and smelting. As mining recovered, Denver prospered. Situated on the open plains with ample space for railroad yards, warehouses, hotels, and stores, and yet relatively close to the mountain mining towns, Denver was an ideal supply center and break-in-bulk point for goods brought from the East. As a result, commerce became Denver's major economic activity and the most important avenue to wealth for its citizens. Of the eighty-four Denver residents whose personal worth was estimated by R.G. Dun & Company credit correspondents to be $20,000 or more in the years between 1864 and 1876, forty had made their fortunes through wholesale or retail activities.[13]

Banking was the second pillar of Denver's economy in these years. The rapid emergence of banking was one of the most impressive features of Denver's early development, helping it to achieve the "initial advantage" that urban geographers regard as crucial to a city's long-term growth. As early as 1860, five banks were operating in Denver, one of which also minted coins. The first bankers were actually merchants who bought gold dust and kept deposits, making loans only as a sideline. But by 1877, Denver had three nationally chartered banks, with combined deposits of $4.8 million, total resources of $5.1 million, and loans and discounts of $3.7 million. Leading bankers, like Jerome Chaffee and David Moffat, of the First National Bank, and Charles and Luther Kountze, of the Colorado National Bank, were among the most prominent individuals in the city.[14]

Railroad development was a third preoccupation of local capitalists. In 1871, a group of Denver investors led by General William Palmer, brought in Thomas Scott and J. Edgar Thomson of the Pennsylvania Railroad and Cyrus Field of New York on a project to build a narrow gauge line along the eastern slope of the Rockies as far south as Mexico City. By 1872, the new Denver and Rio Grande Railroad had reached Pueblo, the site of rich coal fields 110 miles south of Denver. Though the Colorado mining boom of the late 1870s prompted the railroad to build west rather than any further south, the D&RG brought huge profits to its owners and made Denver even more important as a western transportation hub. The city gradually emerged as the node of a vast railroad network, the point of interchange between the trunk lines that crossed the plains and a system of lines (many of them using the narrow gauge system) that penetrated every important mining district in Colorado. Not surprisingly, when delegates to Colorado's constitutional convention threatened to introduce a Grange-inspired program for the regulation of railroads in 1876, Denver's business community reacted with alarm. Fifty of the city's most prominent capitalists petitioned the convention, opposing any governmental interference with the railroads. In a separate petition, John Evans asked the convention to frame a constitution that gave railroads the same protection given to other forms of property.[15]

As their investments in trade, banking, and railroad building indicate, Denver's business leaders held a commercial, rather than an industrial, vision of their city's future. Individuals like Evans, Palmer, Chaffee, and Moffat envisioned Denver standing at the heart of a vast mercantile empire stretching south toward Mexico and west through Utah. They believed that Denver was destined to be a great metropolis. And its greatness would rest on control of trade routes and a flourishing commerce, not on industrial might.[16]

Industrialization remained limited not only by the commercial orientation of Denver's capitalists, but also by the small size of the local market, the high costs of transportation, and the unwillingness of lenders to provide capital for manufacturing. High transportation costs, for example, led Colorado's earliest smelter owners and mining machinery manufacturers to locate their operations in mining towns like Black Hawk and Central City rather than in Denver. To be sure, there had been some manufacturing in Denver from its beginnings and this grew in importance with the coming of the railroads. Typical frontier industries like brick making, flour milling, brewing, and carriage and wagon manufacture all appeared during the 1860s and first half of the 1870s. But manufacturing remained a small-scale activity, peripheral to Denver's primary economic activities. In the view of one writer looking back from the early 1880s it was "questionable whether the city of 1877 had an industry worthy of the name manufactory."[17]

Developments in Colorado's mining districts soon transformed this situation, not only increasing Denver's population but turning it into an important industrial city as well. In 1877, a group of lucky prospectors discovered silver at Leadville, eighty miles southwest of Denver. Over the next few years, Leadville stood at the center of one of the biggest booms in the history of American mining. A few log shacks in 1876, Leadville claimed a population of fifteen thousand by 1880. In the early 1880s, the annual output of silver from this single camp surpassed that of every nation except Mexico. On the heels of the Leadville bonanza came silver discoveries at Aspen, Lake City, Creede, and Silverton. By the mid-1880s, Colorado's mines had become the most productive in the nation.[18]

Though mining remained the primary basis of Colorado's growth, agriculture also grew rapidly on the state's eastern plains in the last three decades of the nineteenth century. Improving railroad connections after 1870 led eastern and European capitalists to invest heavily in Colorado cattle ranching, and irrigated farming was given a strong boost by successful experiments in colonies like that at Greeley. In 1870, the census takers counted only 1,738 farms in Colorado, most of them in the southern part of the territory. Twenty years later, that figure had reached 16,389. The growth of efficient cattle ranching and the spread of irrigation bolstered the agricultural sector of Colorado's economy and made Denver an important grain and livestock market by the end of the nineteenth century.[19]

Denver's population grew rapidly as a result of these developments in its mining and agricultural hinterlands and of its own industrialization. The Leadville boom triggered immediate growth. According to one observer, even with the rapid exodus of many of Denver's residents for "the new Mecca" of Leadville in the early part of 1879, "the city seemed to grow every day, and houses to live in, and stores to do business in, were in greater demand than supply." "Denver was her great beneficiary," wrote a contemporary about Leadville. "It was to Denver that her wealth foregathered, that her people came sooner or later to reside, and where the smelting industry largely concentrated." The U.S. Census found 35,629 residents in 1880, making Denver the largest urban center between San Francisco and Kansas City. In the 1880s, a decade of remarkable urban growth in the nation at large, Denver grew even faster than other cities.

Chicago, Milwaukee, and Detroit all doubled their populations over the decade; Denver's population nearly tripled, reaching 106,713 in 1890. Though its rate of growth slowed in the depression-scarred 1890s, the city still counted 140,500 residents at the opening of the twentieth century.[20]

Denver continued to be an important commercial and transportation center, its trade growing as western railroad building proceeded through the 1880s and 1890s. By the turn of the century, Denver's wholesalers had established a field of operations that embraced not only Colorado, but large parts of Utah, Wyoming, and New Mexico. Banking and insurance also played important roles. Though a number of Denver banks failed during the panic of 1893, the industry rapidly recovered in the later years of the 1890s. By the end of the decade, Denver was, according to one contemporary, "by far the leading banking centre between the Missouri River and the Pacific Ocean" and the headquarters for all of the great insurance, mortgage, and investment companies doing business in the West. The federal government recognized Denver's importance as a financial center in April 1900, when it designated the city the depository of reserve funds for the banks of Wyoming, New Mexico, and Colorado.[21]

But despite the continuing importance of commerce, banking, and transportation, the traditional foundations of Denver's economy, many of its business leaders in the last two decades of the century began to turn toward industry. As early as 1873, Evans, Byers, Kountze, and several other investors had formed an industrial association to explore the possibilities of manufacturing. In the wake of the Leadville boom, this enthusiasm grew rapidly and, in 1882, a National Industrial Convention was held in the city. "The future of Denver will depend on the number of manufacturing interests that are induced to locate here," editorialized the *Rocky Mountain News* in 1884. Following the tradition of concerted action established by the struggle for the railroad in the 1860s, Denver business leaders established a Chamber of Commerce in that year to attract industrial capital and labor to the city.[22]

In the last twenty years of the nineteenth century, Denver emerged as an important industrial city. Between 1880 and 1900, the number of manufacturing establishments in the city climbed from 259 to 1,474, and the value of their product leapt from $9.4 to $41.4 million. Meanwhile, the number of Denver's wage earners employed in manufacturing soared from under three thousand to nearly eleven thousand. Visitors to the late nineteenth-century city observed that "the ringing of Factory Whistles in early morning is almost continuous."[23]

It is important not to overstate the significance of manufacturing in Denver's economy. Though the second most important industrial city in the West, Denver had a far smaller manufacturing sector than did San Francisco, the region's leading industrial city. Less than 10 percent of

Denver's population was employed in manufacturing throughout these decades, compared with approximately 20 percent in New York, Philadelphia, and Pittsburgh and approximately 16 percent in San Francisco. Equally important, the scale of industrial production remained generally small. Only 9 of the 117 manufacturing establishments counted by a state manufacturing census in 1885 employed more than one hundred workers. More than two-thirds of the city's 6,481 manufacturing employees in that year worked in establishments of less than one hundred workers, and a full third in those with less than 25. These numbers should not occasion surprise, for the older local market industries that had originated in the 1860s and 1870s continued to play a highly significant role in this later stage of Denver's industrialization. Four of the six top manufacturing lines in 1880 (brick making, flour, beer, printing) remained in the top six in 1900, all centered on small-scale production and all, with the partial exception of flour milling, remaining geared toward a local, rather than a national, market. There were limits to Denver's industrialization.[24]

In attempting to explain these limits, many contemporaries focused on the discriminatory rates charged by railroads, rates designed to make long hauls more economical than short ones. These rates had the effect of making states like Colorado importers rather than exporters of manufactured goods. To take one example, a Chicago publisher was charged $1.75 per one hundred pounds to ship books to San Francisco in the late 1890s, while a Denver publisher was charged $3.00 per one hundred pounds for the Denver–San Francisco journey. Though the Colorado legislature appointed a committee to investigate railroad rates and eventually created a state railroad commission, nothing could be done to alter the national interstate commerce laws that permitted such practices. Although certainly not the only barrier to industrial growth, discriminatory railroad rates remained a source of bitter complaint among Denver manufacturers and merchants into the twentieth century.[25]

Nevertheless, a number of new industries did appear in Denver in the last quarter of the nineteenth century, differing in important respects from those of the frontier era. First, these industries served a large national market and were often controlled by absentee owners or corporations. Second, they were located mainly at the edges of the built-up areas of the city, where land was inexpensive and rail service available, and the new industries in turn attracted small related shops and services like liveries and teamsters. Finally, the workers of these new industrial districts were often immigrants, who labored in much larger factories or shops than did other Denver workers and had little or no contact with the individuals who employed them. For these workers, if not for Denver's working people more generally, industrial capitalism had lost its human scale.

Far and away the most important of the new industries was the re- duction of metal ores from Colorado's mines. Smelting arrived in the city in 1878, when the Boston and Colorado Smelting Company moved its operations from the mining town of Black Hawk to a site known as Argo, two miles northwest of Denver. Labor, fuel, and raw materials were all cheaper here, and Denver's position as the center of the Rocky Moun- tain railroad network made it possible to process a wide variety of ores from a large number of mining camps. The plant was joined by the nearby Omaha and Grant smelter in 1882 and the Globe smelter in 1887. By the end of the decade, smelting and refining accounted for over half of the value of industrial production in the city. With huge brick smokestacks that dominated the city's skyline and belched sulfurous smoke into its air, these were three of the largest smelters in the world, employing over fifteen hundred men when operating at capacity. Immigrants dominated the work force from the outset. Smelter owners grew dissatisfied with the original Cornish and Welsh workers, because, they said, of "difficulty in enforcing discipline among them," and turned in succession to Irish, Ital- ians, and, in the 1890s, Austrians, Poles, and ethnic Germans from Russia. By the turn of the century, observers agreed that smelting's contribution to Denver's economy "overshadows that of all other industries."[26]

Like smelting, the manufacture of mining machinery also migrated from the mining towns to Denver, becoming its second most important industry. By the end of the 1870s, five mining equipment manufactories operated in Denver. Their number and size grew tremendously over the next two decades. By the turn of the century, the U.S. Census counted 1,169 workers employed in Denver's foundries and machine shops, a number of which were large concerns turning out stamp mills, crushers, hoisters, concentrators, and other tools and machines used in hard rock mining. According to a visitor in the 1890s, Denver was the source for "the best mining machinery in the world, whole outfits of which have been shipped to China and South Africa, to say nothing of Mexico and our own mining regions."[27]

Railroad car and machine building was Denver's third most impor- tant industry. As early as 1883, the Denver and Rio Grande, the Denver and New Orleans, the Denver and South Park, and the Kansas Pacific (these last two now owned by the Union Pacific) maintained machine and car shops on the outskirts of the city. In 1870, William Jackson Palmer had envisioned his Denver and Rio Grande as "a little railroad," in which workers would regard the company as "a family," rather than "some stranger soulless corporation," and in which "there would never be any strikes or hard feelings among the labourers toward the capitalists." But the sheer scale of the D&RG shops, spreading for block after block through the industrial suburb of Burnham by the mid-1880s, rendered

Palmer's vision obsolete, though far more than the smelters, Denver's railroad shops remained complexes of distinct craftsmen's shops rather than fully integrated plants. In 1900, the Pullman Company took over and refitted some of the Union Pacific shops. In that year, the U. S. Census counted 1,006 workers in the industry.[28]

In the 1890s new areas of manufacturing emerged. The Overland Cotton Mill began operations with 250 workers in 1890, producing unprinted cotton cloth. Located on the west side of the Platte River in a tiny industrial village, optimistically named "Manchester," the mill for a while brought profits to its owners, though high debt forced it to shut its doors in 1903. The mill attracted considerable notoriety in Denver because of its employment of women and children, many of whom were recruited from the textile regions of the South. The following year, the Denver Paper Mills Company built what the Chamber of Commerce termed a "magnificent mill with the most modern machinery" in Denver. Also in 1891, the Hitchcock Knitting Mill Company moved its operations from Massachusetts to Denver.[29]

As this last example indicates, outside capital and absentee ownership played a central role in Denver's industrialization. From the very beginning, eastern capitalists had been crucial in the development of the smelting industry—as the name of Denver's pioneer firm, the Boston and Colorado Smelting Company, makes clear—and British investors were also active in the industry. The trend toward absentee ownership and control would become even more pronounced with the emergence of the American Smelting and Refining Corporation (the so-called smelter trust), which took control of Denver's Grant and Globe smelters in 1899.[30]

Colorado's railroads, though originally financed in part by local capitalists also soon came under outside control. In 1880, speculator Jay Gould forced Union Pacific directors to comply with his scheme for buying out both the Denver Pacific and Kansas Pacific. Thus, by the mid-1880s, two of Denver's railroad shops were part of a gigantic New York–based economic empire, one of the largest companies in the world. By 1892, only two of the seventeen roads that entered Denver were locally controlled. Local railroad developers of the earlier era (like David Moffat and the Evans family) increasingly turned away from railroad investments and toward investments in Denver's highly profitable public utilities.[31]

There were some exceptions to this emerging pattern of outside control. Though the manufacture of mining machinery and the milling of flour were dominated by a handful of large companies as early as the mid-1880s, even the largest firms in these lines (like the Colorado Iron Works Company and the Colorado Milling and Elevator Company) were owned by local capitalists. On the other hand, even a local market industry like brewing could come under control by absentee owners, as occurred when a British syndicate bought the large Zang Brewery for $2.5 million in 1889. Similarly, the Rocky Mountain Paper Company, which absorbed the Denver Paper Company in 1900, was controlled entirely by capitalists from New York, Philadelphia, and Wilmington, Delaware. Developments such as these, combined with the well-known role of eastern and British capital in Colorado mining and ranching, led one early historian of Colorado to characterize the state in this era as "little more than a pocket borough of the corporate oligarchy."[32]

Class Formation

Within this context of rapid economic and urban growth and growing outside control, a sizable working class emerged in the city. The process began relatively early in Denver's history. Storekeepers, professionals, and independent artisans had dominated the occupational structure of pioneer Denver. But by 1880, census takers counted eighty-seven hundred wage-earning manual workers in the city, constituting 66 percent of the total work force. Over the course of the 1880s, the number of manual workers climbed to thirty-three thousand—a growth rate considerably surpassing the threefold growth of the city's population as a whole in this decade—and represented 68 percent of the work force in 1890. The number of men and women in working-class occupations fell to 32,000 between 1890 and 1900, but they still constituted 59 percent of the total labor force. Throughout these years, Denver was a working-class city.[33]

An upper class also emerged in Denver in these years. The formation of this class occurred in two stages, with each stage leaving its imprint on the social geography of the city. A commercial elite became visible as early as the mid-1860s, when distinct commercial and residential areas of the town began taking shape. Following John Evans's example, Denver's leading merchants and speculators began building stylish Gothic and Italianate homes, surrounded by lawns and trees, in the area around Fourteenth and Arapahoe streets. By the end of the decade, a clearly defined upper-class style of life had emerged in the city. Upper-class leisure centered on the home, often the site for lavish entertainments within Denver's "society," and thus contrasted sharply with the saloon centered leisure of many laboring men. In 1868, a French visitor expressed surprise at the rapidity with which "comfort, the habits of domestic life, the 'home,'" had emerged among Denver's elite. At a dinner with Evans, he was pleased to find that "the society was select and animated, and we conversed as in a Paris salon."[34]

With the Leadville mining boom and the onset of industrialization after the late 1870s, this older mercantile elite underwent a process of expansion and transformation. The so called "bonanza kings," some of whom had made fortunes overnight through Leadville silver discoveries, now made their homes in Denver, forming political alliances, business relationships, and friendships with members of the old upper class and with newly arrived eastern and European investors like the Scotsman James Duff. The most prominent of the new men of power was Horace Tabor. Tabor had struck it rich in Leadville but was soon purchasing stock in Chaffee and Moffat's First National Bank, actively participating in Republican party politics (he was elected lieutenant governor of Colorado in 1880), and financing some of Denver's largest buildings, including the Tabor Block and the Tabor Grand Opera House. When a group of the city's wealthiest men founded the Denver Club in July 1880, they gave expression to their emerging social identity, an identity they soon inscribed in the city's social geography. Joined by new industrialists like smelter owner James B. Grant, Tabor, John F. Campion, and the other bonanza kings led an exodus of the older elite from their Fourteenth Street moorings to a previously undeveloped bluff, 1½ miles to the east. The extravagant Colonial and Roman architecture of this area, renamed Capitol Hill because of its proximity to the state capitol, dramatically changed the face of the city. Huge stone mansions, filled with polished woods and crystal chandeliers, and bordered by carriage houses and servants' quarters, marked the coming of age of this expanded urban upper class.[35]

Less spectacular but equally important was the emergence of a middle class in Denver. The growth in the ranks of storekeepers, middling professionals, and white-collar salaried people who made up this social class brought with it important changes in the geography of the city. New middle-class suburbs continually pressed upon the boundaries of the city over the course of the 1880s and early 1890s. As factories and workers moved into the central sections of the city, the middle class began moving out, creating neighborhoods like Montclair, Curtis Park, and Highlands along the lines of Denver's expanding street car system. As Denver's area of settlement grew from six square miles in 1874 to fifty-nine square miles in 1902, class segregation deepened considerably. In Denver, as in all the nation's larger cities, middle-class suburbanization was one of the most notable developments of the later nineteenth century.[36]

While middle-class suburbs often took shape to the east, west, and south of the city, working people found homes in densely populated central sections or in industrial areas north of the city. Auraria, the oldest neighborhood in Denver, located across Cherry Creek from the central business district, became an important working-class district in the 1880s, when the Denver and Rio Grande and the Denver, South Park, and Pacific built shops in the area. An ore-sampling plant, the Tivoli Brewery and

John K. Mullen's large Hungarian Flour Mill soon followed, and the area rapidly became the home of numerous railroad men and other workers.[37]

By the 1890s, many other working-class families resided in the crescent of neighborhoods northwest, north, and northeast of the central business district (and literally "on the other side of the tracks"), where neighborhoods like Argo, Globeville, and Swansea offered small cottages close to jobs in foundries, machine shops, and smelters. Some of these, like the twenty-four houses on Sheedy Row (named after Dennis Sheedy, owner of the Globe smelter) were company houses, though employer-provided housing was not generally of great significance in Denver. More mobile workers often resided in the belt of boarding houses, cheap hotels, and saloons surrounding the Union Station. Here, near the heart of the central business district, living conditions deteriorated and slums emerged. Finally, by 1890, an area along the Platte River known as the Bottoms housed approximately eight thousand poor people in tar shacks and tents.[38]

Segregation along class lines was never total. As in many other cities of the late nineteenth century, there remained a good deal of residential mixing among workers, shopkeepers, and small business people. When a working-class woman named Emily French moved into the neighborhood of Fairview, near the Burnham railroad shops, in 1890, her neighbors included a plasterer, a postmaster, a railroad switchman, two carpenters, a teamster, a rag peddler, and a laborer; but also a merchant, a brick manufacturer, two dairy operators, and a farmer.[39]

Large tenement houses, like those of New York, were not present in the city. Investigators for the Colorado Bureau of Labor Statistics in the early 1890s found that most working-class families in Denver lived either in small cottages or in blocks of self-contained terraced houses. In their study of housing conditions in large American cities at the turn of the century, Robert DeForest and Lawrence Veiller concluded that Denver's poor typically lived in small one-story houses, containing from three to six rooms and with plenty of land around. In 1900, 80.5 percent of Denver's families lived in single-family dwellings, a percentage surpassed only by Philadelphia and Indianapolis among the 28 largest cities. Only 5.9 percent of Denver's families lived in dwellings housing three or more families, compared with 82.1 percent of New York's families.[40]

Yet life was often harsh in Denver's working-class neighborhoods. The town of Globeville, which had a population of two thousand by 1900 and which was not annexed by Denver until 1903, did not include the land on which the Globe smelter stood. The resulting impoverishment of the town government made it impossible for Globeville to pave its streets or provide lighting on more than a third of its streets. No public transportation existed in the city, and working people had to walk a long distance and across the South Platte River to catch a streetcar into Denver. The town was dominated by the smelter, which polluted the air and the river, and over the years a slag pile gradually built up covering a great deal of land. Conditions were even worse in the Bottoms. "Children be dyin' down 'ere all the time," one resident told a newspaper reporter in 1890. "It all comes from these piles of dirt. . . . An' nobody comes and takes it away like they do on Capitol Hill."[41]

The still primitive level of domestic technology and the paucity of corner stores in working-class neighborhoods demanded extremely hard physical labor from working-class wives and daughters in this era. In the 1880s, Denver's central business district and middle-class neighborhoods obtained their water from private water companies that provided hydrant, domestic, and commercial services, but, according to the memory of one resident, the working-class districts north of Seventeenth Street "had no domestic water supply save that from a well or two in a block here and there." Working-class women had to make long journeys to the ditches or to the polluted South Platte River for doing their households' laundry and to the wells for drinking water. The task of shopping for a family was made more difficult by the fact that Denver had "few, if any, corner groceries. . . . I can't see how the Denverites stand it," commented one female newcomer to the city in 1888. "They must be long-suffering and kind."[42]

Denver's industrialization, and its role as a dynamic urban center in a region marked by extensive mining and railroad building, created a powerful demand for labor that drew an ethnically and racially diverse working class to the city. Irish-, German-, Scandinavian-, and British-born workers and their children were highly mobile and responsive to regional economic pulls, easily finding their way to a booming center like Denver in the 1880s. By 1890, over half of Denver's manual workers (56.7 percent) were first- and second-generation immigrants or African Americans.[43]

To be sure, there was a good deal of variation in the ethnic and racial makeup of occupations. The printing trades, for example, were dominated by native stock whites: over 63 percent of the city's printers, engravers, and bookbinders were native-born whites of native parentage. At the other extreme, 79.7 percent of Denver's tailors were either foreign-born, of foreign parentage, or black; indeed, a full 64 percent of them had been born abroad, mostly in Germany.

Thus, although the role of white native-stock workers in shaping the city's labor movement can hardly be ignored, life on the shop floor and in Denver's working-class neighborhoods had a distinctly ethnic character. Who were the city's immigrants? Although 38 different nationalities were represented by 1890, the Irish, Germans, British, and Scandinavians were the principal ethnic groups represented in both the city and its working class in that year. Over the course of the 1890s, other European groups joined them, including Italians, Poles, Slovenes, and ethnic Germans from Russia.[44]

Though they would constitute the largest ethnic group in Denver's population after World War II, Colorado's Mexican Americans remained mainly concentrated in the southern areas of the state during this period. Chicanos, however, played a critical role in the region's economic development, as many men gradually left long-established subsistence agricultural communities in New Mexico's Upper Rio Grande Valley for employment in Colorado's mines and railroad camps during the late nineteenth century. Colorado railroad building and maintenance provided the first experience with wage labor for Chicanos from this area. In the 1880s, many Mexican American men worked as track laborers on the Denver and Rio Grande in southern Colorado, though Chicano track workers could also be found as far north as Leadville. By the turn of the century, large numbers of Chicanos and Mexican immigrants played an important role in the coal mining work force of southern Colorado, especially in Las Animas and Huerfano counties, where they made more than twice the wages of track laborers and worked side by side with Greek, Italian, Slavic, and British miners. Chicanos moved to the Denver region in substantial numbers only with the development of the sugar beet industry near the city in the 1910s and 1920s.[45]

African Americans, by contrast, had been residents of the town as early as 1860. By 1880, Denver counted more than a thousand black residents and their numbers grew over the next decade, as migration from the South stepped up and as the demand for labor in Colorado increased. In 1890, there were more than three thousand African Americans in Denver, and nearly four thousand in 1900. As a proportion of the total population, the African American population remained remarkably constant, representing slightly less than 3 percent of the total population throughout these years.[46]

A handful of Denver's black citizens managed to accumulate wealth over these years. Hotelkeeper Barney L. Ford became one of Denver's wealthiest citizens in the 1860s and speculator Lewis Price amassed a fortune in the real estate boom of the 1880s. Yet, even these economically successful African Americans faced discrimination: the Tabor Grand Opera House, for example, had a "long-time rule" that prohibited "persons of color" from occupying seats in the dress circle. But, overwhelmingly, blacks held working-class occupations. Men worked as laborers and porters, while women took in washing or worked as domestic servants.[47]

Denver's Chinese population was considerably smaller than its African American one. Census takers counted the Chinese population as 238 in 1880 and 980 in 1890. Drawn to Colorado by the building of the rail-roads in the 1870s, Chinese immigrants ended up in a variety of service jobs in the city. In the face of a strong and often violent anti-Chinese movement throughout these years, their numbers dropped to 306 in 1900 and declined even further thereafter. Meanwhile, only in the years after 1900 did Denver gain substantial numbers of Japanese immigrants.[48]

The racism facing Asian immigrants and African Americans deci-sively shaped their residential experience in the city. By the 1880s, Chi-nese residents of Denver lived in a highly segregated "Chinatown" along Wazee and Holladay Streets. The development of residential segregation occurred over a longer period in the case of African Americans, but by 1900 the Five Points district of the city had emerged as an almost entirely black neighborhood and an extremely poor one.[49]

Among the European immigrant groups of the late nineteenth cen-tury, on the other hand, no clear pattern of residential segregation emerged. There were small concentrations of Italians, Poles, and Ger-man Russians, but these were far from clearly defined "ghettos." Even so immigrant a neighborhood as Globeville, dominated by laborers in the giant smelting works, contained a variety of eastern and southern Euro-pean groups. Older immigrant groups such as the British, Germans, Irish, and Scandinavians were scattered widely throughout the city's neighbor-hoods.[50]

Whatever their ethnic makeup, Denver's working-class neighbor-hoods housed a population that was to a great extent on the move. Ex-tremely high rates of geographic mobility characterized the American population as a whole in the nineteenth century. Yet out-migration from Denver during the 1870s and 1880s was even higher than the national norm. This pattern resulted from the pull exerted by mining and railroad building in the wider region. News of each new gold or silver discovery in the mountains temporarily depleted Denver's population as city residents rushed to the new mining camp. The railroad's huge demand for construc-tion laborers may have been an even more significant force. Between the fall of 1879 and the spring of 1881, for example, an average of perhaps one thousand men a month passed through the city, bound for grading camps on the Denver and Rio Grande railroad alone. At the opening of the twentieth century, highly mobile ethnic Germans from Russia often worked in the sugar refineries of the upper Arkansas valley during the harvest months and then moved to Globeville to take work in smelters in the winter. For working people, Denver was, as one historian has put it, "a turnstile town." On the other hand, middle- and upper-class groups were much more likely to remain in the city over long periods of time.[51]

As the preceding discussion indicates, the working man who signed himself "Vindicator" was, on the whole, accurate in his observations.

Accompanying Denver's dramatic growth in the late ninteenth century was the emergence of structured social inequality, and for some working people, outright misery. By themselves, these trends did not determine the labor movement's rise or the shape that it took. They did, however, provide the context within which Denver's labor movement emerged and grew.

2 Irish Nationalism and the Ideological Origins of the Knights of Labor, 1878–83

On 1 May 1884, four hundred machinists, yard hands, and freight dock workers at the main Union Pacific Railroad shop in Denver put down their tools and walked off the job in response to a 10 percent wage cut announced that morning. Caught by surprise, the Union Pacific management rescinded the wage cut three days later and the workers returned to the shop, organizing a local assembly of the Knights of Labor that would stand at the center of the city's labor movement through the early 1890s. The short and successful strike, fought against one of the most powerful corporations in America, had an electrifying effect on other groups of working people in the city. In its aftermath, membership in trade unions and in the Knights of Labor began climbing rapidly. "The producers here are awakening from their sleep and are organizing very fast," wrote John B. Lennon, a Denver labor leader and future treasurer of the American Federation of Labor, four months after the strike. The Union Pacific strike marked the beginning in Denver of what Selig Perlman called the Great Upheaval in American labor history.[1]

Before the strike, working people in the city had built two different kinds of organizations, craft unions, and voluntary associations. Craft unionism was a major force in the lives of many skilled male workers by the early 1880s. Although craft unions excluded a significant proportion of the city's laboring people, they were crucial in laying the foundations for the later labor movement. Equally important were the voluntary associations of native and immigrant working people—fraternal orders, benevolent societies, church auxiliaries, marching societies, and the like —that had proliferated in Denver over the course of the 1870s. These associations provided essential economic and cultural services and helped inculcate a sense of mutuality within various parts of the working-class community. The rise of the Knights of Labor in the middle years of the 1880s would build on both of these organizational forms, while extending their range considerably. The Denver Knights would seek to construct an ethic of mutuality not only among the members of a particular craft or ethnic group but among what they called the "producing classes" as a whole. They would build a movement that to an unprecedented degree cut across the lines of skill, gender, ethnicity, and race.

But the Knights would also mark an ideological departure from earlier working-class organizations. Unlike the craft unions or the voluntary associations, the organization developed an oppositional ideology, a publicly articulated system of ideas and symbols that challenged the forces of monopoly, competitive individualism, and—to some extent—the wage system itself, as these had developed in Denver and in the nation at large. The power of this ideology lay in its capacity to present a clear and vivid image of the ills befalling American society and a justification of various courses of action designed to remedy those ills. Its emergence provided an essential part of the Great Upheaval of the mid-1880s.

Neither the broadening of working-class mutuality nor the emergence of an oppositional ideology, however, happened automatically. Rather they were the product of several years of intense intellectual ferment among Denver's working-class activists that preceded the rise of the Knights. This period of intellectual ferment was set off by the appearance and spread of Irish nationalism in the city in the years from 1880 to 1883.

The organization that expressed this nationalism, the Denver branch of the American Land League, commanded considerable attention in the community and played a significant role in city politics in these years. More importantly, the experience of working-class activists within the Denver Land League and the Irish nationalist movement at large provided them with the key ingredients of a powerful ideology that they would carry with them into the Knights of Labor. The Land League cultivated mutualism and promoted mass struggle. In its efforts to ameliorate the bitter religious antagonisms within the Irish American community, the league encouraged political independence from the Catholic clergy and interdenominational cooperation. It also criticized the traditionally subservient role of Irish and Irish American women and encouraged their movement into public life. Finally, the league denounced the Irish monopolistic land system, supported the struggles of Ireland's rural poor, and encouraged support for the single tax reform. Ironically, these ideas developed under the leadership of members of Denver's Irish American middle class, many of whom opposed trade unionism and the Knights and were friendly to Colorado's Republican party. Despite this fact, the league provided Denver's Knights of Labor with the key intellectual materials out of which they constructed their ideology.

Craft Unions

The struggle to build effective craft unions in Denver had been an arduous one, but by the end of 1882 a small group of trade unions had emerged among the city's skilled workers. All of Denver's three large immigrant groups—the English, the Germans, and the Irish—had participated in the building of the trade union movement. Though craft unions drew a rigid line between the skilled and the unskilled worker, the craftsman and the laborer, they represented a powerful form of solidarity that could be broadened substantially as the city's working-class movement grew.

Craft unionism came to Denver early in its history. In April 1860, the five printers who worked on the *Rocky Mountain News* met at the cabin of Charles Semper to organize the Denver Typographical Union, obtaining a charter from the ten-year-old International Typographical Union two months later. Semper had been a member of the New Orleans local of the ITU before coming to Denver and his experience proved essential in the organization of the union. Denver printers faced an uncertain economic future. Though the cost of living in the town remained extremely high, William N. Byers, who owned the *News*, had recently threatened Semper with a 20 percent wage cut. Within days of the union's founding, Byers's foreman, John L. Dailey, sent the men a note "cutting down their wages." The action triggered a short and unsuccessful strike, the first in Colorado's history, while convincing printers of their good judgment in forming a union.[2]

Denver Typographical Union No. 49 had less than a dozen members in its first two years of existence. The town's economic stagnation and the departure of founding president Jack Merrick for service in the Union army brought the union close to collapse. When it lost its charter and funds in the great Denver flood of May 1864, matters appeared very bleak indeed. But the next twelve months saw intensified activity as the printers, like workers throughout the northern states and territories, struggled to keep pace with wartime inflation. By 1865, the union had grown to twenty-eight members and had raised printers' wages by several dollars a week. Even more important, the union began to bring a new element of concerted action into the relationship of printers with their employers. In 1865, for instance, DTU No. 49 put aside its original practice of unilaterally announcing a list of prices and calling upon each printer to quit work in those so-called rat shops that did not meet it. Instead, it began appointing committees to *negotiate* rates with newspaper proprietors. Union leaders believed that this new approach would not only create "better feelings between the employees and employers" but would also allow printers to derive strength from united action.[3]

The new emphasis on collective action and collective discipline led union leaders to condemn the printers' traditional habits of work. The 1860 diary of *News* foreman Dailey provides a window on these older work habits. It shows that while journeymen printers sometimes worked with great intensity, they also frequently came to work late, knocked off early, and mixed a good deal of leisure with their work in the shop. "Boys 'loafed' today," Dailey recorded on 21 April. "I loafed most of the day and Jack [Merrick] all day," he noted on 7 June. Heavy drinking both on and off the job also characterized the printers' style. On 3 July, for example, Dailey and his men were "busy at work to get the paper up. Got to work at it in the evening. Worked at it until late at night and devoured several bottles of choice fluid, the effects of which were to exhilerate [*sic*] the company." On 14 July, a union meeting was followed by "a spree" that lasted "all the next day." This mixing of work and leisure was so common that on 18 June, when printers "stuck to the office all day," Dailey considered it unusual enough to record in his diary.[4]

By the mid-1860s union leaders had come to oppose this work style, regarding it as an obstacle to effective unified action among printers. In July 1864, DTU No. 49 resolved that "we will not and do not countenance the shirking of labor by journeymen" and that "all journeymen employed by the week are required to work their full ten hours each day." Any time printers spent away from work during regular working hours, the union further resolved, "should be deducted from their weekly wages." But the union's effort to exercise collective control over the work habits of *printers* was bound up with an equally strenuous effort to control the actions of *employers*. Thus in December 1864, the union resolved that if Byers discharged, "without the advice and consent of the foreman," any union printer involved in a recent altercation, "all members of the Union will give up their situations and cease work." As this example indicates, though their willingness to quit work remained the foundation of the printers' strength, collective action against employers was also assisted by foremen who, in the printing trades, were often members of the union and to some extent agents of its policies.[5]

The move toward more effective collective action could not be accomplished without a shift in the traditionally individualistic attitudes of the printers themselves. Most important was the emergence of a spirit of mutual support within the craft. Union leaders in these years worked hard to develop institutional mechanisms that would further this spirit. Thus the Denver Typographical Union required attendance at its monthly meetings and fined all members who did not attend. Attendance was also required at the funerals of "our worthy and beloved fellow craftsmen." The goal here was to cultivate a deep loyalty to the union and a feeling of solidarity with the other individuals who belonged to it. A. W. Barnard, president of the Denver organization, made the point dramatically at a union meeting in February 1865. Drawing a parallel between the printers union and that other "Union" now approaching victory in the Civil War, he argued that, just as in the struggle against the Confederacy, "it is absolutely necessary that we should have unity of action and purpose, that all personal jealousies and petty animosities be laid aside, and each one of us labor for the elevation of the Craft, and the welfare and good being, not only of the Union, but for each individual member thereof."[6]

The printers maintained a highly visible public presence in Denver throughout the 1860s and 1870s. On 17 January 1873, their union celebrated the birthday of Benjamin Franklin with what one of Denver's first chroniclers called "a gorgeous banquet at the American House, said to have been second only to the Duke Alexis dinner in the amount of eating and drinking, and speechmaking indulged in by the participants." Union members also played a prominent role in Denver's huge Centennial celebration in 1876, marching as a body directly behind the coach that carried "Miss Liberty." The typographers, in short, were Denver's union pioneers, providing other groups of workers with a body of labor traditions and a public presence for unionism that went back to the very founding of the town.[7]

Until the end of the 1870s, the printers constituted virtually the entire local labor movement. Denver carpenters and painters had tried to organize unions in the 1860s, but without any enduring success. In 1871, a group of custom tailors organized the Journeymen Tailors Union of Denver, but their organization stagnated in the 1870s, reviving again only in the early 1880s. The 1870s did see the establishment of various organizations of railroad workers in the city: engineers in March 1875, firemen in June 1877, and conductors in the following month. The death and disability insurance that the railroad organizations featured were important for workers who faced the prospect of death or dismemberment every working day and whose wages in the 1870s did not permit them to obtain insurance from private companies. But the founding of these organizations did little for the broader local labor movement. The Brotherhood of Locomotive Engineers, though functioning as a union, denounced strikes, proclaimed harmony between capital and labor, and avoided all alliances with other groups of workers. The Brotherhood of Locomotive Firemen and the Order of Railway Conductors were benevolent societies rather than unions. Leaders of Denver's conductors vehemently insisted that their order was "not to be classed among the striking labor organizations."[8]

The years from 1878 to 1883 ended this era of labor quiescence. In five short years, unions of iron molders, stone cutters, carpenters, machinists, and bakers appeared in the city, along with two assemblies of the Knights of Labor. Denver tailors meanwhile rebuilt their local organization, went on strike against a wage reduction in March 1883, received a charter from the newly reorganized Journeymen Tailors Union of the United States the same year, and in the following year helped elect their local leader, John B. Lennon, president of the national union. A new militancy could be seen even among those workers who did not successfully organize. The years from 1881 to 1883 saw strikes among unorganized brick makers, hotel waiters and telegraph operators, as well as among unionized masons, iron molders and tailors. Nearly all of these strikes failed, but they reflected a new militancy that went hand in hand with the creation of effective organizations.[9]

This militancy was made possible by the national economic upswing from 1878 to 1882, an upswing that was intensified in Denver by the great Leadville mining rush of these years. As late as the end of 1883, when unemployment was rising in other areas of the country, construction was still booming in Denver. But as important as economic conditions was the immigration of individuals (comparable to Charles Semper two decades earlier) who had experience with unions in other cities. Thus the craftsmen who organized Denver's branches of the Amalgamated Society of Carpenters and the Amalgamated Society of Engineers in 1882 were British immigrants who had been members of these organizations before emigrating from their homeland. Similarly, the rapid growth of the mining machinery industry in Denver attracted many skilled iron molders to the city, some of whom had been members of the Iron Molders Union in cities further east and helped build the Denver local in the late 1870s. The importation of unionism was especially important among iron molders who were classic "tramping artisans" and whose national union dated to before the Civil War.[10]

But the growth of the labor movement depended on more than a favorable employment situation and the presence of craftsmen with union experience. Although conditions in each trade varied considerably in the late 1870s and early 1880s, certain common problems confronted all skilled workers in the city and encouraged their moves toward organization. Most pressing were the attempts of Denver employers to introduce various incentive pay schemes, especially piecework. While employers favored piecework as a way of increasing productivity, skilled craftsmen, who had been accustomed to a certain amount of workplace autonomy, saw it as a direct attack on their dignity and on established traditions of work. While it might lead to higher wages for some workers in the short run, the long-run effect of the piece system was to create competition among workers that would lead to a decline in pay. By connecting wages to measurable output, the system also greatly enhanced the power of the foreman, at the expense of the craftsman. Thus the abolition of piecework became a central objective for a number of trade unions in Denver and provided impetus for the organization of new ones.[11]

Piecework became a major issue in three of Denver's most important trades: printing, tailoring, and the manufacture of mining machinery. When Joseph Ray Buchanan, a Missouri-born printer who would soon become Denver's most prominent labor leader, arrived in the city in the late 1870s, he found that in some nonunion printing establishments the piece system had created "many opportunities for the practice of favoritism." Some printers were "enabled, through favors shown them by foremen, to make larger bills than men greatly their superiors as compositors," Buchanan later recalled. Piecework in Denver's highly competitive mining machinery foundries encouraged a spirit of competition among workmen that, as one Denver iron molder put it, was "the most expeditious route to hell for the human race." "Both molder and boss help in this competition—this cutting of each other's throats," he proclaimed. "Both are criminals and both are victims." In the manufacture of men's clothing the system assumed its most vicious form: since few Denver employers provided workshops for their employees, tailors worked at home and acted as subcontractors, often systematically exploiting their wives and children.[12]

Piecework was not the only problem facing Denver's craftsmen. Among bakers, brick makers, building trades workers, and some railroad workers, struggles with employers over the length of the working day remained preeminent. But the fight against piecework was crucial to the development of the Denver labor movement because it prompted the assertion of a mutualistic ethos against the acquisitive individualism enshrined in middle-class ideology. Craftsmen built this ethos into the fabric of their union rules, rules that attempted to fix terms of apprenticeship, limit the authority of foremen, and put journeymen on what Buchanan called "an equal footing as to wages and other conditions."[13]

Enforcing this mutuality was not always easy. In the Denver printer's union, it meant the expulsion of so-called rat printers who broke the union's "laws" regarding work practices. Even those who supported the union sometimes found its discipline harsh. In 1882, for example, Buchanan argued that the Denver Typographical Union should grant a pardon to a rat printer who sought readmission to the local. "I believed the union's treatment of him was cruel and uncalled for," Buchanan later recalled, "but men older than I in the union said that his offense could not be condoned." Associated with this harsh discipline, however, was the creation of tight, almost family-like bonds among workers. "I look to the welfare of the Union as I would that of my children," said one printer at a union meeting in 1884.[14]

The establishment of the Denver Trades Assembly marked an effort to extend these bonds of mutuality from the individual craft to the community of skilled workers as a whole. In August 1882, conscious of the rapid growth of local trades councils in cities across the nation, Denver printers appointed a committee to organize such a body in their city. On 12 November 1882, their representatives and those of local tailors, stonecutters, iron molders and bakers formed the Denver Trades Assembly. Richard Watson, a stonecutter, was elected president, narrowly defeating Buchanan, who became recording secretary.[15]

The Trades Assembly was made up of three delegates from each union and met every other week. Over the next two years it played a number of important roles. First, it spearheaded the use of the boycott in Denver labor disputes. The boycotting of employers was a tactic employed mainly by Denver printers and tailors, but in principle it could be useful to all who worked in trades serving a working-class market. Since boycotts required funds and coordination beyond the resources of the individual trade union and depended on the creation of solidarity beyond the ranks of its members, the Trades Assembly was an ideal instrument for the direction of boycotts. In enforcing interunion support, the Trades Assembly helped create bonds of reciprocity among Denver's skilled workers that crossed lines of craft. Its constitution made it clear that once a decision had been made to endorse a boycott or strike, "a call shall be made on all trades and labor organizations to assist the one in difficulty. . . . Any union failing to assist another when called upon by the Assembly shall forfeit its right in a similar emergency."[16]

The Trades Assembly also played an important political role. It actively lobbied the city government and, since Denver was the capital of Colorado, it lobbied the General Assembly (the state legislature) as well. In so doing, it increasingly became the political voice of organized workers in the state as a whole, a role it would play until the founding of the Colorado State Federation of Labor a decade later. In 1883, the Trade Assembly's legislative committee helped defeat an antiunion "conspiracy" bill and fought for a law exempting certain wages from attachment. But the Trades Assembly was political in another sense as well: like similar bodies in cities throughout North America and Europe, it became a center for a variety of reform and radical currents of political thought. It sponsored a weekly newspaper, the Denver *Labor Enquirer*, which served a similar function. With a stated mission "to educate, elevate, and advance the laboring classes" of the city, the *Labor Enquirer* appeared every Saturday until 1888 at a subscription rate of from $1.50 to $2.00 a year.[17]

Joseph Ray Buchanan, editor of the *Labor Enquirer*, quickly became Denver's most prominent labor activist. Buchanan had been born in 1851 in Hannibal, Missouri. The son and grandson of printers and newspaper publishers, he naturally gravitated to the trade and acquired a broad training in newspaper production on a Missouri country weekly called the *Riverside Press*. His father and grandfather had both been Whigs until that party's collapse in the 1850s, and Buchanan inherited from them not only a belief in the potential benefits of industrialization, but also the critique of unbridled individualism, the belief in "community," and the moralistic rhetoric that characterized the outlook of the old Whig party. Though he cast his first vote as a Republican, Buchanan gravitated toward Missouri's powerful Greenback movement in the late 1870s and voted for Peter Cooper, the Greenback presidential candidate, in 1878.[18]

Buchanan was introduced to trade unionism in Denver, where he worked on several newspapers in 1878 and 1879, joining the Denver Typographical Union in the latter year. But it was Buchanan's residence in Leadville during the bitter miners' strike of 1880 that turned him into a self-proclaimed "labor agitator." The evident justice of the miners' struggle and the role of mine owner and governmental violence in the strike convinced Buchanan of the need for broad working-class organization. Upon his return to Denver in 1881, he threw himself into the world of labor activism, representing Denver printers at the ITU's 1882 national convention, helping to organize a Knights of Labor local assembly in November of that year, taking an active role in the Denver Trades Assembly, and editing the *Enquirer*.[19]

Like other working-class intellectuals of this era, Buchanan also avidly sought out reform and radical programs offering long-range solutions to labor's problems. Between 1880 and 1882, he later recalled, he "had been reading everything dealing with social conditions that I could get hold of. I had devoured the writings of the leading political economists and had formed opinions of a just and equitable social and industrial system." Like many others in the labor movement, Buchanan was attracted to the analysis of the Greenback theorist, Edward Kellogg, and that of Kellogg's post–Civil War popularizer, Alexander Campbell. Buchanan felt that Kellogg's book, *Labor and Other Capital* was "one of the ablest treatises" ever written on the labor question. He never became an orthodox greenbacker, however. Rather, he took from Kellogg and Campbell mainly their condemnation of poverty amidst plenty, their sharp distinction between "producers" (workers, farmers, and manufacturers—who were seen as natural allies) and the "non-producing" financiers who exploited them, and their morally powerful labor theory of wealth. Buchanan was attracted to these greenbackers because, like them, he longed for a system that would bring some moral order to the new world dominated by the market and factory.[20]

But the essential text for Buchanan, as for thousands of other working men and women in this era, was Henry George's *Progress and Poverty*, a book that Buchanan believed "the greatest and most comprehensive work on political economy of the age." Again, it was not George's single tax reform program itself that fired Buchanan's imagination. Rather, like most other enthusiasts in these years, Buchanan responded mainly to George's quasi-religious condemnation of the current order and his effort to bring the language of natural rights into the struggle for land and labor reform. It was this side of George's work that made *Progress and Poverty*, after the bible, the most widely bought book of the nineteenth century.[21]

Buchanan, soon to become a key figure in Denver's emerging working-class movement, was thus an old-stock American who brought an updated version of aspects of the American political tradition into his role as a labor activist. That he was no backward-looking opponent of industrialism itself should be clear from his Whig political heritage and his early attraction to the writings of Alexander Campbell, an enthusiast of industrial growth. But Buchanan did seek to recreate in industrializing America the republican vision of a commonwealth of independent citizens, endowed with equal rights. As the motto Buchanan printed in early issues of the *Enquirer* put it:

> We will renew the times of truth and justice
> Condensing in a fair, free commonwealth
> Not rash equality, but equal rights.[22]

Native-born workers were not the sole, or even the most important, builders of the Denver labor movement however. Immigrant craftsmen with different traditions also took active roles in the building of trade unions in the city. The role of British carpenters and machinists in organizing Denver branches of the Amalgamated Society of Engineers and the Amalgamated Society of Carpenters has already been noted. Both organizations predated unions among American-born workers in these trades. In 1882, German bakers in the city established a union that helped found the Trades Assembly, although in the face of employer opposition it collapsed shortly thereafter. While there are no conclusive data on the ethnic composition of other labor organizations in Denver, the fact that the iron molders, the stonecutters, and the first local assembly of the Knights of Labor held their regular meetings at Mitchel Guard Hall, an Irish community center, suggests a significant presence of Irish American workers in these organizations.[23]

On the other hand, the trade union movement was far from inclusive. Skilled African American craftsmen, for instance, found Denver trade unions extremely hostile to their aspirations. In 1869, the Denver Typographical Union turned down a membership application from Henry Wagoner, a leader in the struggle for black voting rights in Reconstruction Colorado, ostensibly because "no one vouched for him," but, in fact, because of his race. Partly as a result of his experience with the Denver labor movement in the late 1860s, Lewis H. Douglass, the son of abolitionist Frederick Douglass, roundly condemned "the folly, tyranny, and wickedness of labor unions" in the mid-1870s. Lewis Douglass had come to Denver seeking work as a typographer but was unable to find regular employment because of his exclusion by No. 49. "There is no disguising the fact—his crime was his color," said Frederick Douglass in a speech denouncing the Denver Typographical Union and locals in Rochester and Washington, which had also denied admission to his son.[24]

Denver's anti-Chinese riot of 1880 represented the most extreme case of white working-class racism in this period. The riot was triggered by an altercation between white railroad laborers and two Chinese men in a saloon, and most of those who participated in the violence were white workers. The immediate background to the riot was one of Democratic party agitation against the Chinese. In the days immediately preceding the 1880 election, the Democratic *Rocky Mountain News* launched a vitriolic campaign against the Chinese, denouncing Republican President Garfield for supporting the unrestricted immigration of "cheap labor." Day after day in late October, the *News* drew attention to the Chinese living in Denver and hinted that violent action was required to remove the "pests." When the riot broke out on 31 October, whites shouted "Garfield's a Chinaman" as they overwhelmed police and fire fighters, destroyed most of Chinatown, and lynched Look Young, a twenty-eight-year-old immigrant from China.[25]

Working-class and labor movement sentiment was not entirely with the rioters. During the course of the riot, a printer named George Hickey risked his life trying unsuccessfully to rescue Look Young from lynching at the corner of Nineteenth and Lawrence streets. "I endeavored to shield him and prevent them from putting the rope around his neck," Hickey later told a congressional investigating committee. "The crowd then commenced kicking him, and said I was a damned Chinaman, and they would hang me if I did not get away, and attempted to put the rope over my neck." Judge J. B. Belford, who would soon be prominently identified with the Denver working-class movement, also denounced the rioters, comparing them to the nullifiers of South Carolina in their disregard for law and human life.[26]

But despite the opposition of some workers and labor movement figures to the use of violence, hostility to the Chinese and opposition to Chinese immigration were dominant themes in Denver's emerging working-class movement. "The Chinese are, directly and indirectly, the cause of more suffering and crime than any other class of people in our state," wrote Colorado's Deputy Commissioner of Labor Statistics in 1890, voicing sentiments that had long been present among Denver's organized workers. "We . . . know of no way to correct the evil, except for all Trades' Organizations to combine against them." From its earliest issues, the *Labor Enquirer* was filled with anti-Chinese editorials and articles. Stephen Vinot, a French immigrant, real estate investor, and sometime Democratic candidate for city office, who became the paper's publisher in June 1883, did much of this writing. "Vinot's hobby was the Chinese question," Buchanan later recalled. "He believed that if the Chinese were allowed unrestricted entrance to this country they would in time dominate the white people in every walk of life, and that American workingmen would be degraded to a coolie level." Though Buchanan himself attacked the "demagogue" Denis Kearney's anti-Chinese campaign in California—believing with Henry George that the hysteria was beginning to distract workers from the more fundamental problem of monopoly—he was nonetheless throughout these years "in hearty sympathy with the opposition to the admission of the Chinese to the country." When questioned on an 1886 speaking tour of California about the contradiction between his stated commitment to "the international brotherhood of man" and his opposition to Chinese immigration, Buchanan responded by redefining his position as a belief in "the Brotherhood of Man, Limited."[27]

Attitudes toward the admission of white women to trade unions showed somewhat more variability. Denver's male unionists recognized the danger posed by employers hiring women workers at lower wages, and they sometimes called for equal wages and the unionization of women. But they also believed women's main contribution should be as mothers and wives; ideally women should be in the home, not in the labor force at all. Thus while the Denver Typographical Union permitted the admission of women members as early as 1869 (though there is no evidence of women actually joining until the mid-1880s), the iron molders remained implacably hostile to the idea of women entering either their trade or their trade union. The tailors' position fell between these two poles. Although one of their "cardinal principles" was to "procure for female workers the highest possible wages," the Denver Journeymen Tailors Union remained a union of male custom tailors and never tried to organize the rapidly growing numbers of poorly paid clothing workers in the city. "If we working girls could get ourselves organized into a union and establish a price list for piece-work, we would be better situated than we now are," a woman dressmaker told Colorado Bureau of Labor Statistics investigators in 1887, complaining of neglect by the Tailors Union.[28]

A deep-seated racism and firm beliefs concerning the roles of women may have accounted for the hostility of trade unionists towards African American, Chinese, and white women workers. The exclusive position of trade unions toward unskilled workers generally, however, sprang from a somewhat different source. It was built into the very nature of craft unions, which derived their strength from the scarce skills possessed by their members. Despite the growth of a spirit of solidarity within the young working-class movement in Denver, that movement remained restricted to skilled workers; on more than one occasion its activists expressed a belief in the craftsman's superiority to the common laborer.

The railroad brotherhoods and their members were famous for this. "The idea of an engineer associating with section men and wipers" was unthinkable for one Denver engineer in the mid-1880s. "Do you consider a man getting a dollar per day equal to [one] who gets four dollars per day?" he reportedly asked a Knights of Labor organizer. "As for me, I consider myself four times better." Although the account of the conversation may have been apocryphal, it illustrates values widely held among what contemporaries called the "aristocracy of labor." Such sentiments were not commonly voiced in the Denver Trades Assembly. Its stated intention "to secure united action on the part of skilled labor" in the city, however, reveals the limits of its ambitions. Even the early Knights of Labor assemblies were restricted in practice to skilled craftsmen. The first, founded in May 1881, was composed of plasterers, plumbers, and other skilled building tradesmen. The second, organized in November 1882, was made up entirely of printers.[29]

Denver's early labor movement, then, was pulled in different directions. On one hand, the trade unions excluded women, African Americans, and unskilled workers from their ranks and launched a full-scale attack on the Chinese. On the other hand, in the course of its growth before 1884—and particularly in its struggles against piecework—the trade union movement developed an ethos of mutuality that ran directly counter to the individualism of the day. Denver's labor activists would later broaden this ethos into a sweeping denunciation of "the selfishness and deadening effects of competition" generally.[30]

Ethnic Associations

The trade union was not the only organizational expression of working-class life in this period. For first- and second-generation immigrants, who constituted the majority of Denver's working class, as well as for African Americans, the fraternal or benevolent association was a far more important institution in the 1870s and early 1880s. The membership of some of these organizations overlapped with that of trade unions. But unlike the trade union, the immigrant society did not foster occupational divisions among its members, and it was more likely to include women in both its membership and its activities. Denver's ethnic societies were central institutions in the working-class community, helping to cultivate mutual support and serving as a kind of incubator for the values the labor movement would soon uphold.[31]

The years following the Civil War saw a flowering of working-class associational life in Denver as throughout the United States. The pioneering immigrant organization in Denver was the *Turnverein*, founded by German immigrants—mainly small businessmen and skilled workers— in 1866. As the city's population grew in the 1870s, increasing numbers of Irish, English, and German immigrants provided the basis for a rich organizational life. In 1872, English immigrants founded a short-lived St. George's Protective Association. By 1874 Irish immigrants had organized the Denver Catholic Benevolent Society and the Mitchel Guards, a semimilitary social club. In the mid-1870s, German-speaking Swiss immigrants founded the *Grutli Verein* and helped form an inclusive German American Association to represent the German-speaking community as a whole.[32]

Voluntary societies like these provided a number of essential economic and social services to working people in the city. In the absence of governmental social insurance, ethnic benevolent societies provided sickness, death, and burial benefits to working-class families, many of them on the margins of poverty. In the absence of any urban recreational facilities save the saloon, they provided a major focus of working-class leisure. Ethnic organizations also provided a sense of community for immigrant workers frequently on the move. As noted in the previous chapter, in the 1870s and 1880s Denver's inhabitants were even more mobile than the nineteenth-century American population as a whole. Immigrant societies did much to ease the loneliness that went hand in hand with high rates of geographic mobility. The experience of Karl Nadler, a clerk, provides a good illustration of this situation. When he arrived in Denver from St. Joseph, Missouri, in 1871, Nadler immediately took his Turner's pass to the Denver *Turnverein*. Over the next few years, he seems to have made the organization the center of his social life, becoming a theatrical director and a gymnastics instructor.[33]

Denver's African Americans also participated in the building of voluntary societies, organizing a lodge of the black Prince Hall Order of Freemasons as early as 1868. Along with the three black churches that existed in the city by 1890, the Masons were a key organization, providing the black community with an important institutional expression of solidarity. The struggle for education played a similar role. In the late 1860s, Henry Wagoner and several other African American leaders established the first adult education classes in Colorado, teaching reading, arithmetic, and government to other members of their community.[34]

The struggle for equal rights in Colorado also served to solidify Denver's African American community. Blacks mobilized effectively to fight for equal suffrage in the years from 1864 to 1866, a fight they won when Congress prohibited territories from placing racial restrictions on the franchise in 1867. In the wake of their achievement, Denver's African American adult males voted in numbers sufficient to provide Republicans with their margin of victory in the Congressional election of 1868. They also fought for school integration, winning this battle in 1873. But, as leaders like Wagoner often observed, legal equality could only be maintained by constant vigilance. Their continuing political activism provided Denver's African Americans with a sense of community as important as their voluntary societies.[35]

Labor activists sometimes criticized ethnic organizations, pointing out their tendency to be led by nonworkers and arguing that they accentuated lines of division between workers of different immigrant backgrounds and between immigrant and native-born workers. "We are all very clannish," wrote Joseph Buchanan of Denver's workers in 1883, "and each clan must have its own club or society to keep us from identifying with the people among whom we have come to live." By this time there had been a proliferation of ethnic organizations in the city. The Irish maintained chapters of the Ancient Order of Hibernians and the Irish American Progressive Society along with the Mitchel Guards. The English, Welsh, and Scots had organized branches of the Albion, Cambrian, and Caledonian clubs. Swedes had founded a Skandia Benevolent Society and Denver's Germans had organized separate German-speaking lodges of the Oddfellows and Knights of Pythias. The German and Irish communities of the city also supported their own newspapers, the *Colorado Journal* and the *Rocky Mountain Celt*.[36]

Nevertheless, Buchanan's view that these societies divided the working class—a view sometimes echoed by later social historians—was wrong. On the contrary, the fraternal and collective spirit that animated the ethnic societies posed an implicit challenge to the individualist ethos of the times that paralleled that of the trade unions. After race, religion, not ethnicity, provided the most important line of conflict among Denver's working people. Internal tensions between Protestants and Catholics were paramount, affecting several immigrant groups. Germans, for example, were divided between Lutherans and Catholics. The division took on an especially bitter character among immigrants from Britain and Ireland. The Irish Ancient Order of Hibernians, for example, restricted membership to Catholics and expressed hostility toward the Protestant immigrants from Ulster. Meanwhile, although there was no Orange Order in Denver, anti-Catholic sentiments flourished in the social clubs of immigrants from northern Ireland, Scotland, and Wales.[37]

Denver's political parties also gave expression to the conflict between

Catholics and Protestants. Although religious differences in Colorado were not as thoroughly intertwined with partisanship as they were in the Midwest and Northeast during the late nineteenth century, it was generally true that the Democrats were the party of Catholic cultural groups while the Republicans spoke for the Protestants. During the 1870s, religion entered the political arena more directly. In 1876, Colorado's Catholic bishop, Joseph Machebeuf, unsuccessfully petitioned the state constitutional convention to provide funding for parochial schools, a move that triggered bitter opposition from Protestants. Two years later, Machebeuf brought the church into politics again, denouncing the rising movement for woman's suffrage in Colorado as the work of "battalions of old maids disappointed in love" and married women seeking "to hold the reins of the family government."[38]

Woman's suffrage was one of the most important reform issues of the Gilded Age, and Machebeuf's tirade reflected what some Denver reformers perceived as Catholicism's implacable hostility to the nineteenth-century reform tradition. Caroline Churchill, Denver's leading middle-class feminist and temperance advocate, for example, frequently used the pages of her weekly newspaper to denounce the church as an opponent of reform. Churchill went beyond anti-Catholicism, ridiculing Irish immigrants, the largest contingent of Denver's Catholics, as a group made up wholly of "criminals" and "paupers."[39]

From the abolitionist crusade to the feminist movement of the early twentieth century, the American reform tradition had been shaped by the powerful currents of perfectionist Protestantism, currents that often contained a good deal of hostility to the Irish. As Eric Foner has convincingly shown, however, the mercurial rise of the American Land League among Irish immigrants in the early 1880s marked a conjunction of the Irish American community and the Protestant reform tradition. Important as this was, in Denver the rise of the Land League accomplished something else as well: it prepared the way for the Knights of Labor.[40]

Irish Nationalism

Organized by Michael Davitt, John Devoy, and Charles Stewart Parnell in October 1879, the Irish National Land League marked what has come to be known as the "New Departure" in Irish politics. Although the league put forward the historic demand for national independence from British rule, its greater significance lay in its efforts to redress the grievances of Ireland's rural poor. Formed against a backdrop of severe agricultural depression caused by crop failures and a weak market, the Land League waged political war against oppressive landlords and raised the slogan, "The Land for the People." Under Parnell's leadership, the organization built an enormous following over the next few years and represented the first genuine mass movement of the Irish poor.[41]

The Land League soon began to play a major role on this side of the Atlantic as well. In 1880, Parnell and Davitt toured the United States to raise funds for their struggle in the Irish American community. They met with immediate success, and in the same year the Irish National Land League of America was founded. By September 1881, there were fifteen hundred branches of the league in towns and cities across the nation. In the United States, however, there were two distinct centers of power within the Irish nationalist movement. The first revolved around the growing Irish American middle class. In spite of their support for the agrarian and national struggle in Ireland, individuals associated with this wing of the movement were not particularly sympathetic to the nascent workers' struggle in the United States. There was also, however, a more radical working-class wing of the movement, represented by the Irish American newspaper editor, Patrick Ford.[42]

From New York, Ford edited a widely circulated weekly, the *Irish World and American Industrial Liberator*. As the paper's name indicates, Ford sought to draw connections between the land struggle in Ireland and the labor struggle in the United States. "The cause of the poor in Donegal," he proclaimed, "is the cause of the factory slave in Fall River." In some areas of the country, particularly the anthracite mining region of Pennsylvania and the industrial areas of New England, working-class branches of the Land League arose that adhered closely to Ford's position, in some cases virtually merging with local assemblies of the Knights of Labor. In these areas, the Land League and the Knights together elaborated a producer ideology that posited a fundamental conflict between the producing classes and monopolists. Ford and his followers saw the latter as posing a fundamental threat to the social order, for they appeared to be coming to control not only the land of Ireland, but American industry and finance as well.[43]

The Rocky Mountain West was a major stronghold of the Land League's working-class wing. Hard rock miners in Leadville, Virginia City, Nevada, and Butte, Montana, provided enthusiastic support for Ford, as did many western railroad workers. On the other hand, the Denver branch of the Land League, organized by Michael Davitt himself on his 1880 American tour, was dominated by the city's Irish American middle class. As will be made clear, however, this fact did not undercut the importance of the Land League for the city's labor movement.

Irish nationalism was not a new phenomenon in Denver. In the closing months of the Civil War, Irish American soldiers posted near the town had organized a circle of the secret Irish Republican Brotherhood, known in America as the Fenians. By 1866, their membership had reached fifty, and they were attracting a good deal of local attention. Denver's Fenians organized Fourth of July celebrations in 1868 and 1869, featuring speeches by some of the leading political figures in Colorado. The Denver organization was probably more important for its social functions than its political activities, and it went into decline in the wake of the abortive Fenian invasion of Canada in 1870.[44]

Nevertheless, Denver's Fenian Circle, like those in other cities, played an important role in bringing Irish Americans into the mainstream of American political culture. No individual who was "averse to the Republican form of government" was permitted to join the Denver circle, for example. When Denver's Fenians took a stand in support of African American suffrage in 1868, they went considerably further in the defense of republican principles than most whites of the city. Equally noteworthy was the absence of religious sectarianism in the organization. Denver's Fenians were nationalist, not Catholic, in their orientation and ruled that "no sectarian or religious principles would be permitted to be discussed" in the circle. They welcomed not only Irish Protestants but non-Irish as well, announcing that "Fenians are not interested in where a man was born, nor what his religious principles were," and that any man could become a member of the circle "provided he was willing to enter into the cause of liberation of that long oppressed and abused people of Erin."[45]

Irish nationalism did not disappear in the 1870s. A circle of John Devoy's Clan na Gael, the most important revolutionary nationalist organization in this decade, maintained a shadowy existence in Denver, putting aside its secrecy to march in Colorado's 1876 Centennial parade. When the Irish revolutionary Jeremiah O'Donovan Rossa sought to finance a campaign of guerrilla warfare in Ireland, he found fifty-one Denver Irish American men and women, loosely organized as the "Bull Whackers," willing to make contributions to his so-called Skirmishing Fund. Though sixteen of these individuals can be identified as skilled or unskilled workers, the growing Irish American middle class was also well represented. Ten of the men in the group were saloonkeepers, businessmen, small proprietors or white-collar workers, presaging the important role Denver's Irish American middle class would play in the city's Land League. Equally significant, six of the Bull Whackers were women, though their class background is not clear. In addition to support for skirmishers, the 1870s also saw the organization of the Irish American Progressive Society, which, like the Fenian Brotherhood, opened its ranks to Protestants, "one of its principal objects being to do away with those religious and section bickerings which have kept Ireland divided in the past."[46]

None of these organizations, however, came close to wielding the kind of influence that the Land League did in the period between 1880 and 1882. Its influence was especially profound among Denver's working people. Like other ethnic organizations, the Land League's membership crossed class lines. Though its leadership ranks were dominated by men of the emerging Irish American middle class, its active members included many individuals from working-class occupations. More importantly, the league maintained a highly visible presence among working people in the city that made it influential beyond its ranks. Its activities were regularly reported not only in the daily press but also in the *Labor Enquirer.* When T. P. O'Connor, an Irish nationalist member of Parliament, spoke in Denver in January 1882, his official sponsor was the Land League, but among those turning out to welcome him were predominantly working-class organizations like the Mitchel Guard, St. Joseph's Catholic Total Abstinence Union, and—most significantly—the Denver Stonecutters Union.[47]

In the early 1880s, the Land League played an important role in influencing thought and action in the city's working-class movement. The organization, for instance, had a profound impact in challenging religious divisions among working people in the city when it attempted to assuage the bitter conflict between Irish Protestants and Catholics. The signal on this issue came from the movement in Ireland itself. As one visiting Irish activist told a Denver league meeting in 1882—with exaggeration to be sure—"Catholics and Protestants in Ireland feel that upon this question of land reform they have one common ground to stand upon, one common cause to fight for, and one common enemy to oppose." In the spirit of this proclamation, the Denver league opened its doors to Protestant members and even elected a Protestant, Robert Morris, as its first president. At a demonstration in 1882, Denver Land Leaguers carried banners reading "North and South" and "Orange and Green." In 1883, the Denver League even went so far as to oppose the celebration of St. Patrick's Day. Though one of St. Patrick's supporters tried to persuade the league to honor him not as a Catholic saint, but rather as "one of the greatest and grandest Irishmen," after considerable debate its members decided that this Catholic holiday threatened to divide a community that included many non-Catholics and would do nothing toward "relieving the suffering of the poor and starving people of Ireland." As a result of the league's decision, Denver saw no celebration of St. Patrick's Day until 1887, when it was revived by the entirely Catholic organization, the Ancient Order of Hibernians.[48]

Though the Land League built on traditions embodied by the Fenians and the Irish American Progressive Society, its deeper roots in the working class gave its attack on religious sectarianism greater impact. Equally significant was the Denver Land League's criticism of the traditionally subservient roles occupied by Irish American women. The cue again came from trends in the wider movement. In what was regarded by some as "the most important step since the start of the movement," Fanny Parnell and Jane Byrne organized the Ladies Land League in New York in October 1880. Anna Parnell began organizing Irish branches a month later, and the movement spread rapidly in both Ireland and the United States. As an early student of the movement noted, "the Land League was the one national movement that availed themselves of [women's] services as citizens, instead of shutting them out like children from the conduct of political business." Indeed, perhaps the most important accomplishment of the league was that it provided a kind of political baptism for a generation of Irish women activists, many of whom would go on to play important roles in later feminist and nationalist movements. In any event, Denver followed these leads. In April 1881, men in the city's Land League began voicing enthusiasm for "working with the Ladies," and in December of that year Irish American women had organized the Ladies Land League of Denver and had elected officers. In Denver, as in Ireland, this marked a massive rupture with the deep conservatism of Irish culture regarding the public roles of women.[49]

The organization of women and Protestants in the Land League was also associated with a growing anticlericalism among Denver's Irish Americans, for a vocal sector of the church hierarchy had expressed strong opposition to both of these moves. Anticlerical sentiments in Denver had been brewing for some time. Although the city's Catholic population was overwhelmingly Irish, its bishop, Joseph Machebeuf, was French. In the 1870s, Machebeuf had aroused opposition from Denver's Irish for his pro-British views and his alleged discrimination against Irish priests. Irish nationalists in the city had also been critical of the church's hostility toward the movement for Irish independence. As one Catholic member of Denver's Irish-American Progressive Association put it, "not only have we England to contend with, but Rome." The Denver Land League thus built on a critical spirit that Irish Catholics had already expressed toward the church hierarchy. But, again, its greater influence enabled it to spread this spirit far more widely than had any previous organization.[50]

The conflict with the church had ramifications far beyond the local situation. It came to a head in June 1882, when Cleveland's politically conservative bishop Richard Gilmour, determined to keep women out of the political arena, censured the Ladies Land League of his city. The Denver branch of the league went into a long and argumentative session to determine a response to Gilmour's action. Although some members believed that "if you open a breach by criticizing the conduct of Bishop Gilmour you will bring nothing but harm and will awaken prejudice [among Catholics] against the League," sentiment generally ran toward strong condemnation. The Irish Catholic judge, John W. Mullahey, for example, did not favor the denunciation of Gilmour "as a man or as a Catholic, but he would denounce the action of any man, whether priest, bishop, or pope, who opposed the Irish people in their struggle for liberty." A formal resolution of denunciation carried the day. As one Land Leaguer put it in a statement reflecting both the deeply rooted republicanism and the growing anticlericalism of the Denver organization, "it was not for kings or priests to dictate to the Land League."[51]

There were limits to the Land League's radicalism however. These limits reflected the fact that, although it played an important role in Denver's working-class community, the branch was led by members of the city's Irish American middle class. By the 1880s, this middle class was a force to be reckoned with. To be sure, in the earlier years of the town, Irish immigrants had been overwhelmingly poor, the men heavily concentrated in unskilled jobs. In 1870, for example, over half of Denver's 143 Irish-born adult males worked as common laborers. Only 7 of these men had accumulated real estate or personal property of $4,000 or more. In the wake of the Leadville mining boom, however, the situation changed dramatically. Denver's rapid growth in the late 1870s and early 1880s provided opportunities for occupational mobility not present in more settled eastern cities. Thus, the occupational structure of the city's Irish American population exhibited increasing diversity. By 1890, nearly 30 percent of Irish-born males in the work force held occupations in the skilled trades, a figure roughly comparable to that for the native-born. Even more important was the emergence of an Irish American middle class. Nearly 15 percent of the Irish-born in Denver's work force occupied positions in business, the professions, or white-collar jobs in 1890.[52]

It was members of the growing Irish American middle class, not Irish American workers, who dominated the leadership ranks of Denver's Land League branch. Its nine officers in 1882 included a land agent, a hotel proprietor, a lawyer, a clerk and Colorado's wealthiest Irish immigrant, flour mill owner John K. Mullen, who served as the league's treasurer. The only manual worker among the traceable officers, a teamster named Michael Ivory, served as sergeant-at-arms. This was a fairly common pattern in larger cities, as opposed to mill towns and mining communities, where workers tended to dominate the league. Thus middle- and upper-class Irish Americans also took the lead in Land League branches in St. Louis, Philadelphia, and Pittsburgh.[53]

Why were middle-class Irish men and women attracted to the Land League? Many were undoubtedly motivated by a deep attachment to what the *Rocky Mountain Celt* called "the old land" and for the preindustrial world they had left behind—as the ancient race summed up in the name of this newspaper indicates. Their nationalism was related to their sense of being "exiles," a theme that Kerby Miller has persuasively placed at the center of Irish American culture in this era. While earlier nationalist organizations like the Fenians and the Clan an Gael had also drawn on this sense of exile, these organizations advocated violent routes to Irish independence that repelled those Irish Americans seeking respectability and acceptance within the American middle class. The nationalism of the Land League, on the other hand, while adding land reform to the call for independence, broke sharply with Fenian and Clan na Gael violence. Moreover, the league's most famous leader, Parnell, was an eminently respectable Protestant landlord, revered by many shapers of American middle-class opinion. Thus, through the Land League, Denver's middle-class Irish Americans could rally to a deeply felt cause without facing ridicule as dynamiters or criminals.[54]

Not surprisingly, given the social composition of its leadership, Denver's branch expressed little sympathy with Patrick Ford's radical producer ideology. Explicitly rejecting Ford's efforts to draw parallels between social conditions in the United States and Ireland, the Denver organization was much more impressed with the contrasts. Denver Land Leaguers applauded, for example, when a speaker argued that unlike "feudal" Ireland, "America is the hope of every enslaved nation, a land of promise in which the ark of freedom shall securely and forever rest." As Robert Morris, president of the Denver organization, stated forcefully, "the Land League was not a revolutionary organization."[55]

This stance was reflected in the hostility expressed by the Land League's leaders toward the labor movement. The epitome of what contemporaries called the "self-made man," Land League treasurer John K. Mullen had little sympathy with those seeking sweeping social reform and over the years he had numerous disputes with unions among his employees. C. E. McSheehy, an important figure in the Irish movement and the editor of the *Celt*, used the editorial columns of his paper for a running attack on trade unionism and the Knights of Labor. Connections with the most antilabor sector of Denver's elite were cemented by the liberal contributions to the Land League treasury by Colorado's Republican governor, Frederick Pitkin. Pitkin had called out the state militia to crush the Leadville miners strike in 1880.[56]

Pitkin's association with the Land League also illustrates the role of party politics in its development. Throughout the early 1880s, the Denver League maintained a close relationship with Colorado's dominant Republican party. This relationship was furthered by the arrival of Michael Boland in the city in August 1883. Boland, along with Chicago's Alexander Sullivan and D. C. Feeley of Rochester, formed the Clan na Gael's so-called Chicago Triangle, which would soon attain notoriety for financing a dynamiting campaign in England. According to the Irish nationalist John Devoy, the Triangle also sought to turn the Irish nationalist movement into "an American political machine to secure jobs" for Irish Americans within the Republican party. Whether or not one accepts Devoy's characterization of Boland as "a crooked lawyer who fleeced his clients in Louisville and had to get out because no one there would trust him," his analysis of the latter's political inclinations was on the mark. One month after his arrival in Denver, Boland and Judge John W. Mullahey, an officer of the Land League, organized an Irish American Republican club to orchestrate support for the party within the Irish American community.[57]

The basis for this strategy had actually been worked out earlier, in the Denver municipal election of 1881. Robert Morris, president of the Land League, ran for mayor of the city on the Republican ticket and won the election. Although he had been born in Ireland, Morris was both a well-to-do businessman and a Protestant; nevertheless, his candidacy drew wide support among Denver's Irish Catholic workers. Despite their traditional allegiance to the Democratic party, an estimated four-fifths of Irish voters supported Morris, according to the *Rocky Mountain News*, "because of his relations to the various national organizations of his countrymen." Middle-class leaders of the Land League were delighted with the election returns. Immediately after the election, John K. Mullen praised Morris and the Land League for "creating a bond of sympathy which has united Irishmen as they have never been before."[58]

But for all of its antilabor sentiments and Republican party connections, the radicalism of the Land League was far from a sham. And, because of its importance in Denver's working-class community as a whole, the Land League's openness regarding women's participation, its attempt to put aside the traditional animosity between Catholics and Protestants, and its growing independence from the Catholic hierarchy established an ideological legacy of tremendous importance for the city's working-class movement, the Knights of Labor in particular. In 1883, for example, Joseph Buchanan began calling for the organization of Denver working women into the Knights, thus breaking decisively with the notion of the labor movement as the special preserve of highly skilled males. In support of his position, he quoted Henry George to the effect that "in the Irish Land League cause the best men were the women, and . . . they would prove to be in every emancipatory cause, if they were given the opportunity."[59]

Buchanan's weekly, the *Labor Enquirer,* also built upon the Land League's efforts to overcome religious differences among Denver's working people. Although the columns of the newspaper were strongly influenced by the rhetoric of Protestant perfectionism, it showed none of the anti-Catholicism characteristic of reformers like Caroline Churchill. Indeed, Buchanan praised Catholic organizations, like the St. Elizabeth's charity society, whose members, he held, had "done much for the unfortunate of this city and are unostentatious." Individual priests also won his praise on occasion.[60]

But if Denver's labor activists treated individual priests with sympathy, they shared with the Land Leaguers an antipathy toward the meddling of the Catholic hierarchy in the affairs of their movement. They found that the Land League had effectively prepared the way. When Bishop Gilmour turned his attacks from the Ladies Land League to the Knights of Labor in the mid-1880s, Denver labor leaders could respond forcefully without fear of alienating their large Irish Catholic following. Burnette G. Haskell, who took over the editorship of the *Labor Enquirer* in 1887, went so far as to proclaim that the Catholic hierarchy in the United States had become "part of the machinery of oppression" and so naturally opposed the Knights. This extreme point of view was probably not shared by Denver's Irish Catholic Knights as a whole but, in Buchanan's view, "most of these hold the opinion that the Church has no right to interfere in the matter."[61]

Obviously, Denver's labor activists could not abide by the Land League's connections with the Republicans or its antilabor stance. The *Labor Enquirer* played an essential role in criticizing these aspects of the league. Yet even as it did so, the paper reflected the influence of Irish nationalism. Although he was himself an old-stock American and had been raised as a Protestant, Buchanan followed the Irish land struggle closely. This was true of a great many non-Irish labor activists across the nation—especially those influenced by the single-tax theorist Henry George. George had thrown himself into the work of the Davitt-Ford wing of the Land League, publishing an influential pamphlet on *The Irish Land Question* in 1880 and sending a series of widely read dispatches from Ireland to the *Irish World* in 1881 and 1882. Following George's lead, Buchanan proclaimed that "the downtrodden people of Ireland" had been subjected to wrongs which entitle them to the sympathy of every man and woman in the world, of whatever nationality or belief." The columns of his paper were filled with news of both the Denver and the national Land Leagues and with the progress of the struggle in Ireland itself. By mid-1883, it was a rare Denver gathering for the Irish cause that did not find Buchanan in a prominent place in the hall.[62]

Yet it was Buchanan who led the initial attack on Denver's middle-class Land League leaders. Throughout the 1880s, the editor sought to construct an independent "anti-monopoly" political movement in Colorado. This led him to denounce the Republican machinations of the Land League—particularly those of Judge Mullahey, whose "disgraceful conduct should be a lesson to the working men and should teach them that it is best not to be swayed by feelings of compassion and personal friendship when selecting men for positions of prominence and responsibility."

When Mullahey and Boland organized the Irish American Republican Club, Buchanan warned "all workingmen, and particularly the sons of Erin" to beware; as for himself, he was "sick and tired of party 'clubs.' "[63]

The challenge to Denver's Irish political leaders was extended to the Irish press as well. In 1883, Buchanan began a series of diatribes against the "hypocrisy" of the *Rocky Mountain Celt*. While denying any personal animosity toward its editor, he sought "to call attention of the patriotic printed-in-green advocate of the oppressed poor that its policy of crying out against existing wrongs and urging their overthrow [in Ireland] don't jibe very well with the long and prevaricating tirades upon trade unionists." In Buchanan's view, "the editor of the *Celt* knows about as much of what are labor's rights as he does of the 'make up' of a newspaper."[64]

Reflecting the influence Irish nationalism had on him, Buchanan counterposed Patrick Ford's radical producer ideology to that of Denver's Irish American middle class. Throughout 1883, excerpts from Ford's *Irish World* appeared in every issue of the *Enquirer* and the paper was made available to Denver's working people in a reading room that Buchanan maintained in his editorial offices. But an even more effective criticism of the Land League's middle-class leaders was offered by the Irish-born Joseph Murray, a local labor activist of equal stature to Buchanan. "Plain and substantial in his language, as well as in his apparel and his life," Murray provided Buchanan with an indispensable ally. And, even more clearly than Buchanan, he demonstrated the influence of Irish nationalism on the ideology of the Knights of Labor.[65]

Murray had lived a life worlds apart from the lawyers, politicians and businessmen who dominated Denver's Land League. Born in poverty near Dublin in 1843, he emigrated to Manchester with his family, where he labored in the mills and acquired an education in a night school for workers. As a youth, Murray became active in the Irish nationalist movement in Manchester. But he also became a corresponding member of Garibaldi's *Carbonari* and in 1859 left Manchester to fight with the Redshirts for Italian independence. He returned to England in 1860, but in the following year was commissioned as a officer in Thomas Francis Meagher's 69th New York regiment, the so-called Irish Brigade. Like other Irish nationalists who migrated to the U. S. to fight for the Union Army, Murray sought to defend republican principles in America, while simultaneously preparing his countrymen in arms for the coming battle to establish an Irish republic.[66]

After the war, Murray moved to New York, where he worked as a bookkeeper, married, and joined the city's Fenian movement. But his social views took a new turn in the late 1860s. He became a follower of Horace Greeley, attracted by the editor's belief in organized cooperation as "the application of Republican principles to Labor, and the appointed means of reducing laboring classes from dependence, prodigality and need." In 1870, Murray took up farming in Colorado, as a founding member of the Union Colony at Greeley (and one of its few Irish Americans). Although the Greeley colony was never a full-fledged cooperative enterprise, and although Murray himself moved to nearby Fort Collins in 1873, his experience there had a tremendous impact on him. Temperance, which was a founding principle of the colony (the town of Greeley remained "dry" until 1969), became one of Murray's deepest commitments. The colony's successful cooperative efforts in the area of irrigation led Murray to a belief in the potential benefits of larger-scale cooperative enterprises that he took with him into the Knights of Labor and the Farmers Alliance. The intensive direct democracy practiced at Greeley, revolving around mass meetings, lyceums, and farmers clubs, strengthened Murray's democratic commitments and gave him considerable experience in public speaking. Finally, intellectual exchange with other colonists, among whom were included ex-Chartists, abolitionists, free thinkers and financial radicals—providing, in short, a hothouse of reform ideas—led Murray to take his thinking on social questions in even more radical directions.[67]

As his thinking developed, Murray began to play an active role in the labor and political reform movements that were growing in Colorado in the late 1870s and early 1880s. In 1878, along with many others in Greeley and Fort Collins, he left the Republican party to join the Greenbackers, standing for Congress on the Greenback ticket two years later. By 1881 he was active in the Knights of Labor, working as an organizer for District Assembly No. 43, which at the time embraced all of Colorado. Still at heart a republican—Murray was "opposed to kings, queens, landlords and all their supporters"—he now regarded working-class organization and struggle as essential to fulfilling the republican vision.[68]

Murray's life history illustrates two important points. First, his political career reveals a gradual shift from middle class republicanism to a working-class version of that ideology, the turning point coming in his 1878 decision to leave the Republican party. Second, though, there was an important element of consistency in Murray's career. "A soldier of liberty on the battlefields of two continents," as one admirer put it, Murray was never a narrow Irish nationalist, but rather a fighter for national self-determination as an international principle. Murray's commitment, like Patrick Ford's, was to a *global* vision of "human liberty."[69]

An event at Denver's Tabor Opera House in the winter of 1883 illustrates both strands of Murray's political outlook and serves as a measure of his growing influence among the city's Irish-American workers. The house was packed for a speech by Thomas Brennan, an important figure in the Irish movement, who was received with enthusiasm by the audience. At the conclusion of Brennan's speech, however, "a unanimous cry" went up for a response by Murray, who had been discovered in the dress circle. As the *Labor Enquirer* reported it, Murray disagreed with Brennan "that the struggle in Ireland is one of race," arguing instead that "it is a class war." As Murray saw it, "it was not only the poor of Ireland who were suffering from the tyranny of despotic and capitalist rule but that the poor of all countries were enslaved thereby; and that the cry would soon be—is now in fact—for the equality of all mankind." About half the audience followed the example of a number of the league's officers on stage ("specialistic liberators," Buchanan called them) in walking out of the hall, while those who remained broke into loud applause.[70]

Less than five months after the Tabor Opera House incident, the Union Pacific shop workers went on strike, triggering a labor upsurge that spread quickly through the city. The Knights of Labor were the main beneficiaries of this upsurge. They grew from two assemblies with less than two hundred members in 1883 to thirteen assemblies representing nearly twenty-five hundred members in 1885. In 1888, Cornelius J. Driscoll, deputy commissioner of the new Colorado Bureau of Labor Statistics, put forward an explanation for this impressive growth. Denver's workers, he observed, "perceiving the benefits derived from organized efforts on the part of the Union Pacific employees, began to unite, and assemblies of the Knights of Labor sprang rapidly into existence." Although statistics are lacking, evidence points toward the widespread participation of Irish American workers in the Knights. Indeed the Irish American Driscoll had himself been active in the order before his appointment as deputy labor commissioner.[71]

Changing economic conditions played a major role in what John B. Lennon called the "awakening" of 1884–85. As the economy turned downward in these years, Denver employers attempted to cut their labor costs by slashing the wages of their workers. These attacks on their living standards, however, prompted resistance and organization among Denver's working people.

But while economic conditions can explain the context of working-class militancy, they can explain neither the form that militancy took nor the ideology that underlay it. The form was set by the example of the Union Pacific shop workers, whose new organization, Knights of Labor District Assembly No. 82, included both skilled and unskilled workers and embraced Germans, Irish, and old-stock Americans. The ideology revolved around antimonopoly ideas and the powerful idea of the producing classes.

From where had such practices and ideas come? The early craft unions and the ethnic associations had laid some foundations, for both encouraged a growing sense of mutuality among Denver's working people. But neither form of organization led to the broad working-class solidarity and antimonopoly ideology that the Denver Knights of Labor would uphold during the middle years of the 1880s. It was, rather, the Denver Land League and Irish nationalism generally that prepared the way for the Knights.

When Henry George observed that "the Irish land question has educated a class of our people who might not for years have been reached by any other influence," he was referring to the growing working-class support for the single tax. But for Denver, his point could be couched in broader terms. The process, as we have seen, was complex and contradictory: working-class activists enthusiastically embraced some ideas put forward by Denver's middle-class Irish nationalists while criticizing others. Nevertheless, for all its complexity, the "Irish land question" was central to the ideological origins and character of the Great Upheaval in Denver.[72]

3 The Knights of Labor and the Fight against the Saloon, 1884–86

The autumn of 1886 saw a political upheaval in the ranks of the American labor movement. Spearheaded by Henry George's mayoral campaign in New York and drawing on the increasing strength of the Knights of Labor, independent working-class parties sprang up in towns and cities across the nation, raising a massive challenge to local political elites everywhere. Denver experienced this political upheaval but with a significant difference. Here, a number of key labor activists mounted their challenge not through a labor party, but rather through an alliance with Colorado's two-year-old Prohibition party. Joseph Buchanan, now not only Denver's most visible labor agitator, but also a national leader of the Knights, gave full support to the Prohibition crusade and Joe Murray, the state's preeminent Irish labor radical, stood as the party's candidate for Congress. "I am a Socialist myself," Murray declared during the campaign, "and think more of my standing as a Knight of Labor than anything else." But as Murray saw things, prohibition was essential because "it was necessary to get men sober before he could awaken them to the greatness of the labor and industrial question."[1]

The existence of temperance sentiments among groups of workers in the nineteenth century, and within the Knights of Labor's leadership in particular, is now well known. Such sentiments, however, are often seen as emerging solely from an ideology revolving around moral uplift and self-help. This ideology, without question, played a role in the support that Buchanan and Murray gave to the Prohibition party. But other concerns predominated. They sought, above all, to undermine the influence of the urban saloon, an institution they believed hindered the growth of a unified labor movement and served as a key social base for a corrupt and antilabor political machine. Their efforts to stamp out the saloon were also part and parcel of the labor movement's efforts to build a movement culture within which Denver's organized workers could fulfill their needs for companionship, recreation, and education. Such a movement culture, labor leaders believed, would help cultivate and strengthen working-class solidarity. An examination of the Prohibition campaign thus provides a window on the emerging working-class movement, particularly the Knights of Labor.[2]

Yet the 1886 campaign proved to be a dismal failure. Not only did the main body of the city's labor movement—including the rank and file of the Knights of Labor—refuse to support the Prohibition party, but the campaign itself greatly exacerbated emerging tensions within the movement. Most organized workers rallied around the leadership of John B. Lennon, a key figure in both the Knights and the trade union movement, who advocated support for Colorado's Democratic party in the election of 1886. The Democratic-labor connection would gradually evolve over the next two decades, emerging as the dominant strain in Denver labor politics by the early twentieth century. The fight over Prohibition thus illustrates the limits of the Knights' efforts to reshape working-class life. Nonetheless, the effort to construct a movement culture was far from over. It would go on to play a central role in early twentieth-century labor radicalism.

The Knights of Labor

Between the spring of 1884 and the autumn of 1886 a labor movement of impressive dimensions emerged in Denver. With the Union Pacific shop workers providing the example, the Knights of Labor grew rapidly, climbing from two assemblies with 180 members in 1883 to thirteen assemblies with 2,447 members in 1885. Though figures are not available, accounts indicate that the order added even more members in 1886. Trade unionism also saw significant growth in these years, with the number of local unions climbing from seven to thirteen. The election of Buchanan to the General Executive Board of the Knights in 1884, and of Lennon as president of the Journeymen Tailors National Union in the same year, gave Denver a new visibility in national labor circles. No longer hanging on to a tenuous existence in a handful of highly skilled trades, Denver's labor movement had come of age.

The Knights of Labor's early existence in Denver had been precarious, giving little hint of the rapid growth that was to follow. In October 1880, the city boasted two local assemblies of the order with a combined membership of 89, but by the end of 1881, one of these assemblies had collapsed and membership in the other, Local Assembly 1424, had fallen to 33. The Knights' policy of extreme secrecy in these years—not even the name of the order was allowed to be spoken—may have hurt it. In 1881, the General Assembly of the Order shelved its secrecy policy, and the Denver Knights began to pick up strength. Eight months later, membership in L.A. 1424 had climbed back to 60, and the addition of L.A. 2327 in November 1882 enabled the city's Knights to count 180 members by July 1883. But withdrawals and a large number of suspensions for nonpayment of dues led to a decline in the membership in these two assemblies to 154 over the next twelve months. In late 1883, Terence V. Powderly, the Grand Master Workman of the Knights, complained that "we bring men into the Order to educate them [but] they do not remain with us. They go almost as fast as they come." His observation applied perfectly to Denver.[3]

Despite the turnover in membership, the existence of these two local assemblies established the base upon which the Knights would build. L.A. 1424, the Montgomery Benevolent Assembly, would be the longest-lived Knights of Labor organization in Denver, remaining in existence until 1894. Equally important was L.A. 2327. Dubbed the Union Assembly, because all of its charter members were also members of various trade unions, it included Buchanan and the journeymen tailors' leader, Lennon, among its founders. Buchanan's *Labor Enquirer* also championed the principles of the Knights throughout 1883 and the first half of 1884. Though the weekly paper did not attract much of a readership in its first eighteen months, it would play a central role in the Denver Knights of Labor in the mid-1880s. Like the founding of the two local assemblies, the birth of the *Enquirer* helped establish the institutional framework for the later growth of the Knights.[4]

Rapid growth of the Denver Knights began in the wake of the Union Pacific railroad strikes of May and August 1884. The May strike was a classic example of the spontaneity that characterized many strikes of the early 1880s. Faced with falling traffic, an increase in competition, and a drying up of new investment, the Union Pacific Railroad experienced a crisis of profitability in 1884. Gross earnings fell by 15 percent and dividend payments ended. In an effort to improve the company's position, the UP's managers decided to cut labor costs and strategically targeted unorganized shop workers, rather than the unionized engineers and firemen, to bear the brunt of the cuts. The fact that Union Pacific shop workers made higher wages, averaging $2.25 a day in Denver, than shop workers on other western roads also induced management to cut the pay of these workers. When they came to work on 1 May 1884, Denver's UP shop workers, along with those in the company's shops throughout the West, found notices announcing wage reductions of from 10 to 15 percent.[5]

But the UP's managers had badly misjudged the mood of these workers. Paradoxically, the railroad's high wages, far from making the men content, had helped give them a sense of independence and an ability to survive at least short periods of unemployment that spurred their re-sistance. Not only the severity of the cut, but also the absence of any advance announcement of its implementation angered the workers, for this flew directly in the face of their sense of independence. After working a few minutes, one machinist put down his tools, saying he would quit before accepting a cut like this on such short notice. Other men in the machine shop gathered around him and word quickly spread through the shops that the machinists had struck. Within an hour, the entire work force of four hundred machinists, yard hands, and freight dock workers had quit work. They called a mass meeting to plan their next step. By the afternoon another two hundred workers in the shops of the UP's South Park Division had joined the strike, marching in a body through down-town Denver to join the men who were meeting in a Larimer Street hall.[6]

Although strike meetings, according to Buchanan, were marked by "radicalism, denunciation of employers, threats, and incendiarism," the workers showed impressive discipline and a determination to avoid vio-lence. Strikers asked yard watchmen to remain on duty to guard company property and even offered to pay them for the extra work. They also kept in check those within their ranks who called for "bashing" scabs' heads.[7]

As in other industrial conflicts of this era, the shop workers rapidly created organizational forms to coordinate the strike. On its first day, they selected representatives from the various departments, who then called Buchanan in to advise them; held a large meeting where they passed and signed resolutions refusing to return to work until the reduc-tions were withdrawn; and formed committees to take charge of picketing and various other tasks. On the second day, while the strike spread along the UP lines in Kansas, Nebraska, Wyoming, and throughout Colorado, the Denver shop workers formed the Union Pacific Employees Protective Association of Denver. But before things could move much further than this, the strike was over. As soon it began to spread across the system, Union Pacific second vice president Silas H. H. Clark in Omaha wired president Sidney Dillon for direction. Receiving no reply, Clark rescinded the cut on his own. By 4 May, the Union Pacific shopmen were back at work.[8]

For the shop workers, though, the quick victory raised more ques-tions than it answered. Some of them now opposed the creation of a permanent organization. The independence and high wages that had con-tributed to their militancy now proved an obstacle to organization, as did their quick success. According to Buchanan, these workers argued that "they had gotten along all right without organization before the cut, and had shown that it was a simple matter to secure united action when nec-essary." Continuing to see matters through the prism of the boom years of

1878–83, they did not believe that a radically changed economic situation would lead the railroads to attempt again and again to cut labor costs.[9]

Other shop workers, however, had had experiences that led them to the opposite point of view. Thomas Neasham, a forty-three-year-old boiler maker, had been a trade unionist and cooperative organizer in the north of England, emigrating to the United States in 1880 only after being blacklisted for union activities in his native country. Neasham, machinist Julius N. Corbin and several others argued the necessity for permanent organization not only in the Denver shops but, if possible, all along the Union Pacific lines. Only this kind of thorough organization, they believed, would prevent further efforts of the railroad management to reduce their wages.[10]

In the end, their arguments proved persuasive. On 6 May, Denver's Union Pacific shop workers founded Knights of Labor Local Assembly 3218 and organizers were dispatched to other towns on the UP line. Within a month, assemblies had been formed in a large number of towns. In June and July, E. P. McPhilomy, a Denver Knights of Labor organizer, traveled along the line, organizing nine local assemblies in railroad towns across Idaho, Utah, and Wyoming. Buchanan, who was commissioned as an organizer for the Knights of Labor in the aftermath of the strike, helped organize assemblies in Omaha and a number of other shop towns in Nebraska. In February 1885, all of these local assemblies were consolidated as Knights of Labor District Assembly No. 82, the Union Pacific Employees Association.[11]

The Union Pacific shop workers chose the Knights as their organizational vehicle partly because of the absence of alternatives. The Machinists and Blacksmiths Union, which had once represented Union Pacific shop workers, and craft unions of boiler makers and molders had all collapsed by the time of the strike. The railroad brotherhoods were uninterested in organizing shop workers and opposed their militancy. The Knights, on the other hand, though still small, were decentralized, flexible and had the potential to organize broad community support behind railroad workers. They seemed to be on the move. The fact that the respected Buchanan was associated with the order was significant for the shop workers as well. Finally, the Knights' slogan, "an injury to one is the concern of all," suggested a strategy far more effective than that provided by the narrow and exclusive railroad brotherhoods. The Knights, in sum, seemed to offer protection to a group of workers increasingly aware that their position was endangered by the power of the large railroad corporation.[12]

The wisdom of this organizational strategy was put to the test in August. In the wake of the May strike, reports surfaced that the Union

Pacific management (along with that of the Denver and Rio Grande) was planning to institute gradual reductions on a department-by-department basis. On 11 August the company announced a 10 percent wage cut for fifteen machinists in Ellis, Kansas, and in Denver fired twenty men, all of them active in the May strike and several of them union leaders. Though railroad officials maintained that these actions reflected only economic necessity, members of L.A. 3218 were convinced that the firings marked an effort to destroy their new organization. They called a strike for 13 August along the entire line.[13]

Again caught off guard and now under the new management of Charles Francis Adams, the Union Pacific ended up not only retracting the wage cut and reinstating the Denver workers, but making a number of other concessions as well. It agreed that no members of the union were to be discriminated against and that no other changes in wages or the size of the work force would be made unless the executive board of the union was notified and then only after collective bargaining. If negotiations failed to produce a settlement then the dispute was to be submitted to binding arbitration. "The successful termination of this affair is one of the greatest victories ever achieved by organized labor," Buchanan proclaimed, "and it will go far toward awakening the sleepy heads on other Western railroads." While he may have overstated the case a bit, it did launch the Union Pacific Employees Association on a decade-long career as the most powerful industrial union of railroad workers before the American Railway Union. It also indicated the way in which wage struggles in these years could quickly escalate to become struggles over issues of managerial authority and workers' control.[14]

The two successful strikes triggered a rapid growth in the Knights of Labor among workers in Denver. By the time of the Philadelphia General Assembly of the order in September 1884, there were four local assemblies of the Knights in the city, with a combined membership of over five hundred. Buchanan represented these assemblies at Philadelphia and, partly because of his reputation as a successful strike leader, was elected to the five-member General Executive Board of the order. Buchanan's election not only added to his own emerging stature as a national labor leader, but also increased the visibility of the Knights in Denver and throughout the Rocky Mountain region. By the end of 1885, there were thirteen assemblies of the Knights of Labor in Denver, embracing nearly twenty-five hundred workers. Although nearly half of these were railroad shopmen at the Union Pacific and Denver and Rio Grande shops, the Knights also embraced trade assemblies of clerks, building trades workers, leather workers, and a number of mixed assemblies representing a wide variety of occupational groups in the city.[15]

Though overshadowed by the dramatic rise of the Knights, trade unions also experienced significant growth in these years. In addition to the railroad brotherhoods, there were thirteen unions in Denver by the end of 1886. Members of the building trades led the way in new organizing, with carpenters, bricklayers, plasterers, and granite stonecutters all organizing new unions in the years between 1884 and 1886, but other groups of workers, such as cigar makers and horseshoers, established unions as well. Meanwhile, union locals that had already been established in Denver continued to grow. By August 1885, for example, despite having to accept a slight wage reduction throughout the city and then fight a lockout in four establishments against further reductions, the Journeymen Tailors Union claimed seventy-two members, making it the sixth largest local in its national union. The reelection of the Denver tailor John B. Lennon as a national officer in 1885 indicated the local's continuing importance.[16]

Close connections existed between the unions and the Knights in this period. The Knights' Union Assembly had been founded entirely by trade unionists. Trade union leaders like the tailors' John B. Lennon and the printers' O. L. ("Yank") Smith worked actively for the order in Denver, and Buchanan later argued that "the phenomenal growth of the Knights of Labor, which culminated in 1886, was in great measure due to the affiliation of trained, able, and active trades-unionists, which began in 1882." On the other side of the equation, by the end of 1884, four Knights local assemblies had affiliated with the Denver Trades Assembly. To be sure, there was never total harmony within the movement. Thus in December 1884, L.A. 3218, the UP shop workers' assembly, withdrew from the Trades Assembly, alleging that "certain members of the assembly were acting in a manner calculated to injure the cause of labor." But at this date such conflict was rare. The combination of organizational growth and effective unity among different organizations was impressive.[17]

Labor's unity and strength was symbolized by a large demonstration held on Washington's Birthday, 22 February 1885. Despite the snow that fell through the afternoon, the workers' gathering, beginning with what the *Denver Tribune-Republican* called "one of the most imposing and respectable parades that ever moved through the streets of Denver," attracted over four thousand men and women, representing Knights of Labor assemblies, trade unions, and railroad brotherhoods. Although called by the Trades Assembly to lobby the state legislature for a variety of labor bills, the demonstration's main effect was to increase the visibility of the labor movement generally and the Knights of Labor in particular. "The labor movement was in the public eye of Denver," Buchanan later recalled, "and the situation was ideal for the labor agitator."[18]

The demonstration proved to be extremely beneficial for the Knights. There had been eight assemblies in Denver at the time of the parade.

In the next two weeks, four new ones came into existence, bringing the total to twelve. This was a period in which the Knights of Labor were growing throughout the country. Nonetheless, the rapid local growth of the organization was unusually impressive. According to Buchanan, at the order's national headquarters Colorado was being referred to as the Knights' "banner state" in the early months of 1885. Denver workers were full participants in the surging labor movement growth of the mid-1880s known as the Great Upheaval.[19]

As the term implies, the labor movement's growth was punctuated by conflict in these years. Denver proved no exception. The twelve months following the Union Pacific workers' second victory in August 1884 witnessed not only the organization of trade unions and Knights of Labor local assemblies, but also a wave of strikes. Eight strikes occurred in the city in this period, more than in the entire previous four years. Five of these, all ordered by unions, successfully fought employers' efforts either to cut pay or increase working hours. Although economic conditions did not permit offensive industrial action at this point, the clear success of union-called strikes in resisting wage cuts and a lengthening of the working day added to the growing prestige of the labor movement.[20]

An important exception to this pattern, however, was the long and bitter strike of shop workers on the Denver and Rio Grande Railroad, which began in May 1885 and ended in a major defeat for the workers. The immediate cause of the strike was management's dismissal of ten members of the Knights, who, following the UP workers' example, had organized a local assembly of the order in the railroad's shops. Underlying the conflict was a demand for an increase in wages, increasingly common among Denver workers by the spring of 1885.[21]

The shop workers, however, were unprepared for the determination of the D&RG management to resist their demands. Since the railroad was in receivership and Judge Moses Hallet of the U.S. District Court had already ruled in the receiver's favor, federal marshalls were called in to arrest strikers. Some of the strikers, charged with having "interfered with the receiver in the management of the railway property," were given sentences of up to six months by Judge David Brewer, who also gave them a short lecture on the benevolent laws of supply and demand. The D&RG attempted early on to open the shops, employing strikebreakers with police protection. This move, though, provoked considerable violence, with the wives of strikers taking the lead in attacks on scabs.[22]

By midsummer, the railroad had made some headway in recruiting strikebreakers: in August, sixty-four members of L.A. 3217 were expelled from the Knights of Labor "for scabbing in the D&RG shops while members of the assembly were on strike." As the hopes of victory faded, the level of violence increased on both sides of the dispute. Several explosions occurred during the summer, resulting in the destruction of several locomotives and some track. These "outrages" were blamed on the Knights of Labor—and Joseph Buchanan in particular—and were followed by the formation of a "vigilance committee" of local businessmen which threatened a resort to lynch law. Although never called out, the Colorado National Guard remained in a state of readiness until late summer, when L.A. 3217 finally admitted defeat.[23]

The strike's outcome was a major blow to the Denver labor movement and caused considerable hardship to the strikers, many of whom were blacklisted, unable to get work on any railroad again. The tragedy of their defeat was highlighted by a letter from a railroad telegrapher in San Francisco, blacklisted after walking out in support of the Denver and Rio Grande shopmen, to Terence V. Powderly, Grand Master Workman of the Knights:

> I have tried to get employment at my profession but every where I am blacklisted and can not get it. I am 42 years old, been at the business of telegraph operator since I was 14 and am good for nothing else. In Denver I had a house built by a Building Association, was paying so much a month for it but getting out of employment I was unable to meet the monthly dues and in consequence have lost it. My two little girls 11 and 8 years of age are in the House of the Good Shepherd being taken care of by the good sisters until I can do something for them, my little boy 10 years is getting his food for what he can do in a restaurant and my wife when I last heard from her was in the Sisters Hospital sick. All in Denver and myself here a homeless wanderer.[24]

Knights of Labor believed that an economic and social order that could do this to a family was fundamentally immoral. And questions of morality and immorality were central to the rise of the Knights. Although they stood at the center of a number of large industrial conflicts and sometimes constructed powerful workplace-based protective organizations like the Union Pacific Employees Association, the Knights of Labor always had larger goals. Much of what they sought can be summed up by the term *morality*. At one level, the Knights sought to infuse American industrial capitalism with a new morality through structural measures such as land and currency reform and the establishment of producer cooperatives. At another level, they sought to bring a new morality to working-class life by "uplifting" workers through education and temperance. These two levels of social change were always linked in the Knights' social vision. "I believe that every man should be free from the curse of slavery, whether that slavery appears in the shape of monopoly, usury or intemperance," intoned thousands of Knights throughout the country when they took the so-called Powderly Temperance Pledge in the mid-1880s.[25]

Cornelius J. Driscoll, a carpenter and KOL organizer in the D&RG shops who went on to become Colorado's first Deputy Commissioner of Labor, believed that the order's stated goal "to make industrial and moral worth, not wealth, the true standard of industrial and National greatness" accounted for its broad appeal among Denver's workers. But the Knights sought not only this long-term fundamental reordering of American values. They also sought to improve the concrete material and cultural conditions of American working people, "to secure to the workers," as the order's preamble put it, "the full enjoyment of the wealth they create, sufficient leisure in which to develop their intellectual, moral and social faculties; all of the benefits, recreation and pleasures of association; in a word, to enable them to share in the gains and honors of advancing civilization." These somewhat more concrete aims also accounted for their appeal.[26]

But by the mid-1880s, many Denver workers felt that the achievement of these goals had been threatened by the development of large-scale industrial capitalism. "Monopoly," the term Knights commonly used to sum up the vast economic changes that had taken place since the Civil War, had undermined the independence that significant numbers of white male workers in the North and West had once been able to attain through hard work and self-denial. As Joseph Buchanan put it in 1886: "Twenty years ago the mechanic could, by being industrious and economical, raise himself from the days-pay condition to a little business of his own; to-day the opportunity to start in his business for himself has been thrust from him by the greedy hand of the great manufacturers who make their wares by machinery with the help of labor organized on a colossal scale. . . . The man who can rise from the wage condition in these days must catch a windfall from his uncle or a bank unlocked."[27]

This view was a central one for many of those who joined the Knights of Labor in the 1880s. But even Buchanan's statement did not fully describe the extent of the problem for, as the Knights understood the world, the undermining of the independence of a virtuous citizenry threatened to undermine the American Republic itself, which they saw as resting on that independence. The corruption of the state by powerful capitalists, reflected in so-called class legislation favoring business interests, only increased the political threat. When Denver labor activists chose Washington's Birthday as the date for their 1885 demonstration, they testified to the influence of these ideas, which some historians have called labor republicanism. Many of the banners that Denver workers carried in the parade offer further evidence of this influence. Among the banners were those reading: "We Are Free-Born Men and Not Slaves"; "Justice to All—Partiality to None"; "Where Liberty Dwells our Country is Free"; "Equal Rights—Equal Burdens—Equal Privileges"; "We Do Not Ask Class Legislation—but Simply Fair Play"; and, in the most direct and powerful statement of the republican tradition, "Liberty, Equality, Fraternity."[28]

Yet another dimension of the Denver Knights was highlighted by the presence at the Washington's Birthday demonstration of Reverend Gilbert DeLaMatyr who, as Buchanan remembered years later, "softly and tenderly pleaded for the blessing of Almighty God upon the hosts of toilers who 'eat bread in the sweat of their faces.'" According to Buchanan, "a truly religious sentiment pervaded the entire assemblage." Indeed, the Denver Knights as a whole were pervaded by this "religious sentiment," which gave added moral force to their republican critique of American industrial capitalism.[29]

Almost everywhere the Knights were characterized by a religious orientation, an orientation that usually took a Protestant form despite the large numbers of Irish Catholic workers in the order. The Denver Knights went a step further than those in other communities by recruiting two of the city's most well known Protestant ministers into the order itself. DeLaMatyr was one of these ministers. Born in New York state in 1825, he had joined the Greenback party while a clergyman in Indianapolis and in 1878 had won election to the House of Representatives on the Greenback ticket. Between 1882 and 1887, he was the pastor of Denver's Methodist Episcopal Church, but despite the wealth of his congregation, Joseph Buchanan believed DeLaMatyr to be "a noble and a brave Christian man" and "an outspoken champion, in the pulpit and out of it, of the workingman." Buchanan even named his son Gilbert after him. He also went to great lengths to recruit DeLaMatyr to the Knights, reporting it triumphantly to Terence Powderly when he had successfully done so.[30]

Myron W. Reed, pastor of Denver's First Congregational Church, was another recruit. Reed had been born in Vermont in 1836, a descendant of seventeenth-century New England settlers. In the 1850s, after varied experience as a sailor, a farm laborer and a reporter, he applied to Horace Greeley for work and found a position with the New York Republican state central committee. Reed enlisted in the Union Army in the second year of the Civil War and ended the war as a captain. Only after the war did he decide upon a career in the clergy, graduating from the Chicago School of Theology in 1868. After several pastorates, including one in New Orleans, where he married a northern abolitionist school teacher, Reed came to Denver in 1884 to take charge of one the wealthiest congregations in the city, though he announced upon his arrival that his chief mission would be to plead the cause of the poor. A nationally known exponent of the social gospel, and later a self-proclaimed Christian Socialist, Reed sympathized with the Knights of Labor. Buchanan persuaded him to join L.A. 2327, the Union Assembly, in the second year of its existence.[31]

The membership of Protestant ministers in the Knights of Labor points to one of the most distinctive aspects of the order, its organizational expansiveness. Though in practice the Knights were overwhelmingly a working-class organization, the only occupational groups specifically excluded from membership in the Order were stockbrokers, lawyers, bankers, gamblers, and saloonkeepers. At least in theory, individuals in all other occupations were considered part of the producing classes. This broad conception of its membership brought to the order workers who had not previously participated in the labor movement. Denver store clerks, for example, formed a Knights' assembly, L.A. 3639, soon after the Washington's Birthday parade. Charles Machette, a clerk in a notion store making $9 a week, had been an early supporter of the Knights and in 1883 had sold his watch to make a much-needed $20 contribution to Buchanan's *Labor Enquirer*.[32]

The expansiveness of the order can be seen even more clearly in the welcome it offered to white working-class women, both wage earners and those the census takers listed as "at home." Over the course of the 1880s, Denver's female work force leapt from under two thousand to over eight thousand, representing a climb of from 10.7 to 15.4 percent of the total work force. Yet employment opportunities in Denver were extremely limited, with 59 percent of employed women in Denver laboring either as domestic servants or in the sweated clothing industry in 1890.[33]

Conditions were very hard in such occupations. The black, foreign-born, and second-generation immigrant women who constituted over three-quarters of Denver's female domestic workers in 1890 earned higher wages than many other women workers in the city. But they also worked up to fifteen hours a day, did a great deal of hard physical labor, such as attending furnaces and carrying coal, along with cooking, washing, and cleaning, and suffered social isolation and frequent affronts to their sense of dignity. Moreover, as one domestic worker explained, "no matter how bad we feel, so long as we can drag around at all, we must do the work set out for us or lose our place." In a perhaps even more difficult position were women clothing workers—dressmakers, shirtmakers and seamstresses—who worked on piece rate in their own homes or in shops run by large downtown stores. Having to pay not only room and board, but also up to $2.50 month for the rental of sewing machines, these women labored under what sympathetic contemporaries called "the starvation wage-plan."[34]

Responding both to these conditions and to the harsh existence suffered by many of Denver's working-class housewives, thirty-seven women organized Knights of Labor L.A. 3314, the Hope Assembly, in July 1884. By the time of the February 1885 demonstration, L.A. 3314 boasted over a hundred members. It did not act as a trade union, but was rather a mixed female assembly that drew members from a number of occupations as well as from the ranks of working-class wives. Led by Emma App, a clerical worker who later became a printer, the assembly sought to create institutions that would better the lives of the city's working-class women generally. In 1885 and 1886, it established a boarding house and an employment agency for the city's single women wage earners. Even more important, in the cooperative laundry and cooperative store it helped set up with other KOL assemblies, the Hope Assembly created institutions that responded directly to the needs of housewives, still the majority of working-class women.[35]

The Knights' concern with the needs of working-class women should not be confused with a belief in women's equality. In the 1885 parade, Hope Assembly members rode in twenty-four carriages provided by the city's male labor organizations under "the escort" of L.A. 1424, suggesting a firm belief in the importance of gender distinctions. On the other hand, women writers—both residents of Denver and those from other cities— were frequent contributors to the columns of the *Labor Enquirer*, indicating that the Knights had greater respect for women's intellectual abilities than did society at large. Joseph Buchanan's wife, Lucy Buchanan, took over the editorship of the paper for a while in 1887. And though the Denver Knights may not have endorsed full equality for women, they did support the vote. "Are you advocating female suffrage as a true Knight should?" asked John W. Hornby, a Denver Knight, writing in the order's national paper, the *Journal of United Labor*, in 1888.[36]

On the other hand, there was considerably less movement on the question of race. In endorsing an 1884 strike of southern Colorado coal miners who were, in part, protesting the employment of Italians and Mexican Americans in the mines, Buchanan's *Labor Enquirer* characterized both groups as "degraded," inevitably willing to work for low wages. The Denver Knights also continued to exhibit extreme anti-Chinese sentiments, supporting a so-called abatement campaign designed to remove Chinese immigrants from all western work sites by force. In the wake of the horrific 1885 massacre at Rock Springs, Wyoming, where white miners employed by the Union Pacific railroad killed twenty-eight Chinese laborers, Denver Knights' leader Thomas Neasham defended the miners whom he had earlier helped to organize in the order. The charge of UP officials that the Denver Knights had actually planned and instigated the massacre was unfounded. But the event, far from creating revulsion among Denver's Knights, instead heightened anti-Chinese feelings among organized workers in the city.[37]

Nevertheless, in some respects, the Denver Knights were influenced by the movement toward more egalitarian policies that the order was developing nationally. Thousands of African Americans in the South had organized KOL assemblies during the 1880s and, by the end of the decade, the order had become to a great extent an organization of black agricultural laborers in the region. This upswing of African American unionization affected race relations in Colorado. During the 1884 strike in the southern coal fields of the state, mine operators hired a number of black miners from the South, but when the African Americans realized they were being employed as strikebreakers, most of them quit. Though no data exist on black membership in the Denver Knights, Buchanan claimed that in the 1885 Washington's Birthday parade "there was no color line" and that "several" African American men marched. Though his conclusion from this fact that "the workingmen of the world are uniting" was an overstatement, black participation in the labor parade represented a significant departure from previous exclusionary practices.[38]

The rise of the Knights of Labor was thus an extremely dynamic feature of Denver life in the mid-1880s, altering a number of traditional practices and assumptions in the labor movement and drawing the attention of the press, the pulpit, and the middle class. The Knights also tried to alter important aspects of daily life for working-class people in the city. This dimension of the order can best be appreciated by examining the opposition of some of its key leaders to the urban saloon.

The Fight against the Saloon

When labor activists took on the saloon, they were challenging an institution with deep roots in working-class life. "The saloon exists in our town because it serves a want—a need," wrote a working man to the Denver-based *Miners' Magazine* in the early twentieth century. "It offers a common meeting place. It dispenses good cheer. It ministers to the craving for fellowship. To the exhausted, worn out body, to the strained nerves—the relaxation brings rest." As this writer indicated, the social functions of the urban saloon went far beyond the provision of alcohol. Denver's saloons provided a least three distinct services to their working-class customers: they offered food and lodging at reasonable prices, served as meetings halls for various ethnic and labor organizations, and provided a principal setting for male working-class recreation.[39]

Food and lodging assumed particular importance in the late 1870s and early 1880s, when the Leadville mining boom and the burst of Colorado railroad building turned the city into what a contemporary called "the temporary abiding place of multitudes of strangers and immigrants" bound for mines and grading camps. This floating population, overwhelmingly male, came to rely on the cluster of boardinghouse-saloons and small hotels near the city's Union Station. Providing inexpensive lodgings, these establishments also offered companionship and frequently a meal for the price of a nickel beer.[40]

The gradual emergence of stable immigrant communities added a new dimension to the saloon's functions. The immigrant clubs and benefit societies that proliferated in Denver over the course of the late 1870s and 1880s required meeting space and, as in other American cities, Denver saloons often provided that space. The Irish American Progressive Society, the Irish Fellowship Association, and the Ancient Order of Hibernians all held their meetings in the city's drinking establishments. Turner Hall, the meeting place of the *Turnverein*, was a major cultural center for the city's German community: in addition to a saloon, it housed exercise rooms, equipped through financial assistance from German-owned breweries, and, for a while, the largest lecture hall in the city. Not only benevolent and fraternal organizations, but also trade unions that drew their members from particular ethnic groups, gravitated to the immigrant saloon. The German bakers who organized a union in the early 1880s held their meetings at Turner Hall. The Amalgamated Society of Carpenters, composed of British craftsmen, held their weekly meetings at the Little Emma.[41]

The requirements of space naturally provided a major consideration in the choice of the saloon as a meeting hall. The typical Denver working-class family in these years resided in a three- to six-room, one-story house, hardly adequate for holding large meetings. Yet space was not the only consideration, for the great strength of the saloon lay in its ability to provide a meeting hall and meet the needs of recreation simultaneously. The significance of this third function of the urban saloon should not be underestimated. While fraternal societies did provide a focus for recreation, Denver workers also sought less demanding forms of leisure. And, as even city boosters had to admit, Denver was "sadly deficient in places of legitimate amusement" at the opening of the 1880s. Although increasingly excluded by ordinance from the new middle-class suburbs, and generally off-limits to women, the corner saloon in Denver's working-class neighborhoods served as a primary locus of male sociability.[42]

The last two decades of the nineteenth century saw the rapid development of new forms of recreation that constituted at least potential alternatives to the saloon. In 1883, the first professional baseball game was played in Denver and the popularity of the sport grew rapidly over the next twenty years. Also in 1883, the intra-urban Denver Circle Railroad constructed Jewell Park at the end of its line in an effort to attract Sunday fare-payers, thus initiating a trend that would culminate in Denver's two large "streetcar amusement parks" in the 1890s. The latter development was particularly important for it represented the movement of women and children into the world of public urban recreation.[43]

The saloon, however, was not ready to give up its place in urban life. During the 1880s, a new type of drinking establishment grew up alongside the neighborhood tavern and the immigrant saloon. Concentrated in the tenderloin district near the central business district, a group of larger saloons began to attract considerable numbers of working-class customers. In part their appeal stemmed from sheer display: Ed Chase's Palace Saloon was famous for the rows of silver dollars embedded in its floor and for its elaborately crafted bar. Equally important was the provision of musical and dramatic entertainment. The "concert halls" and variety theaters of Denver's tenderloin added a new dimension to patterns of urban leisure. It is not surprising, then, that the Denver saloon grew in importance during the 1880s. At the opening of the decade, there were 353 residents for each saloon; at its close, the figure had dropped to 334.[44]

The saloon, however, generated considerable opposition, particularly within Denver's middle class. The "Blue Ribbon" campaign of the late 1870s and the activities of the Woman's Christian Temperance Union and the Anti-Saloon League in the 1880s and 1890s represented major efforts on the part of middle-class reformers to alter the habits of working-class drinkers. Some of Denver's large employers, hoping to strengthen industrial discipline among their workers, gave support to these efforts. The Union Pacific Railroad, for example, had assisted the Young Men's Christian Association by establishing boarding houses and reading rooms as alternatives to the saloon for railroad workers along its lines. In the last two decades of the nineteenth century, the managers of both the Denver Tramway Company and the D&RG followed the UP's example by providing reading rooms at their Denver shops for workers whose punctuality and productivity, they feared, were threatened by nearby saloons. In their selection of books for such reading rooms, these companies also had the opportunity, as one historian has put it, "to indoctrinate readers with knowledge that bespoke management's problems, if not its high ideals."[45]

Even when they were not directly hostile to the labor movement, middle-class temperance advocates made few efforts to build alliances with Denver's labor movement. Disturbed by the growing social heterogeneity of the city and increasingly drawn to programs for the social control of the poor, organizations like the Colorado Woman's Christian Temperance Union seemed to find the labor movement as threatening as the immigrant saloon. Thus, although the WCTU established a department to consider "the relation of temperance to labor" in the late 1880s, the topic remained a low priority. In 1890, the department superintendent called for a joint WCTU—Knights of Labor meeting in Denver but complained afterwards that "it was very poorly attended by the temperance people." Her exhortation to the WCTU that "we need to understand the labor question just as much as they do the temperance question" seems to have fallen upon deaf ears.[46]

Leading figures in the Denver Knights, especially Buchanan and Joe Murray, had already given considerable thought to the temperance question. Like the middle-class temperance advocates, they attempted to construct substitutes for the saloon during these years. On the other hand, the underlying dynamic of the middle-class antisaloon movement, the drive for industrial discipline and social control of the poor, was noticeably absent from the Knights' temperance project. A very different dynamic was at work here. In their establishment of reading rooms, workers' meeting halls, and recreational alternatives to the saloon, temperance advocates in the Knights attempted to build the foundations of a movement culture that would challenge, not legitimize, existing patterns of social inequality.

The struggle to establish a workers' meeting hall was central to their project. An alcohol-free environment for conducting labor's business was only part of Buchanan and Murray's concern here. Ethnic fraternal societies might rely on the meeting space provided by the immigrant saloon, but the Knights, which theoretically embraced all members of the producing classes, needed meeting places that were free from divisive cultural influences. In 1883, Buchanan lamented the absence of suitable meeting halls for workers' organizations in Denver and offered the offices of the *Labor Enquirer* as a possibility. "The room is small," he admitted, "but fifteen or twenty can be comfortably accommodated and writing material, copies of various trades and labor constitutions, and other little conveniences will be freely tendered." The Denver Knights, however, never established a permanent meeting hall. Although city directories included listings for a "Knights of Labor Hall" in 1884, 1885, and 1886, these were actually three separate halls at different addresses, indicating a failure to establish a central meeting place for the working-class movement. In May 1884, a meeting of the Denver Typographical Union began in the Knights of Labor Hall, but after a few minutes adjourned to the liquor-serving Turner Hall. The Knights' building had been "deemed unsafe."[47]

Knights' activists met with more success in building alternative forms of recreation, focusing on three vehicles designed to carry working men out of the saloon: the "sociable," the day excursion, and the reading room. The first Knights' sociable, or ball, was given by the Union Assembly in August 1883. Music and other entertainment was offered and nonalcoholic refreshments were served "by the ladies," wives and daughters of Union Assembly members. Thereafter, the Union Assembly tried to hold sociables on a schedule of one every two weeks. Although sometimes these were fund raisers (in April 1886, for example, a Knights of Labor ball was held "for the benefit of strikers on the Southwest system"), most were purely recreational in function. Among its other purposes, the Knights provided a focus for Denver working people who simply wanted to get together and enjoy life.[48]

The importance of the sociable in the movement culture of the Knights should not be minimized. It was a form of recreation that clashed at every point with that revolving around the saloon. Again, alcohol was not the only issue involved. The culture built around the saloon was primarily a male culture that excluded women and threatened the stability of the working-class family. The Denver Knights, on the other hand, sought to create recreational forms that strengthened family and community. It is notable that in a period in which recreation for Denver's middle-class was marked by a clear pattern of separate spheres for men and women, the Knights sought to create patterns of leisure that brought men and women together. These concerns, as much as a concern with the effects of alcohol use on family life, shaped the Knights' emphasis on the sociable as an alternative to the saloon.[49]

The day excursion was another such alternative. In July 1883, the Denver Knights held the first of a series of annual picnics at Argo, "one of the nicest resorts in the state." For fifty cents, an individual could purchase a ticket for the outing, which included round-trip rail fare and admission to the park. Unlike the saloon, the day excursion involved the entire family while simultaneously providing respite from an increasingly oppressive urban environment. Family-oriented recreation, of course, did not need to be organized by the labor movement. "I find, working eight hours," a Denver working man reported to the Colorado Bureau of Labor Statistics in 1888, "that I can get time to become acquainted with my family, and plan things that will interest them, which I never could before." But the Knights' railroad excursions, like their sociables, brought the family together in the context of a wider working-class movement. For all their talk of "hearth and home," Knights activists conceived of the family not as an isolated haven from the world, but rather as the cornerstone of the working-class community.[50]

The tactical need to build a movement culture, of course, was not the only reason for the balls and picnics sponsored by the city's labor movement. To a great extent, they were designed simply for the enjoyment of working people, to fulfill their needs for companionship and sociability. Nor does the existence of these events reveal much about rank-and-file working-class attitudes toward either temperance or the various strategies recommended by labor leaders for reforming American society. What can be concluded is that to some unmeasurable extent, the ongoing cultural activities of the Knights and the unions encouraged temperance, while cultivating a sense of mutuality among diverse groups of working people in the city.

From the standpoint of the Knights' leaders, the reading room was the most important alternative to the saloon. "An imperative want of the working people of Denver is that of a reading room," noted Buchanan in 1883, "where the different trades and occupations can meet for social converse, to read such books and periodicals as may prove of interest to them." Reading rooms were hardly new to Denver. The institution had played an important role in the efforts of employers and middle-class temperance advocates to instill self-discipline and loyalty among workers in the city. When the Knights established their central reading room in Denver in May 1885, the local press compared it to earlier efforts, especially those of the YMCA.[51]

Upon close examination, however, differences appear far more salient. A statement by Buchanan, who set up a reading room in his editorial office in 1883, illustrates the nature of the differences. "We extend to every workingman in the city who believes in fair pay for fair work an invitation to make himself at home in the *Enquirer* office. Plenty of the right kind of reading matter always on the table." Buchanan's notion of the "the right kind of reading matter" can be gauged by the writings recommended in the columns of the *Labor Enquirer*. These included Laurence Gronlund's *The Cooperative Commonwealth*, works by Marx (who was compared to Newton and Galileo in scientific importance), and Henry George's *Progress and Poverty*. Thus for Buchanan, liberating working men from the saloon was only the first step in the development of leisure time activities that would stress self-education in political economy and strategies for social change.[52]

Whether Denver's organized workers actually read the works Buchanan recommended is impossible to determine. Like rank-and-file Social Democrats in Germany, faced with similar reading lists prepared by their leaders, Denver's Knights and unionists may very well have preferred fiction to social science. Yet, it is also true that there was a notable intellectual engagement with a wide variety of issues of the day that could be found among working people in this era. Rachel Wild Peterson, a Protestant missionary in Denver in the 1890s, recalled being questioned to the point of irritation by a railroad brakeman and conductor on topics such as the debate over Moses' body, the existence of a hell, and the doctrinal differences among the various Protestant denominations. Though Peterson herself felt such issues were "none of my business" and that the main thing was simply "to love one another," the conductor and brakeman obviously took considerable pleasure in the discussion. Many other workers brought precisely this sort of intellectual engagement into the Knights of Labor and its struggle for social change.[53]

The Knights of Labor's vision of social change was far-reaching. "The great object of the Order is a complete change in our social and economic environment," wrote John W. Hornby, a Denver Knight. "The Order . . . proposes to abolish the competitive system under which we now live and in its place substitute the cooperative system." There can be no doubt that education, and self-improvement generally, were seen as essential preconditions for the abolition of competition; hence the importance of reading rooms in the Knights' activities. But self-improvement in the service of social change bore little resemblance to self-improvement as conceptualized by the YMCA and its business supporters. The 1887 attack that the *Labor Enquirer* launched on what it called the "Young Men's Capitalist Association" for its connections with Jay Gould should make this clear.[54]

The best indicator of the gulf between the middle-class temperance project and that of the labor movement is the strong support that Denver's organized socialists gave to the struggle against the saloon. In 1883, Buchanan became a socialist and the Rocky Mountain organizer for an organization called the International Workingmen's Association. Though it claimed direct descent from the Marxist First International, which had gone by the same name, this organization had actually been founded by Burnette G. Haskell, a San Francisco lawyer, in 1881. The IWA, shrouded in secrecy and ritual, apparently failed to attract many supporters in Denver. But Buchanan continued to give socialist ideas an important voice in the city until he moved to Chicago in 1887. His tireless propaganda efforts bore fruit in December 1885 when between thirty and forty Denver socialists organized the Rocky Mountain Social League for the purpose of "propagating their doctrines."[55]

The membership of the League was drawn from the broad social group that the Knights called "the producing classes." Its charter members included a printer, a house painter, a dentist, a tailor, and an undertaker. Primarily a discussion group, the League held meetings every Sunday evening over the next two and a half years. Although prominent ministers and politicians occasionally addressed these meetings, more typical were speeches like that given by a Denver iron molder on "Why I am a Socialist." Buchanan maintained that league members were "intelligent propagandists of the doctrines of modern socialism" and that they formed "a strong socialist element in the [KOL] assemblies and the unions."[56]

The Rocky Mountain Social League played a major role in shaping the attack on the saloon. Like the leaders of the Knights, activists in the league believed that movements for social change required sobriety and self-improvement. "Socialism is a science," claimed Buchanan, "and science does not attract the ignorant, grovelling herd who can comprehend nothing but that which ministers to their gross animal appetites." Thus the Rocky Mountain Social League took a strong position against the saloon and the broader culture of which it was part. In April 1886, "Comrade Ann Bartlett delivered a sermon she said was intended for a temperance meeting, but that it could be applied to the League." Opposition to the saloon extended to kindred vices, and in February 1886 the league voiced "extreme dissatisfaction with the action of the mayor and city council in granting licenses to the gambling halls, as contrary to the good morals of this city."[57]

The Social League not only took formal positions against the saloon; its weekly meetings also provided practical alternatives to it. These meetings involved not just men but entire families and attempted to combine political agitation, self-improvement, and recreation in a single institution. The flavor of a League meeting is best conveyed by an entry in the diary of Anna Haskell, who came to Denver in 1887 with her husband, the Californa socialist leader Burnette Haskell:

> I said Victor Hugo's "To the Rich and the Poor" at the meeting tonight, and I think I said it very well. The audience seemed to think so. The meeting was very interesting. They have adapted appropriate words to well known music—and there are a number of good singers among them. The baby was awful funny. In the meeting he went and sat himself down on a big black dog and while Burnette was speaking he went and stood directly in front of him and had everyone in the room laughing.

It was this mixture of politics and poetry, of education and family-oriented recreation, that gave the Social League its appeal to Denver's working people. Institutions like this were at the core of the movement culture the city's labor activists were attempting to build.[58]

Thus the opposition of Buchanan, Murray, and other KOL leaders stemmed not only from their belief in temperance, but also from their efforts to construct a movement culture. These efforts also led them to face with great unease emerging forms of urban leisure, particularly professional sports, the new popular press and the variety theater.

Associated with the rise of professional sports in late nineteenth-century America was the growth of a number of widely read popular publications devoted to the coverage of sporting events. The most important of these was the New York–based *Police Gazette*, which combined sporting news with a sensationalized coverage of major crimes and scandals. Knights of Labor activists watched the growth of such publications with considerable anxiety for they seemed to threaten directly the cultivation of a movement culture based on self-improvement and education. For example, Julius Corbin, one of the leaders of the Knights in the Union Pacific shops, maintained that the order was essentially "a school room." The *Union Pacific Employees Magazine*, which he edited, a monthly journal giving attention to political economy, religion, current events, and science—as well as to conditions on the railroads—represented an effort to put this vision into practice. Not surprisingly, Corbin denounced the *Police Gazette* and other examples of what he called "the debasement of the popular press."[59]

More problematic for the labor movement was the growing popularity of baseball. When Knights of Labor organized teams at Denver's main railroad shops, they were using baseball's popularity to cultivate workers' loyalty to the labor movement. But, as a spectator sport, baseball could draw workers out of the orbit of the labor movement and could, on occasion, even hinder its efficient working. In 1884, for example, the members of the Denver Typographical Union imposed a fine on their delegates to the Trades Assembly when they discovered that, despite "knowing that there was important business in the interest of the Union to be transacted," the delegates "did not remain in the hall over half an hour, but attended a baseball game in Athletic Park."[60]

Finally, the variety theater seemed threatening to the labor movement. Even if some theaters admitted women, they destroyed the delicate balance between family and community which the Knights of Labor sought to establish and encouraged a passive and noneducational approach to leisure. The saloon, in sum, was only one part of a larger complex of urban recreational patterns that seemed to challenge the movement culture Knights' leaders sought to build. "The whiskey drinker and variety theater attending workingman who reads the *Police Gazette* is also the one who says he has no use for socialism," growled Buchanan. "Let us give thanks for that—thanks that it attracts only men whose minds are raised above the rumhole and the haunts of vice."[61]

Nevertheless, the saloon remained the central target for Buchanan, partly because its essential character seemed to reflect the process by which the rise of monopoly undermined community life. In the years between the Civil War and the opening of the twentieth century, the United States witnessed a major alteration in drinking habits, with the consumption of fermented liquor, especially beer, supplanting that of distilled spirits. This trend was reflected in Colorado, where the production of beer increased tenfold between 1878 and 1893. Here, as elsewhere, the growth in production was accompanied by a trend toward concentration in fewer establishments. Although twenty-three breweries were operating in the state in 1880, only eleven were in existence ten years later. Small local breweries were increasingly displaced by emerging Denver-area breweries like Zang, Tivoli, and Coors, which came to dominate the market. Colorado brewing was undergoing the same processes of consolidation and concentration as that affecting many other American industries in these years.[62]

These developments affected not only the production of beer but retailing as well. In the early 1880s, larger breweries began the practice of paying for the licenses of Denver saloons and then requiring that only their product be sold. This practice, along with the outright ownership of saloons by breweries, dramatically altered the position of the saloon within the urban environment. For many Denver residents, as one historian has noted, "the neighborhood tavern became an extension of impersonal corporations," its bartender "no longer a long-time friend and familiar merchant but a person hired by unknown owners." Because of these developments, the Knights' antimonopoly rhetoric found a clear target in the brewing industry and the urban saloon.[63]

Joe Murray, the Irish nationalist, socialist and Knights of Labor organizer, who ran for Congress on the Colorado Prohibition party ticket in 1886, brought many of these themes together in his speeches. Murray pointed to the importance of the movement culture that working people could build as an alternative to the saloon, noting that "we are building [cooperative] mills, a public hall and reading room in Stout [Colorado]: in short, doing what all people can do by remaining sober and industrious." More to the point, he argued that the growth of the working-class movement in general would be furthered by the destruction of the saloon. "I organized the first Knights of Labor organization in the state, and I hope to live to see the cause triumph," Murray told his listeners, adding that "as soon as the people are educated up to sobriety . . . then all the working men will be Knights of Labor." Finally, he struck the antimonopoly note, when he argued from the vantage point of the Prohibition hustings that "the only great question today is one of classes—the producing poor, the idle rich," including those who controlled the liquor industry in the latter category. Murray brought the producer ideology into the movement for prohibition.[64]

But it was a very large jump from temperance to prohibition. Murray's decision to stand for Congress as a Prohibitionist and Buchanan's decision to support him ended up costing the Denver labor movement a good deal. While the sociables, day excursions, and reading rooms may have encouraged temperance among working people, they did not necessarily lead to support for Prohibition. The main body of the Denver Knights of Labor backed the Democrats, not the Prohibitionists, and the election led to a bitter fight within the Denver order.

The Pitfalls of Politics

To understand why Murray and Buchanan turned to a political attack on the saloon, it is necessary to understand saloon politics. The Denver saloon was not only an example of the trend toward monopoly in economic life. As in many other American cities during the late nineteenth century, it was also a political institution of considerable importance. Specifically, the Denver saloon provided a major base of operations for the Republican party's political machine in the city. This point is crucial in explaining the move of Murray and Buchanan from the advocacy of temperance to the call for total prohibition. Their attack on the saloon was also an attack on its closest ally, the Republican party.

From 1878 to 1893, in the words of an early student of Denver politics, the Republican party "was the actual government of both Denver and Colorado," usually controlling the governorship and majorities in the state legislature and the Denver city council. While the charge that the party was simply a tool of large corporate mining and railroad interests was somewhat exaggerated, it was true that the Colorado GOP saw its central mission as that of providing a suitable political environment for capital accumulation. This led the party in the early 1880s to oppose virtually all of labor's demands—the prohibition of child and convict labor, the eight-hour day on state and municipal work, effective mechanics' lien laws—as "class legislation." The harshest dimension of the Republican stance toward the labor movement was revealed by Governor Frederick Pitkin when he called out troops to crush the Leadville miners' strike in 1880.[65]

Colorado Democrats tried to use the antilabor position of the GOP to their advantage, putting forward their own party as the friend of the working people. After a bitter fight, for example, the Democratic convention of 1880 passed a resolution condemning Pitkin's use of the militia at Leadville. Nonetheless, the party in these years generally opposed strikes like that on the D&RG, claiming that "the worst enemies" of the working people were not capitalists but "the leeches styled professional workingmen," that is labor leaders like Buchanan. Not surprisingly, then, Murray could argue that "there was no distinctive difference between the two parties . . . the leaders of both parties knew little about political economy and cared less."[66]

Yet Denver's working-class third-party activists had little to show for their efforts. In the municipal elections of 1883, the Trades Assembly put forward a "workingmen's ticket" that included a stonecutter and a tailor as aldermanic candidates. In the following year, some support was generated within the city's labor movement for the Greenback-Labor party, and an officer of the Trades Assembly was represented on the party's ticket for state office. Neither effort was successful however.[67]

In 1885, labor's political initiatives began to show more results, at least at the local level. In the spring of that year, Cornelius J. Driscoll, an Irish American carpenter in the Denver and Rio Grande shops and a leader of the local Knights of Labor, was elected alderman from the Seventh Ward. In the same election, O. L. ("Yank") Smith, a printer and president of the Trades Assembly, was elected to the county board of supervisors. But although both men were elected with strong labor support and both worked effectively for labor-backed ordinances during their two-year terms, neither endorsed third-party efforts: Driscoll was a Democrat and Smith a Republican.[68]

A number of factors accounted for the third-party failures and the continuing Republican domination of Colorado politics. First, the Republicans' emphasis on accumulation, while running against the specific program put forward by the Denver labor movement, gave them some basis for claiming Colorado's prosperity as their own creation—although the claim must have sounded increasingly hollow in the depressed years of the mid-1880s. Second, the fact that a large proportion of Denver's citizens had migrated from the free-soil states of the Midwest gave the GOP an edge in a period in which the "bloody shirt" of the Civil War had not yet lost its persuasive powers. Finally, despite its growth, the city's labor movement still lacked the financial or organizational resources to effectively contest for political power.[69]

Nevertheless, by the mid-1880s, some labor activists were beginning to believe in another key to Republican strength at the Denver polls: the saloon. In fact, saloon keepers and brewery owners had good reason to take an active interest in Denver politics. Continuously threatened by higher licensing fees and stricter closing ordinances, if not by outright prohibition, brewers and saloon keepers attempted to maintain close connections with both of the major political parties. Philip Zang, the city's largest brewer, had served one term on the city council, and throughout the late nineteenth century, there was almost always at least one saloon keeper on the governing body. Standing very close to the center of Republican politics in Denver was Ed Chase, the proprietor of the Palace saloon.[70]

If the Palace was representative of the new, large-scale drinking establishments reshaping urban leisure patterns during the late nineteenth century, its owner was almost an archetypal saloon politician. Although Chase had been a member of the Denver city council during the 1870s, he gave up his position to work for the Republican party behind the scenes. Political influence was of great importance to Chase: his business activities included gambling and prostitution, activities for which cooperation from city authorities was essential. In exchange for such cooperation, Chase provided two important sources of Republican strength in Denver. First, he coordinated financial contributions from saloon keepers to the party, reaching his peak with a $25,000 party fund for the close municipal election of 1889. Second, Chase coordinated the mobilization of Republican voters. On election days throughout the 1880s, the Palace became a center of intense activity as the poor and often transient men of Denver's First Ward were rounded up, provided with free beer, and directed to the polls. Chase, to be sure, was an unusual political figure and his influence may well have been exaggerated by reformers. Nevertheless, the publicity that his activities received encouraged at least some support within the labor movement for total prohibition. The move toward prohibition represented not only an attack on the saloon but an attempt to dismantle a power base of the city's Republican party.[71]

Colorado's Prohibition party shared the hostility to the Republicans. Although Prohibitionists frequently compared their efforts with those of the original "free soil party," they argued that the GOP was now bankrupt of "high moral ideas." From its founding in 1884, moreover, the Prohibition party in Colorado had advanced a broad program of reform extending far beyond the liquor question. It advocated the state ownership of irrigation ditches, the free coinage of silver, and an end to railroad pools and rebates, standard antimonopoly positions that drew support within the Denver Knights of Labor and trade unions. But the real key to the party's appeal to workers was its nomination of Joe Murray as its candidate for Congress in 1886. Murray's biography reads like a history of the Denver labor movement: in addition to being Colorado's leading Irish American radical, he had been a founder of the state Greenback party, the organizer of the first KOL local assembly in the state, a leader in the Trades Assembly's workingmen's ticket campaign, and a charter member of the Rocky Mountain Social League. His candidacy gave the Prohibition-Labor party, as it was styled in 1886, an enormous amount of prestige within the labor movement.[72]

In 1886, however, the Prohibitionists were not alone in their effort to woo the labor vote. The Democrats, who had been making unsuccessful appeals to Colorado's working-class voters since the 1870s, now put into the congressional race a genuinely prolabor candidate, the well-known Congregational minister and Knight of Labor, Myron Reed. Despite Murray's popularity, most Denver Knights and trade unionists came to feel that while Reed actually had a chance to win, "a vote for Murray is a vote wasted—a vote in the air." The individual most responsible for organizing labor support for the Democrats was John B. Lennon, leader of Denver's tailors and a key figure in the local Knights. The final weeks of the 1886 campaign were dominated by a bitter struggle between Lennon and Buchanan—once close friends—over how workers should vote.[73]

Born in 1850, Lennon had grown up in Hannibal, Missouri, where he may have actually gone to school with Buchanan, one year his junior. Moving to Denver in 1869 and following his father's craft by becoming a tailor, Lennon had helped organize the Tailors Protective Society of Denver in 1871. In 1884, he was elected president of the Journeymen Tailors Union of America. But as a charter member of the Union Assembly, a close associate of Buchanan's, and a coordinator of labor support for the D&RG strikers, Lennon was also one of the most important figures in the Denver Knights. In January 1886, he proclaimed himself a socialist and helped organize the Rocky Mountain Social League, serving as the chair for several of its meetings over the next few months.[74]

But Lennon's socialist convictions did not lead him to embrace the third-party strategy advanced by Buchanan and Murray. On the contrary, as early as March 1886, in a speech to a Denver antimonopoly convention, Lennon broke ranks with them by declaring his opposition to building a new political party. There were enough of these already, he maintained. Instead, Lennon argued that labor organizations should formulate clear positions on issues, appeal to both of the main parties to adopt these positions, and then "pledge ourselves to vote unanimously with that party that shall come the nearest to adopting our views."[75]

Lennon, outlining his beliefs a number of years later, argued that there was a "proper" role for independent labor politics at the municipal level. The local political victories of Smith and Driscoll in 1885 and their subsequent effectiveness as supervisor and alderman may have convinced him of that. But he also believed that the vast patronage power of the two main political parties—the "spoils system," as Lennon called it—would inevitably corrupt any attempt to build a labor party at the state or national levels. At this level, the "old parties" would inevitably remain supreme, and organized workers should support that party with positions closest to their own in any particular contest.[76]

In the 1886 election, Lennon decided that it was the Democrats who best fit this bill, and the party's nomination of Reed for Congress greatly strengthened his conviction. More importantly, Lennon rallied not only Denver trade unionists but many of the local Knights of Labor to his point of view. In October a meeting of "the Knights of Labor of Denver, in joint session," presided over by Lennon, gave support to the entire Democratic ticket and called on Murray to withdraw from the race for Congress. Over the next few weeks several Denver Knights' assemblies disassociated themselves from the action of the joint session and voiced support for Murray. Nonetheless, the majority of Knights backed Lennon, Reed, and the Democrats, not Buchanan, Murray and the Prohibitionists.

And although both labor-backed candidates lost the state-wide election to the Republican incumbent, Reed ended up carrying Denver by five hundred votes.[77]

The most important result of the 1886 election, however, did not lie in the returns. Its greatest impact was that of heightening tensions within Denver's labor movement. These tensions came to a head on 10 October, when the Trades Assembly officially severed its connection with the *Labor Enquirer* and passed a resolution of censure against its editor, Joseph Buchanan. While the Trades Assembly conceded Buchanan's right "to advocate or oppose any political party or candidate, and indulge in the organization of new departures," it nonetheless felt obliged to protest "against any attempted deception on the part of any one in conveying the impression that the organized workingman of Colorado will cast his ballot as directed by any alleged labor leader."[78]

The 1886 election ended the Denver labor movement's experiment with prohibition. Although efforts were made to unite the Prohibition party with Colorado's Union Labor party in 1888, these proved to be unsuccessful. Reverend Gilbert DeLaMatyr, who had been active in the Prohibition campaign of 1886, became the ULP's gubernatorial candidate in 1888, reflecting the movement of many prohibition-laborites into the broader organization. And even more significantly, Lennon's advocacy of support for the Democrats in state and national politics emerged over the next two decades as the dominant view within the Denver labor movement. Lennon, not Buchanan had carried the day. On the other hand, the struggle of Murray and Buchanan to construct a movement culture, a struggle that had been thoroughly intertwined with the prohibition experiment, continued to live on among the city's labor activists, coming to the fore especially in early twentieth-century labor radicalism.[79]

4 Trade Unionism and the Beginnings of Syndicalism, 1887–92

On the first Monday of September 1892, the Denver Trades Assembly sponsored a picnic and parade to celebrate Labor Day, which had been declared a state holiday by the Colorado General Assembly in 1889. The Trades Assembly had cause for celebration, for the late 1880s and early 1890s had witnessed a dramatic rise in the strength of trade unionism in the city. The years from 1887 to 1892 had seen an impressive economic boom in Denver, producing conditions that allowed successful organizing among the skilled trades. The number of trade unions climbed from thirteen to forty-one in these years. Unions now embraced between 7,000 and 8,000 of Denver's 33,000 manual workers.[1]

The times had been harder on the Knights of Labor in the city. The order continued to make strides among coal miners and railroad workers in other parts of Colorado, but in Denver it experienced a sharp decline, the result of employers' antilabor activities and internal division, that began in 1887. The number of local assemblies of the Knights in Denver fell from thirteen in 1886 to three in 1892, with total membership dropping from approximately twenty-five hundred to less than one thousand. Joseph Buchanan, the Knights' leading figure, left Denver for work in what he called "the larger field," Chicago, in January 1887. His newspaper, the *Labor Enquirer*, which had done so much to advance the cause of the Knights, continued on after his departure, but finally ceased publication in May 1888. By the early 1890s the Denver order was a shadow of its former self.[2]

Joe Murray, the order's pioneer organizer in Colorado, personified the decline of the Denver Knights. In the late 1880s, as the organization he had worked so hard to build began to decline, Murray drifted away from the world of labor reform. The autumn of 1888 found him in Indiana, stumping the state for Benjamin Harrison and the Republican party. Murray spent the next several years in Alaska, where he had been rewarded with a federal job, but he returned to Colorado in 1892 to campaign for the GOP, saddening many of his former friends and admirers in the Denver Knights and the host of other reform and radical movements he had once championed. When he died in 1898, I. D. Chamberlain, a national officer of the now moribund Knights, remarked that the story of individuals like Murray reminded him of "the old story of Jonah—tired, discouraged and worn out, because results are slow, they fall asleep, and then get angry because a worm has eaten the root of their shade, and the gourd is withered."[3]

Denver's experience in these years was far from unique. In cities and towns across the nation, assemblies of the Knights collapsed, while new trade unions sprang up, many affiliated with the American Federation of Labor, which had been founded by Samuel Gompers, Peter J. McGuire, and several other prominent craft unionists in 1886 and which soon emerged as the voice of the country's organized skilled craftsmen. In Denver, skilled craft unionists represented the leading edge of the labor movement after 1886, and the organizations they built were more narrow in membership and policies than the Knights. Still, in a number of respects, these unionists held fast to the Knights' vision of sweeping social reform and sought to place it on more solid foundations. Their main political creation, the Union Labor party of 1887–88, marked a kind of synthesis of the reform tradition in Colorado politics, though many Denver trade unionists remained closely involved with the two established political parties.[4]

In the late 1880s, Denver's socialists drew very close to this dynamic trade union movement and to the workers embraced by it. At the same time, socialist ideology in Denver began to take a new shape. By 1892, the beginnings of what would eventually be called syndicalism could be seen in the radical wing of the city's labor movement. Like later syndicalists, Denver's labor radicals had come to see the institution of the trade union as both the main engine of social transformation and the germ of a future socialist society. Although they were a minority, these protosyndicalists proved to be a vital part of the city's labor movement, providing some of its most active union organizers and engaging mainstream leaders in an on-going dialogue about the character of the social order and paths to social change.

Knights and Unions

The decline of the Knights of Labor in Denver was rapid. As early as 1888, ten of the thirteen local assemblies in the city had disbanded. But important pockets of strength remained, especially among the workers at the Union Pacific shops. In 1889, a committee of the Denver Chamber of Commerce attempted to secure new Union Pacific repair shops in the city. Walter Cheesman and a group of other local investors had purchased a tract of land and were willing to donate it to the company, on the condition that shops be built. But the UP's director, Charles Francis Adams, refused to consider Denver as a site for the shops because he believed the Knights of Labor were too strong in the city. The Chamber of Commerce acknowledged that among railroad shop workers the Knights were stronger than ever, though they maintained that Denver's Knights were not as radical as those in other cities.[5]

The Knights' continuing strength in the city's railroad shops illustrates a point perhaps more important than the decline in membership: the character of the organization was changing. At its peak in 1885 and 1886, membership in the Denver order had embraced working people in an extremely wide variety of occupations. Though some of Denver's local assemblies were "mixed assemblies," which brought together workers from several occupations, others, "trade assemblies," represented workers in specific trades and often sought to act like trade unions. In 1887 and 1888, some groups of workers began to leave the latter assemblies, organizing trade unions that had considerably more independence on matters of policy than could be found within the Knights. The experience of retail clerks in the city provides a good example. Most clerks worked six twelve-hour days a week, and their central concern was that of obtaining shorter hours. A group of Denver clerks organized an "Early Closing Society" in the early 1880s. In March 1885, they affiliated with the Knights of Labor, becoming Local Assembly No. 3639, with forty-nine charter members. The great advantage of affiliation with the order was that it enabled the clerks to generate support among other Denver workers in their struggle for shorter hours. But, from the point of view of the clerks, the Knights were less than an ideal institution in other respects. For example, the order paid no sickness or funeral benefits, which the clerks saw as a useful organizing device. Thus in 1887 the clerks let their Knights of Labor charter drop, reorganized as the Clerks Benevolent and Protective Association, and three years later became one of the seven local societies to form the Retail Clerks National Protective Association, affiliated with the AFL.[6]

Other groups of Denver workers, such as brewery workers, cigar makers, and various building trades workers, followed the same course, leaving the order to establish their own independent trade unions. But in areas of the local economy where the Knights assemblies continued to exist, they did so by becoming, for all practical purposes, trade unions themselves. The Union Pacific workers represented the clearest example. From 1886 to 1894, Denver's UP shop workers were part of District Assembly No. 82. Usually referred to as the Union Pacific Employees Association, the district assembly was in fact a powerful industrial union of shop workers on the UP, with locals in Kansas, Nebraska, Wyoming, and Idaho, as well as throughout Colorado. Although remaining part of the order, D.A. 82 made its own decisions regarding strikes, engaged in collective bargaining with the Union Pacific management, published its own monthly journal, and in general displayed the characteristics of an independent union.[7]

Denver's Local Assembly No. 3714, which continued to exist through 1892, also functioned as a union, representing workers in the city's leather industries, embracing shoemakers, harness, saddle and collar makers and tanners. Not a large local, it reported seventy-three members at the end of 1886. But organizing work picked up in early 1887, and a year later, while other Knights assemblies were collapsing, this local was in what its recording secretary called "a prosperous condition." This should not be seen as surprising, for the local was now part of Leather Workers National Trade Assembly, No. 240, founded in 1886, which—like D.A. 82—was an independent and effective national union operating within the framework of Knights. In 1889, N.T.A. 240 had a national membership of eighteen thousand, a treasury of $10,000, and its own weekly journal. As with other trade unions, it also had a national working card and was seeking to equalize wages across the country, bringing eastern wages up to the level of those in western centers like Chicago and Denver. Thus, though Denver's leather workers may have been attracted to the Knights' broad vision of social reform, they also sought to better their working lives through trade union action. "I have pulled the cords of affliction upon a shoe-bench until 12 o'clock at night long enough," said W. A. Holman at a meeting in March 1887. "Now I'm going to organize to better my condition."[8]

But the best example of the changing character of the Knights was the emergence of a new local assembly in 1890. This was an industrial union of overworked, poorly paid, and largely immigrant street railway employees—a group of workers no trade union had yet attempted to organize. By 1892, the Colorado Bureau of Labor Statistics reported the local assembly as having a large membership and in a "flourishing" condition.[9]

It is difficult to gauge the overall strength of the Knights of Labor after 1885, the last year in which official membership figures were given. But it is certainly possible that individual assemblies continued to grow, even as the number of assemblies fell. Denver correspondents to the order's national paper, the *Journal of United Labor*, claimed that the Knights were growing again in the city in the late 1880s. Their ranks were sufficiently large, in any event, to persuade the order's leadership to hold its annual General Assembly meetings in Denver in November 1890. Whether out of curiosity or commitment, over five thousand Denver residents turned out to hear a speech by Terence V. Powderly, general master workman of the Knights, at the opening of General Assembly.[10]

But whatever its strength, the working-class orientation of the Denver order was clear. This is not to say that middle-class reformers were totally uninvolved with the Denver Knights. At the 1890 General Assembly, Mrs. Anna Steele, a middle-class leader of the Denver Woman's Christian Temperance Union, gave a spirited address on the saloon question. By the following year, Steele had risen to a position of leadership within the Colorado Knights, representing them at the order's General Assembly in Toledo. But on the whole—and in marked contrast to the view that the Knights adopted a "middle-class" ideology after 1886—in Denver the organization became smaller but more clearly *working class* in its outlook: more oriented toward issues of wages, hours, and working conditions, in short, more "job conscious." In light of this, it is not surprising that the Denver Knights spoke the same language of workplace militancy spoken by trade unionists in these years. While in some localities the Knights may have attempted to abolish strikes, relying instead on the "middle-class" panaceas of education and arbitration, Denver Knights of Labor saw no contradiction between the two approaches. "General Grant once said, 'perpetual peace can be attained only by runs through conflict'" noted a writer in the *Union Pacific Employees Magazine* in 1886. "In a like manner arbitration will only be made possible by repeated strikes." In a juxtaposition of terms that flew in the face of efforts to see "strikes" and "education" as strategic opposites, the writer went on to note that "considered as educators, strikes are a stirring power; they waken thought and attract attention when peaceable means would be sneered at with contempt. . . . Strikes are never total failures, and each one brings us nearer the culmination point and final solution." Significantly, even Denver's single surviving mixed assembly, where one might expect to find the most opposition to strikes, contributed funds to help striking miners in the summer of 1889.[11]

Just as the Denver Knights of Labor upheld the workplace-centered militancy of the trade unions, so the city's trade unions continued to put forward broad programs of social reform that are usually identified with the Knights. Thus, in November 1887, the Trades Assembly demanded that "more educational facilities be offered the poorer classes" of Denver and called on the city's board of education to establish a system of night schools for workers "who may wish to avail themselves of the opportunity to improve their education." Cooperative enterprises, as well as education, continued to command support from trade unionists after 1886. Although the Colorado Cooperative Mercantile Association, a cooperative store that operated in Denver through March 1887, seemed to draw most of its activists from the Knights at the Union Pacific shops, its secretary was John B. Lennon, president of the Journeymen Tailors Union. Even the Knights of Labor's emphasis on temperance and the control of the liquor industry was continued by the trade union movement in Denver. As late as 1891, the Denver Trades Assembly passed a resolution calling for the nationalization of the American liquor industry, a proposal designed to end the corruption caused by licensing, eliminate the element of profit from the liquor traffic, and undermine the role of the saloon in political life. Lennon himself was a life-long temperance advocate and in 1909, as treasurer of the AFL, supported a move to establish an antisaloon fellowship within that body. Meanwhile, the Denver Carpenters Union, Local No. 55, allowed ten minutes every meeting for discussions of the single tax.[12]

Perhaps most impressive was the continuing support for women's rights within the trade union movement. This support can clearly be seen in the large meeting of workers to raise money for the Sisters of Mercy's home for impoverished working women in November 1890. Held during the Knights of Labor's General Assembly, and with Powderly featured as one of the speakers, the meeting nonetheless was dominated by trade unionists. On the platform sat not only the printer's leader and president of the Denver Trades Assembly, W. H. Montgomery, but also official representatives from the Brick Molders and Setters, Carpenters Union Local No. 55, the Hod Carriers, the Machine and Wood Workers, the Granite Cutters, the Journeymen Barbers, the Clerks, the Bookbinders, and the Union Pacific Employees. The crowd applauded not only when a speaker called for "equal wages for equal labor for all time" but also when Myron Reed voiced a broader view in favor of "equal rights for men and women," placing particular emphasis on the vote. Two months later, another Denver union, Carpenters Local No. 460, went on record in favor of woman's suffrage as well.[13]

But while there was significant labor support for women's rights, it should also be noted that working-class women no longer played the central role they once had in Denver's labor movement. As the workplace assumed a greater importance as a focus for labor struggles and the rich social life of the labor movement in the Knights era began to decline, married women's labor activism was relegated more and more to the trade union auxiliary. Though the Denver Typographical Union and the city's Journeymen Tailors Union admitted women to membership, the numbers of applicants were few. The collapse of Hope Assembly in 1887 marked a significant loss to the city's once broad-based labor movement. Though KOL organizer Leonora Barry organized a new women's assembly on a trip to Denver in 1889, it proved short-lived.[14]

A similar retreat could be seen in the relationship of African American workers to the labor movement. The retreat was far from total. Black and white hod carriers, for instance, worked together to organize a union in the city in the late 1880s, partially winning a three-week strike for higher wages in May 1888. It was at least one occupation where "white and colored men walked shoulder to shoulder in the common cause," according to the *Rocky Mountain News*. Both Lennon (who moved to New York in late 1887, when he was elected general secretary of Journeymen Tailors Union of America) and Adam Menche, a cigar maker and representative of the Denver Trades Assembly, spoke forcefully at the AFL's 1890 convention against admitting southern locals of the National Machinists Union that excluded black workers. These views must have been shared by at least a portion of other Denver labor activists.[15]

On the other hand, exclusionist practices clearly existed among Denver labor unions. Menche's own union, though without a formal color bar, was composed overwhelmingly of white males, and organized only cigar makers and packers, not the cigar factory operatives or stemmers, whose numbers were growing in Denver and who were much more likely to be women or nonwhite men. As in earlier years, when Lewis Douglass, Henry Wagoner, and other Denver black rights leaders had struggled against exclusionist practices, African Americans voiced strong protests against trade union discrimination. In August 1892, for example, a convention of blacks meeting in Denver to fight for "more just, equal and untrammeled opportunity" formally resolved to "condemn all labor organizations which condemn a laborer because he is black." The continued exclusionist practices of unions may have been one factor leading to the emergence by the early 1890s of a small black nationalist movement in Denver, whose leader, J. N. Walker, called on the city's "exiled children" to "return to the fatherland," specifically Liberia. In any event, the decline of the Knights of Labor marked a shift away from the labor movement's more inclusive stance toward African Americans.[16]

Still, experience in local assemblies of the Knights of Labor had been a formative one for many of the Denver workers who built trade unions in the late 1880s and early 1890s. While many came to reject the order as the appropriate vehicle for working-class action, they brought a number of its concerns and emphases into their new organizations. Thus, the Knights' cardinal principle that "an injury to one is the concern of all" did not die with the order's decline. Rather the principle continued to underline thought and action in the trade union movement throughout the 1880s and 1890s, receiving perhaps its clearest expression when Denver trade unionists took the lead in founding the Colorado State Federation of Labor in 1896. As Harvey Garman, a Denver printer and one of the founders of the State Federation recalled in the 1930s, "while the Knights of Labor perhaps did not have any direct bearing on the formation of the State Federation, many of the men who had previous experience in those assemblies were old members of that organization and had ideas of joint action gathered through their assemblies." [17]

Moreover, Denver trade unionists demonstrated little of the lingering hostility to the Knights that characterized trade unionists in some parts of the country. It is true that by 1887 the remaining local assemblies of the Knights were no longer attached to the Denver Trades Assembly. But relations between the assembly and the Knights were generally close. When the Denver Trades Assembly received its charter from the AFL in 1889, its members apparently did not see this as a total rejection of the order and its principles. In 1891, the Trades Assembly instructed its delegate to the AFL convention "to support any measure not inconsistent with trade unionism looking to an adjustment of the difference between the American Federation of Labor and the Knights of Labor." [18]

As the wording of the instructions reveal, however, Denver trade unionists did fear that an alliance with the Knights might be "inconsistent" with trade union principles. There was a historical basis for such fears. In 1886, the Knights' general master workman, Terence V. Powderly, acting out of a deep conviction that trade unionism was a retrogressive force, helped transform a local dispute between the Cigar Makers Union and a group of New York City Knights called the "Home Club" into a national conflict between trade unions and the order. At the General Assembly held in Richmond, Virginia, in late 1886, Powderly managed to put through a measure expelling from the order all cigar makers who refused to give up membership in their union. The International Cigar Makers Union rallied trade unionists to their side and a virtual war began to break out between the Knights and the unions. [19]

The cigar makers' struggle was only the tip of the iceberg. A number of other characteristics of the Knights troubled trade unionists. The Knights' willingness to admit employers to membership and the failure of the order's national leaders to support strikes and wage demands greatly disturbed them. The apparent hostility to trade unions, combined with growing factionalism within the national leadership and the intensity of the employers' counterattack against the order, led many skilled workers to turn to the growing trade union movement instead. As a result, national membership in the order fell from a high of over seven hundred thousand in 1886 to under two hundred thousand in 1890. Though it was far from the only conflict, the cigar makers' struggle seemed to many to symbolize the problem. It left bitterness in the mouths of many trade unionists. [20]

In Denver, however, the leadership of the Knights vigorously opposed Powderly's order against the cigar makers, and this explains in part why feelings between Knights and trade unionists in Denver continued to be what an observer in 1888 called "most friendly." Joseph Buchanan, who had represented twelve of Denver's thirteen assemblies (under the umbrella of D.A. 89) at Richmond, had been one of the most vocal opponents there of Powderly and the antiunion Home Club. On his return to Denver, he wrote a long report to Denver's Knights, explaining his refusal to enforce the order. It was true, Buchanan admitted, that there was some common ground between his position and that of the Home Club:

> We have both wanted to do away with the Trade Unions, as a *distinctive class organization;* the difference has been that I want, by a system of education and friendly agreement, to amalgamate the Unions with the K of L in the form of Districts. My opponents in the [General Assembly] have wanted to "wipe out"—their own words—the Unions, and the crowd of "wipers out" have brought disgrace upon the Order in New York city, by their idiotic, ineffective war of conquest. I still hold to the idea of friendly combination, and I leave the case with you.[21]

D.A. 82, the Union Pacific Employees Association, did come quickly to Powderly's defense. At its annual convention in Denver in January 1887, the district assembly passed resolutions "endorsing every action taken by Mr. Powderly in the settlement of the Southwestern and Chicago strikes, as well as his views regarding trade unions." The assembly "pledged its members to stand by him in his work." L.A. 3714, the leather workers assembly, also went on record in support of "our great leader."[22]

But, on the whole, the Knights assemblies in Denver rallied to Buchanan's position. Indeed, in the first half of 1887, Denver emerged as one of several storm centers of opposition to Powderly's control of the order. Upon receiving Powderly's circular against the cigar makers, L.A. 2327 carefully considered it but responded that, because it clearly ran against the constitution of the order, "we are unable to comply." Instead this local assembly, one of the most prominent in Denver—it counted not only Buchanan, but Lennon, printers' leader Charles L. Merritt, and the ministers of the social gospel, Reed and DeLaMatyr, among its members—adopted a resolution condemning both the officers of the Knights and of several national trade unions for encouraging the conflict. The resolution went on to deny that the rank and file of the Knights were antiunion and called on the Knights' General Executive Board to heal the breach. Meanwhile, the *Labor Enquirer* launched a series of attacks on the general master workman's "autocratic" control of the order, implying that he had become a tool of large capitalists and the Catholic church. This attack had the effect of driving a wedge between the Union Pacific assembly and other Knights of Labor assemblies in the city, weakening the labor movement through internal conflict. On the other hand, it demonstrated the crucial links that trade unionists and *many* of the Knights local assemblies had built in the city.[23]

The internal conflict within the Denver Knights culminated with a visit by Powderly to the city in May 1887. Powderly had promised Denver Knights a visit as early as 1885, but what would have at one time been a triumphant organizing visit turned into an event that looked more like an inquisition. On May 10, the general master workman spoke before three thousand people at a public meeting sponsored by D.A. 82 and attended by the mayor, the governor, and Bishop Machebeuf. Here he was very well received. The following evening, however, he made an appearance before the city's rebellious Knights. Burnette G. Haskell, the new editor of the *Labor Enquirer*, had prepared in advance fifty questions to which he demanded satisfactory answers from Powderly. These were wide-ranging and involved Powderly's handling of particular strikes, his refusal to support the Haymarket accused, and his relationship with the Catholic hierarchy and certain large employers. But many of the questions focused on his antagonistic position toward strikes and trade unions. Although the details of the encounter were never published, Powderly was clearly unable to placate his opponents. Haskell soon announced that his answers were unsatisfactory, the attacks in the *Enquirer* continued, and four months later a group of Denver trade unionists were still celebrating what they called Haskell's historic "victory in debate and diplomacy over Terence V. Powderly."[24]

By the end of 1887, the Powderly forces had clear control of the Knights. A key showdown took place at the October General Assembly in Minneapolis, which was dominated by a fight over a resolution urging clemency for the condemned Haymarket anarchists, whose scheduled executions loomed a month away. Powderly managed to defeat the resolution by denouncing all radicals within the order as anarchists, blaming them for the employers' counteroffensive, and even claiming that they had threatened his life. As part of this general attack on radicalism, the convention's credentials committee prohibited Buchanan from taking his seat, ostensibly because his local assembly had failed to pay its dues. Burnette Haskell, Detroit's Thomas Barry, and a number of other dissidents were expelled the following year, and other anti-Powderly activists gradually drifted away from the Knights. The events of 1887 in Denver, however, remain of great significance. They indicate that the city's trade unionists did not leave the Knights willingly and continued to support the broad reform vision that the order upheld. They could not, however, remain part of an organization that refused to accept their commitment to building strong and independent trade unions. As J. J. Callahan, a Denver iron molder and socialist, put it following the Minneapolis General

Assembly, there was now no choice but to leave the "rotten" Knights of Labor and rally behind the AFL, which not only had "a bright future," but had also been "founded on broad principles and a recognition of the interdependence of all who work for wages."[25]

Over the next five years, the trade union emerged as the central institution of the working-class movement in Denver. The first stage of this development was appropriately signaled by AFL president Samuel Gompers himself, who spoke to a large meeting of Denver working people in February 1888. Gompers emphasized "the necessity of organization," advised workers to "organize along trade lines," and argued that strikes should only be called when preceded by thorough organization. Denver unions did in fact experience what Gompers called "a labor boom" in these years, with organizations in the building trades and on the railroads growing especially strong. Economic conditions in both cases facilitated growth. On top of the general economic upswing of these years, Denver was in the midst of its greatest building boom ever. Railroad construction was also undergoing tremendous expansion, with eight hundred miles of track being constructed in Colorado in 1887 alone, and Denver emerging as a central point in the western railroad network. By 1892, forty-one trains entered the city every day. Given the organizational foothold already established by workers in the construction industry and in railroading, the conditions for union building here were ideal.[26]

Denver's unions became increasingly deliberate and more thoroughly collective in their dealings with employers in these years. By the early 1890s, for instance, carpenters' work rules were made not by individual local unions but by a citywide carpenters council, to which the locals sent delegates. The council, well aware that only thorough organization could back up the enforcement of rules, also took new initiatives in the area of organizing. In July 1891, it endeavored to draw up a list of all non-union carpenters in the city, then inviting them to a meeting to explain the benefits of unionization.[27]

Even more impressive was the control over work rules exerted by the Union Pacific Employees Association. According to Edward Dickinson, general manager of the Union Pacific, from the formation of D.A. 82 through the early 1890s, the shop workers—not the managers—instituted the work rules. "I don't know as we were over-awed or subdued exactly," he stated in 1894, "but we were given to understand that they would insist upon the rules they submitted, and without saying so directly the intimation was thrown out that they would carry their point some way or other." As the nerve center of the District Assembly, the Denver shops demonstrated this tendency most clearly. After an inspection of the Denver yard in 1890, UP president Charles Francis Adams was appalled. "Our employees are running the properties," he sputtered, "and it is difficult to find any one in our service who approaches an issue with them, except . . . with the feeling that he is whipped in advance."[28]

Dickinson and Adams may well have overstated the situation. More importantly, the level of control exercised by the workers did not go uncontested on the shop floor. The columns of the *Union Pacific Employees Magazine* throughout these years were filled with bitter condemnations of "tyrannical, domineering, slave-driving" foremen and of those workers "who try to curry favor" with them. But the UP situation was in sharp contrast with the shops on other western lines in the years after the Knights of Labor defeat in the great Southwest strike of 1886, where, as machinists leader P. J. Conlon later recalled, "there was no such thing as a shop committee and the master mechanic as general rule was a czar and monarch of all he surveyed." In marked distinction to a pattern that included the massive hiring of semiskilled workers, the introduction of piecework, and the widespread demand for bribes by foremen, Union Pacific workers were able to win the company's agreement to a body of rules governing the relationship of workers and management, institute a uniform wage scale, sharply limit the power of foremen, and build up a system that "gave no class of workmen any special recognition." The contrast with other shops was not lost on the Union Pacific workers or on other groups of workers in Denver: they understood that the key differentiating factor was the presence of the union.[29]

The centrality of the union was also reflected in the patterns of strikes in Denver in these years. In the period from 1881 to 1886, strikes in the city had been marked by two important characteristics. First, six of the nineteen strikes recorded by U.S. Commissioner of Labor for Denver in these years (that is, nearly one-third) lacked the benefit of trade union direction and discipline, either preceding organization, as in the Union Pacific strike of 1884, or taking place without union or Knights of Labor endorsement. Second, the overwhelming majority of strikes in Denver (fourteen out of the nineteen) grew out of wage disputes. They were fought most often either to protect workers against wage cuts or to advance wages.[30]

From 1887 to 1892, however, the character of strikes in Denver underwent a significant transformation. To begin with, trade unions now played the key role in planning and carrying out strikes. Every one of the fourteen Denver strikes recorded by the U.S. Commissioner of Labor in these six years had been called by union officials. Second, with this dramatically greater role of union coordination and discipline came a sharp rise in the proportion of strikes related to enforcing union rules, strengthening unions, or supporting other groups of workers. Only four strikes stemmed from wage disputes. Two—one of painters and one of carpenters—were strikes for shorter hours, reflecting the centrality of this issue to building trades workers in this era. But six of the strikes—over one-third—were fought over neither wages nor hours but rather to enforce union rules, discharge oppressive foremen or nonunion men, or reinstate union members who had been fired. They were, in short, what historians have termed "control strikes," part of the attempt of skilled workers to impose or retain a level of control over the organization of work. Very much related to this increasing aggressiveness were the two Denver strikes called "in sympathy with strikes elsewhere."[31]

Thus, railroad switchmen, who had organized a union in 1886, conducted a two-day strike in 1888 to have a yardmaster named Burns ("an abusive, brutal, overbearing specimen of humanity," one worker called him) discharged and to have the size of the labor force increased. In September 1890 they went out again, demanding the removal of another resented yardmaster. In the following year, the Denver switchmen struck a third time. This dispute was not centered on Denver issues but was rather a sympathy strike with railroad switchmen in Lincoln, Nebraska. The Lincoln workers claimed that the Burlington Railroad had discriminated against union members there, and switchmen in both Denver and Omaha lent them support "by going out in a body." This sympathy strike was, like their earlier strikes, part of a struggle for workers' control; but it may have also reflected the switchmen's view that, as the labor journalist John Swinton put it, the sympathetic strike was "the highest and noblest expression of fraternity." Though none of these strikes were successful, they illustrate the increasing aggressiveness of unionized skilled workers in this era. As a friendly railroad shopworker noted of the first switchmen's strike, "the men considered that patience had ceased to be a virtue."[32]

Even more dramatic was the 1892 strike of engineers and firemen on the Denver and Rio Grande. This was the biggest strike on the railroad since the bitter conflict of 1885 and the largest railroad strike in Colorado in the early 1890s. The underlying issue was a company order, issued 24 August, which eliminated a meal stop at Glenwood Springs. Two days after the issuance of the new order, an engineer named William Gordon, who was slated to take a west-bound freight from Minturn to Grand Junction, called the trainmaster up on his engine and informed him that unless the order was rescinded, he would not leave Minturn with the train. According to the trainmaster, Gordon "said that he didn't care a d——n if he never worked another minute, he would not go until it was recalled, and for me to go in the office and tell them so."[33]

In a disciplinary hearing on the matter held in September, Gordon did not dispute the trainmaster's account, but stated simply that "the bulletin was unjust." Though the division superintendent thought that the case merited dismissal from the service, N. W. Sample, the general superintendent of the road in Denver, imposed only a thirty-day suspension. Nonetheless, a meeting of engineers, firemen, conductors, and brakemen on 7 October demanded the reinstatement of Gordon and stated that unless he was reinstated in a week, they would "positively refuse to handle trains on Second division." The company's engineers and firemen based in Denver participated in this strike which, marked by tight discipline and a total absence of violence (the workers stationed guards at all the yards to protect railroad property), shut down east-west traffic on the road for four days. At that point, the company agreed to arbitration, which eventually led to Gordon's full reinstatement.[34]

As Denver's unionized workers' became more aggressive, and their actions more coordinated, deliberate, and focused on control issues, employers organized in response. Their counteroffensive, when combined with the determination of the workers, almost guaranteed there would be violence. Thus, in April 1891, the Brick Manufacturers Exchange, representing fifty-two manufacturers in the city, introduced a new schedule that increased daily output and decreased wages. When the city's twelve hundred brick molders and setters, who had organized a union in 1886 and fought a successful strike in 1887, went on strike against the schedule, the manufacturers attempted to open the yards with strikebreakers, leading to an exchange of gunfire at the Larmon brickyards in West Denver. On 11 May, a much larger confrontation at City Park between brick makers and a manufacturer, F. N. Davis, led to the shooting deaths of two strikers and the permanent crippling of strike leader Frank Surber. A dramatic procession of several thousand trade unionists and Knights of Labor followed the hearses of the deceased to the cemetery and the Trades Assembly placed an assessment on all organized workers in the city to "aid prosecution of F. N. Davis and his hired assassins." But the outcome was not satisfactory. The brick makers were forced to call off their strike after fifty-six days, and in January 1892 a jury acquitted Davis and several others of murder.[35]

Employer organizations grew up throughout the city in these years, attempting to resist what the local press increasingly referred to as "labor tyranny" in industry. In 1889, for example, Denver contractors organized a Builders' Union to fight the building trades unions, especially their demand for the eight-hour day. In 1890, the city's merchant tailors organized the Merchant Tailors Exchange. Two years later, the organization declared a lockout against the Journeymen Tailors Union, after its 218 members refused to accept a new bill of prices proposed by the Exchange. After a lockout lasting 196 days, the matter was finally settled with employers imposing their schedule in sixteen of the twenty-four affected shops. The Denver tailors, John B. Lennon later complained from his New York vantage point, "had not the least conception of the resistance they would have to meet" and had exhibited "the very worst kind of generalship."[36]

But, if, as Lennon's statement implied, this was war, overall the momentum lay with the unions. Strike activity in the late 1880s and early 1890s was characterized by a growing assertiveness over working conditions and by an attempt to limit managerial prerogatives. With the advent of the sympathy strikes, cresting in Denver in 1894 with a massive walkout of railroad workers in support of the Pullman boycott, Denver's workers also gave clear expression to the old Knights of Labor belief in working-class solidarity. The difference was that this belief was no longer expressed through spontaneous strike actions or through vague pronouncements at meetings of local assemblies. Rather it took the form of disciplined strike action that had been planned in advance and sanctioned by the union leadership.

Workers and Politics

The central place of the trade union in working-class activity in these years did not necessarily preclude an interest in political action. Denver trade unionists engaged in nonpartisan political lobbying and many of them were active in the mainstream political parties as well. Some trade unionists also backed independent third-party parties. But the central place of the trade union in the working-class movement meant that when Denver trade unionists engaged in independent political action, they did do so through a political party that accepted the institutional primacy of the trade union. Thus Denver's major independent third party in the late 1880s was neither a Greenback nor a Prohibition party, but rather an organization called the Union Labor party.

The Colorado Union Labor party began its life as the Denver United Labor club in January 1887, shortly after the divisive labor defeat in the 1886 election. Interestingly, individuals identified both with the Democrats (like Lennon) and with the Prohibitionists (like Buchanan and the shoemaker, O. L. Shove) participated in the new movement from the outset. Though a delegation of Colorado farmers attended one early meeting, arguing for planks on free water and regulation of the water monopoly, unionized workers played the dominant role. Indeed a public call in February to join the club indicated that membership was open only to "bona fide workingmen who are members of labor organizations, in good standing." When club members decided to send a delegate to the convention of labor party clubs to be held in Cincinnati in February, they unanimously named Buchanan as their delegate and subscribed $50 for his expenses.[37]

Denver's trade unionists were encouraged by the results of the Cincinnati convention. Though farmers dominated both the convention and the party's national executive board, the platform of the new organization, calling itself the National Union Labor party, endorsed nearly all of the demands of the Knights of Labor preamble, many of which (like the call for shorter hours) had as much appeal for trade unionists as for Knights. Also significant in shaping the outlook of trade unionists was the shift in the position on independent politics by the Federation of Organized Trades and Labor Unions (the immediate precursor of the AFL). At its convention late in 1886, the organization had hailed the rapid growth of political action among workers and urged "a most generous support to the independent political movement of the workingmen."[38]

But one should not overstate the importance of the national context. As James Wright has argued, the Colorado ULP operated "within a general antimonopoly, prolabor framework" established by earlier third parties in the state; its program "was a synthesis of the reform impulse as it had existed in Colorado prior to 1888." Like earlier parties, the ULP sought to recapture the republican social ideals that it argued had been undermined by the spread of monopoly and its attendant corruption of government and political life. Specifically, the party called for state construction of new reservoirs, the acquisition of existing corporate irrigation projects and the nationalization of railroads and telegraphs. None of these were new demands. Indeed, one Colorado newspaper claimed that the ULP was simply the old Greenback party in a new guise.[39]

There were significant differences between the ULP and its forerunners, however. Though drawing votes from Denver's working-class neighborhoods, and among key trade union and Knights of Labor leaders, both the Greenback and Prohibition parties had built their strongest base of support in the agricultural areas of northern Colorado, particularly Weld, Larimer, and Boulder counties—not in Denver. This fact was reflected in their candidates for office. On the Greenback ticket for Congress and various state offices in 1880, for example, only one out of six candidates resided in Denver. On the 1886 Prohibition ticket, the figure was two out of eight. (Though he was closely identified with the Denver labor movement, Joe Murray, who appeared on both tickets, was a resident of Fort Collins, not Denver.) In 1888, by way of contrast, four out of the ULP's eight candidates were Denver residents, including its nominees for governor (the minister of the social gospel, Gilbert DeLaMatyr), lieutenant governor, and congressional representative—that is, the whole top of the ticket.[40]

There is some evidence, in fact, that the entire base of the ULP lay in Denver. In the state election of 1888, the party polled slightly over twelve hundred votes, a very disappointing showing that spelled the end of the party as an important force in Colorado politics. But in the earlier Denver municipal election in the spring of 1887, the ULP had received fifteen hundred votes, demonstrating an impressive base in that city. But the real achievement of the party never lay in the election returns. Rather the ULP's accomplishment was twofold: it helped to unify various strands of the Denver working-class movement in a period marked by internal conflict, and it helped to strengthen and pass on the producer ideology of the Knights of Labor in a period when the order itself was in decline.[41]

The 1887 municipal elections, held shortly after the founding of the National ULP, saw labor tickets in over fifty cities around the country, including Chicago, Milwaukee, Cincinnati, and St. Louis. In some of these cities, the rise of the political movement set off internal warfare in the labor movement. But in Denver, the ULP effort had a unifying effect, healing wounds resulting from other conflicts. Thus leading officers of the Denver Trades Assembly were put forth as candidates for mayor, city treasurer, and city clerk. But representatives of the Knights of Labor stood as candidates for street and water commissioners. And in an effort to mend fences in the city's working-class movement, Burnette G. Haskell, Powderly's most vociferous critic, nominated Thomas Neasham for the position of city auditor. As leader of the Union Pacific Employees Association, Neasham was the general master workman's most loyal defender. The role of Haskell in the ULP also indicates the enthusiasm of the city's socialists for the new movement.[42]

"We, the organized working people of Denver, declare the first principle of Americanism is that he who will not labor neither shall he eat," read the preamble to the Denver ULP's municipal platform in 1887. "We approve this doctrine and further declare that the produce belongs to the producers, the tools to the toilers and that the speculators must go." Here was a classic formulation of the producer ideology, one usually associated with the Knights of Labor. Yet for all its attempts to build unity with the declining Knights in Denver, the ULP was the creation of the trade union movement in the city. Its state organizer and the secretary of the Denver club was John B. Lennon, Denver's leading exponent of trade unionism. Lennon's movement from the Democratic party to the new third party illustrates both the growing political assertiveness of the city's trade unionists and their desire to carry on the antimonopoly traditions of the Knights.[43]

As in Chicago, where the fear of a ULP victory led the two mainstream parties to fuse, denouncing the labor candidates as bomb-throwing anarchists, Denver's two parties reacted with alarm. Labor parties were "anti-American," proclaimed the Democratic press. More important, in the wake of the 1887 election, a group of middle-class "good government" reformers began a drive to take city government "out of politics" altogether. Their efforts were rewarded in 1889 when the state legislature established a new appointive commission, a Board of Public Works, to manage and control all municipal works in the city of Denver. Combined with the creation two years later of a Board of Fire and Police, the effect of this reform was to transfer large parts of municipal administration from city officials to the state governor, who appointed all members of the Boards. The Denver reform leader Platt Rogers liked to emphasize the way these changes helped end municipal corruption, telling the National Municipal League in 1894, for example, that the Board of Fire and Police was instituted "to prevent the debasement of the fire and police force by the mayor" and that Board of Public Works was created "to prevent the public improvement moneys being squandered by the City Council." But they also reflected one of the more general effects of the political upheaval of the 1880s. As in other cities, this upheaval, of which the rise of the ULP was one expression, had triggered the emergence of a deep mistrust of local democratic institutions by middle-class and business-oriented reformers, who used their influence in state capitals to shift political power upward, away from city governments that were seen as too vulnerable to working-class influence.[44]

Though the reforms may have been motivated in part by fear of a Union Labor party political victory, Denver's ULP was both something more and something less than a traditional political party. Over the course of its two-year existence, the ULP did not at all restrict itself to electoral activity and was fully prepared to take on what would later be called "direct action" to redress the wrongs facing the city's working people. By late May 1887, for example, the rapid growth of Denver's population had led to a sharp rise in the rents that landlords could charge their tenants. The ULP denounced "the so-called boom as a piece of commercial gambling and robbery, designed for the purpose of wringing from the poorer classes an unjust proportion of their earnings." Rather than taking action at the polls, however, the ULP resolved "that as a means of resistance, we, rent-payers of Denver, hereby severally pledge ourselves to at once purchase tents and secure ground upon which to pitch the same . . . locating our tents in a body together." Although this demonstration was apparently unsuccessful in lowering rents, it considerably broadened the scope of action normally associated with a political party.[45]

But the other side of this enthusiasm for direct action was a deep suspicion of politics and politicians. The ULP offered Denver voters a broad political platform during the municipal election of 1887, which included demands for a more equitable system of taxation, a reduction of the size of the police force, and the eight-hour day for city workers. Yet, paradoxically, the distrust of the political process that characterized the views of many in the American labor movement in these years also found expression in the ULP. While believing that some political action might be necessary to free government from the corrupting influence of monopoly, many laboring people believed that truly meaningful social transformation could occur only through the activities of working-class institutions themselves, especially trade unions and cooperatives. Many Denver workers probably agreed, at least in part, with the anarchist Dyer D. Lum who wrote a letter to the *Labor Enquirer* as the national convention of the ULP approached. Although he expressed qualified support for the new party, Lum cautioned workers that "we will not win our economic gains by 'working' at the ballot box. The ballot box can but abolish; it is powerless to construct. Freedom to the serf to economic bondage can only come by cooperative action." And Lum, at any rate, looked forward to the day when "there will be no longer government, for none would be governed." The ULP organizers indicated their ambivalence about politics more directly when they called on "every wage worker, who is not a professional politician" to join their movement.[46]

This skepticism toward political action, politicians, and the state had been associated with Denver's labor movement for several years. In 1884, Joseph Buchanan, dissenting from a central demand of the American labor movement, had even opposed the establishment of a federal Bureau of Labor Statistics. "Talk about 'concessions to the demands of the labor organizations' is allright," he admitted, "but it is not empty 'concessions' we want, but a fairer share of the world's goods—our products and the gifts of nature." No federal agency could accomplish this task. If it could, Buchanan pressed, the bill to establish the bureau "would never have received the sanction of the lower house of the capitalists' Congress." It is difficult, of course, to measure the influence of Buchanan's ideas among Denver's working people. He probably reached the height of his influence in 1886, when the *Labor Enquirer* was the official organ of both the Trades Assembly and the Denver Knights, and when both organizations encouraged their members to subscribe to it. Throughout this year, readers encountered Buchanan's suspicion of electoral politics in a slogan appearing weekly on the editorial page: "Equality in the ballot box is a mere juggle when there is social and industrial inequality all around."[47]

The Union Labor party thus played an important role in unifying various strands of the working-class movement of Denver and in preserving the Knights of Labor's broad reform vision. Nonetheless, the party did poorly in the county election of November 1887 and collapsed following its poor showing in the 1888 election, when it received only about 1,000 of the 91,000 votes cast in the gubernatorial election, less than half the votes won by the Prohibitionists this year. There were a number of reasons for this poor showing. First, the continuing resonance of the old political issues—the bloody shirt and the tariff—hurt all third parties in Colorado. Second, the antiradical themes that first surfaced in the 1887 Denver election continued on and gradually took their toll. Third, the disappointing returns reflected the ULP's inability to build support outside the ranks of Denver's organized trade unionists. Although its platform was designed to appeal to broad sectors of Colorado's citizens (and especially to farmers) the party's dominance by urban trade unionists hindered its ability to appeal to voters outside the ranks of Denver's organized working class. And the very distrust of politics felt by some of its activists stood in the way of their making changes that would have put the party on a stronger footing.[48]

But the biggest problem confronting the ULP was that by 1888 the mainstream of the Denver labor movement's leadership had come to reject independent labor party politics. Although they had been willing to experiment with independent initiatives at the municipal level, Denver trade unionists approached state politics mainly by engaging in nonpartisan lobbying of the legislature. The Denver Trades Assembly had been engaging in such lobbying since its formation in 1882, but for the first four years did not have much to show for its efforts. The difference in the late 1880s was that—partly perhaps because of the threat of independent political action in the wings—lobbying activity began to show some signs of success. "The [Colorado] General Assembly is having much attention from the circles of organized labor," observed a Denver railroad shop worker as the 1887 session of the legislature opened, "and we expect much from our representatives."[49]

On the whole, he would not be disappointed. The General Assembly in this session passed no fewer than five bills supported by labor. It established a state bureau of labor statistics, prohibited the employment of children under fourteen in mining, established the first Monday in September as Labor Day, outlawed the blacklist, and prohibited the hiring out of convict labor. Though not every labor-backed bill was passed, these were significant legislative victories. Ironically, though these victories appeared to validate the nonpartisan strategy increasingly recommended by AFL president Samuel Gompers, the threat of the ULP may have provided the impetus for the legislation. Significantly, the antiblacklisting and labor day bills were passed on the very eve of the Denver municipal election.[50]

The 1889 session of the legislature, which went down in Colorado history as the "Robber Seventh" because of its notorious corruption, nonetheless saw more labor victories, including an anticonspiracy law, a compulsory education law, and a mechanics lien law. To be sure, some Denver workers had doubts about the efficacy of these laws. While the editor of the *Union Pacific Employees Magazine* believed that the intentions behind the antiblacklisting bill were good, for instance, he believed that railroad workers "doubt very much its effectiveness, on account of the difficulty of getting proof that one company in refusing to employ a man, is doing so by the wish of another company." Despite such doubts, the legislative victories of the late 1880s undercut the ULP and encouraged the continued reliance on nonpartisan lobbying.[51]

Still, not all of Denver's trade unionists were nonpartisan. Both Republicans and Democrats could claim a following among labor activists in these years. A key Republican was O. L. Smith, a printer, Knight of Labor, and old friend of Buchanan's, who, in 1889, was elected president of the Denver Trades and Labor Assembly. In 1885, Smith had been elected to the Denver county Board of Supervisors, as a Republican. Well into the 1890s, he gave his time and money to the Republican party and frequently served as a delegate to party conventions. Also identified with the Republican party were the Irish-born Balfe brothers. Patrick Henry Balfe, a plumber who had served as the master workman of the Colorado Knights of Labor in 1881–82, was an active Republican, serving as a delegate to city, county, and state conventions as well as on local committees. Lawrence Balfe, also a plumber, had come to Denver in 1886 and held every office in the Denver plumbers local before being elected third vice president of the international union in 1897. An activist in the Ancient Order of Hibernians and the Irish American Progressive Society as well as in his union, Balfe was also a Republican, serving as a delegate to county and state conventions.[52]

It is not hard to see why some labor leaders would gravitate to the Republican party. From 1876 to 1890, the Republicans thoroughly dominated state government, losing gubernatorial elections only twice in these years, mainly because of factionalism among their own leaders. The party also dominated Denver municipal politics, virtually unchallenged by the Democrats. Any labor leader who wanted to be close to power at either the municipal or state level needed to be close to the GOP.[53]

In addition, some state Republican leaders, such as Judge James B. Belford, an ex-congressman, made more direct approaches to the labor movement. Belford defended the Denver and Rio Grande strikers in 1885 and spoke at a meeting of the Rocky Mountain Social League in 1886 and at an Independence Day labor demonstration in 1887. Even Buchanan considered him to be one of the "friends of the movement," though not all Denver's labor radicals agreed with his assessment. At the municipal level, Republicans made even more efforts to cultivate good relations with organized labor. While state GOP leaders like Edward Wolcott denounced engineers and firemen during the great Burlington Railroad strike of 1888, for example, Wolfe Londoner, a Denver merchant and local Republican who would run successfully for mayor the following year, publicized his support for the railroad workers. Local Republicans attempted to build on Londoner's success by nominating a politician named Milburn for the office in 1891. Though Milburn, according to the *Union Pacific Employees Magazine*, "has long been identified with organized labor in the city and is personally a respectable citizen," he was defeated by the middle-class "good government" reformer Platt Rogers.[54]

Not to be outdone, the Democratic party also tried to make appeals to organized workers in these years. Democrats were greatly hampered by their distance from political power, of course, but they made up for this by adopting more forcefully prolabor positions than Republicans. At the 1890 Knights of Labor General Assembly in Denver, the local lawyer and Democratic leader Charles S. Thomas gave a speech which, as the *Journal of the Knights of Labor* reported it, was a "genuine surprise" to those present:

> It was eloquent, sympathetic, and gave evidence of a life-long study of the labor problem. Knights of Labor have often heard lawyers discant upon the industrial problems, but it was an agreeable surprise to find one who had made it the enthusiastic study of his life, and who was beyond all question as deeply in earnest as any member of a labor organization could be in his advocacy of the claims of the wealth creators to the results of their toil. Clear cut, incisive, with every word the result of study and conviction, Mr. Thomas' address was pronounced by those who heard it one of the best labor speeches they had ever listened to.[55]

The speech undoubtedly improved Thomas's standing among Denver working people and he would be elected governor with labor support in 1898. But Thomas was not alone among Democrats in using the Knights' meeting to score points among workers. While the *Denver Republican* was ambivalent in its welcome to the Knights, praising them only for "the moderation and the conservatism of the leaders" and going on to denounce "radicalism," the Democratic *Rocky Mountain News* used the opportunity to offer a ringing denunciation of "the great combinations of wealth and corporate power" and especially "the policy of disruption which has been adopted by the corporations, and pushed by such infamous means as smuggling Pinkerton spies into labor unions to promote discord."[56]

The tradition of wariness regarding political action, the success of nonpartisan lobbying efforts, and the continuing influence of the mainstream parties combined to shape the Denver labor movement's early relationship with the only third party that achieved success in Colorado, the People's party. Though it was organized by members of the Grange and the Farmers Alliance in Colorado, by 1892 there was some urban working-class support for the new party. Knights of Labor in Denver's Union Pacific shops, for instance, rallied to the Peoples party. L.A. 3218, the Union Pacific assembly, had featured the famous Farmers' Alliance orator from Kansas, Mary Ellen Lease, at its seventh anniversary celebration in June 1891, where she was cheered for her denunciations of the old parties' rule. The *Union Pacific Employees Magazine* strongly supported Davis H. Waite, the party's gubernatorial candidate in 1892, and in the city elections of April 1893, the magazine's editor, Julius Corbin, who had attended the Populist state convention in 1891, ran unsuccessfully as the Populist candidate for city clerk. Other labor movement figures joined in. W. F. Hynes, a Denver leader of the Brotherhood of Locomotive Firemen, who was, according to the *Union Pacific Employees Magazine,* "well known among railroad men throughout the country," won election to the state legislature on the People's party ticket in 1892.[57]

But, in general, Denver's labor activists remained aloof from the new movement. In sharp contrast with the city's Union Labor party, which had been dominated by trade unionists, the leadership ranks of the county central committee of the People's party in 1892 contained not one labor figure. Of the seven members of its executive and finance committees, only one was a manual worker, and he was a cook who was apparently not active in the union movement. Two lawyers, two agents and a contractor made up the other identifiable members. This profile of Denver's Populist leaders roughly paralleled that of the state party leaders, whose most common occupations lay in the areas of real estate, retail marketing, law, and education.[58]

Though Waite and many other Populist candidates were swept into office in 1892, the Peoples party lost Denver, along with the other large cities of the state, Pueblo and Colorado Springs. Undoubtedly, the main cause of their poor showing here was the continuing importance of old political loyalties. But an additional factor was the suspicion of potentially sympathetic trade unionists who held back from full support. Many of Denver's organized workers must have agreed with the position of an Omaha labor paper, the *Western Laborer,* on the Populist movement. Noting that some Populist editors had criticized trade unionism while simultaneously trying to get organized workers to "throw their whole soul into the People's party," the paper argued that "the new party is a great improvement on the old ones in many respects, but it cannot expect the undivided support of union men if it continues to belittle their organizations." Populists needed to understand that "union men are leary of promises and do not propose to jump at conclusions." In a statement that beautifully captured trade unionists' notion of the relationship between the union and the political party, the *Western Laborer* went on to proclaim that "a People's party paper which 'roasts' the union is much like the man who curses his Maker."[59]

The years from 1887 to 1892, then, marked the emergence of a relatively consistent outlook on political action among trade unionists in the city. Though generally oriented toward the mainstream parties, many labor activists were prepared to support a third party like the ULP, which recognized the need to maintain and protect the independence of the trade union, increasingly seen as the central institution in the working-class movement. But they were also deeply suspicious of those "politicians" (even reformers) who would subordinate the trade union movement to some other political cause.

Working-Class Radicalism

The suspicion of independent politics that has been traced here was characteristic of the trade union movement across the country in these years, and it goes far toward explaining the growing isolation of socialists from the mainstream of the labor movement. One of the key features of Daniel DeLeon's wing of the Socialist Labor party—the main socialist organization in this era—was that it *reversed* the relationship between trade union and political party that even *socialist* trade unionist activists (the carpenter's national leader, Peter J. McGuire, for example) felt proper. Rather than conceptualizing the political party as an adjunct of the trade union movement, DeLeon argued that the trade unions should be satellites of the socialist political party—DeLeon's party, to be precise. DeLeon's position was a controversial one in the SLP and came under strong attack from other party leaders, like Morris Hillquit and Max Hayes. Nevertheless, his 1895 founding of the Socialist Trade and Labor Alliance as a federation of unions in direct competition with the AFL, the logical extreme of his position, badly hurt the cause of socialism in the organized labor movement. The experience of socialists in the Denver labor movement, however, was rather different. Socialism, to be sure, was never more than a minority trend within that movement. But socialists in the city, far from experiencing the isolation of the SLP, drew closer to the city's trade unions and exerted considerable influence within them.[60]

The Socialist Labor party had virtually no presence in Denver in these years. There were individual members of the SLP in the city, as well as supporters of its positions among members of the German-speaking Independent Socialist Club and the Rocky Mountain Social League. But a Denver section of the SLP was not organized until 1894. Only in 1896, when the party put forward a full slate of candidates for state offices, did it become a force among working-class radicals.[61]

On the other hand, socialist activity among English-speaking workers had a history in the city going back to 1883, when Joseph Buchanan accepted a commission as organizer for the International Workingmen's Association. The IWA drew few recruits in Denver, but with the founding of the Rocky Mountain Social League in January 1886, socialism in Denver obtained its first public forum. The League's weekly meetings, devoted to lectures, discussions and song, attracted considerable (and—surprisingly—often favorable) attention from the press, the pulpit, and aspiring politicians. With Buchanan's departure from Denver and the arrival of Burnette G. Haskell, the Social League took on a somewhat different character. While continuing to publicize socialist ideas through meetings, the League also suddenly emerged at the center of the trade union organizing drive in Denver. Far from holding a philosophy hostile to trade unionism, the League's members put forward views that were simply radical versions of accepted trade union practice. These views represented an early version of what would be known in the twentieth century as syndicalism.[62]

To be sure, a wide variety of radical intellectual currents flowed through Denver working-class life in the late 1880s. Both the single tax reform and greenbackism continued to generate support among trade unionists. Christian socialism, ably represented by the Reverend Myron Reed, had some followers. In the early 1890s, Carpenters Local No. 460 in South Denver endorsed resolutions presented by the local Bellamite Nationalist club and nationalist ideas were also endorsed by S. W. Harmon, the editor of a short-lived Trades Assembly weekly newspaper. Though anarchism had no clear local following, Carpenters Local No. 55 was sufficiently interested in the subject to host the Chicago revolutionary Lucy Parsons on one occasion. Nevertheless, for all of this range of views, it was the IWA and the Social League that dominated the sphere of organized radicalism in the city.[63]

Neither organization drew a large number of adherents in Denver during this period, probably one hundred at most. Until the red scare that followed the Haymarket bombing in May 1886, Denver's middle class tolerated socialists as a group of "cranks." At least one Denver socialist, a machinist at the Denver and Rio Grande repair shops, embraced the description with enthusiasm. Drawing a metaphor from his own trade, John Swank noted that just as "there could be no revolution in mechanics without a crank, neither could there be in social advancement." His point was well taken, for despite their small numbers, Denver socialists of the 1880s and 1890s proved essential in building the intellectual foundations of twentieth-century labor radicalism in the West. They did so by providing a radical interpretation of the central force in the labor movement of these years: trade unionism. Denver socialists not only accepted the principles of independent trade unionism but also did their utmost to further those principles. By taking this position, they avoided the political isolation experienced by the SLP and left an important mark on the city's labor movement as a whole.[64]

The IWA had shared the trade unionists' suspicion to politics and politicians from its earliest days in San Francisco. "Members engaged in party politics or who intended to affiliate with political wire pullers were requested to surrender their cards at once to the Division Secretary," noted the minutes of an 1884 IWA meeting in that city. While rejecting the anarchists' idea of "propaganda by deed," the IWA was equally opposed to the single-minded party-building of the SLP. "We are revolutionary socialists," Haskell declared in 1885, "and cannot accept the tactics of the Socialistic Labor Party who believe in the ballot." Indeed, because IWA members believed that "participation in politics, as at present conducted, not only corrupts the leaders, but the rank and file as well," one of their foremost goals was "to eradicate the impression that redress can be obtained by the ballot."[65]

Buchanan and his comrades in the Denver IWA and Rocky Mountain Social League, on the whole, agreed with this basic outlook. Their opposition to political activity was far from dogmatic. Buchanan supported Benjamin Butler's presidential campaign in 1884 and the Prohibitionists in 1886, and Social League members threw themselves into the Union Labor party in 1887. But on the whole, they placed their main hopes for socialism in the building of independent working-class institutions, such as trade unions and Knights of Labor local assemblies, and in the development of a cadre of socialists within these institutions.[66]

During 1887, the Rocky Mountain Social League, under Haskell's leadership until he left Denver in September, embarked on two projects. The first was participation in the establishment of a cooperative colony at Topolobampo Bay in the state of Sinaloa, Mexico. Though the brain child of entrepreneur Albert Kimsey Owen, many of the most enthusiastic members of the colony were railroad shop workers, blacklisted after the Denver and Rio Grande strike in 1885. Although the project finally collapsed in 1894, it attracted considerable attention among "advanced social reformers" in Colorado throughout the late 1880s and early 1890s. The main purpose of the colony was to establish a model socialist community, based on Owen's concept of "integral cooperation," that would inspire the socialist movement in the United States.[67]

Throughout 1887, the *Labor Enquirer* provided thorough descriptions of life in the colony. Although individuals there continued to own their personal property, the means of production and distribution (that is land and tools) were under communal ownership and control. The colonists also strove to transform cultural life: thus the colony had, in the words of one member, "no secret societies, no saloons, and no churches." As originally conceived, the colony was not supposed to have workers' organizations either. Albert Owen's ideas regarding labor were thoroughly paternalistic, drawing on, among other models, that of Pullman, Illinois. But the two hundred colonists from Denver, many of them with experience in both the Rocky Mountain Social League and in the Knights of Labor assembly in the Denver and Rio Grande shops, had very different ideas. Some of them, at least, brought an emphasis on working-class self-organization and a concern with how work itself should be organized. Upon arrival at Topolobampo, the Denver contingent organized themselves into labor groups, democratically elected their own foremen, established the principle of equal pay for all work, and began a system of rotating jobs. In short, they made workers' control an essential part of the venture, completely undermining Owen's paternalistic approach to labor.[68]

In late February 1887, a smallpox epidemic and a dangerous shortage of food led to the first of many crises in the colony. Two of its directors deserted, one of them allegedly carrying $600 of the colony's funds with him. But Thomas Young, one of the blacklisted railroad workers and an activist in the Rocky Mountain Social League, assured his friends in the Denver labor movement that there was no panic at the Topolobampo Bay colony, while simultaneously giving expression to its democratic political vision. "We, the colonists, are united and in earnest, and have no time to act as the tools of any self-interested director who may have come here with a big head on him," Young wrote to the *Labor Enquirer*. "We are able to direct ourselves." By May, the colony had emerged from crisis, and Young took the opportunity to contrast political life in the new community with that in Denver. In Topolobampo, elections passed quietly, no advance nominations were made, and each individual simply filled out a ballot listing his or her—for women had the vote here—choice for colony officers. "We trust in the people to do their own thinking, and not allow packed caucuses and conventions to do it for them," Young wrote. Combined with the emphases on worker self-organization and workers' control, this radically democratic political practice, growing in part from the experience of workers like Thomas Young in Denver's trade unions and Knights of Labor assemblies, had a tremendous impact on the thinking of working people and their allies in Denver and in other places. Topolobampo was far from a "backward looking" effort to roll back industrial capitalism. Rather, while a long way from full-blown syndicalism, it pointed in that direction.[69]

The second project that the Rocky Mountain Social League undertook in 1887 flowed logically from this protosyndicalist perspective. Regarding trade unionism as an embryonic form of socialism, the League spent much of its energy organizing trade unions. Consequently, it was able to make a tremendous contribution to the rapid growth of unions in Denver in the late 1880s.

Regarded by Buchanan as "brilliant but erratic," Burnette G. Haskell emerged at the center of the trade union organizing drive in Denver in 1887. Haskell made speeches to unions and workers attempting to organize unions all over the city, while his *Labor Enquirer* hammered again and again at the need for organization. By one account, Haskell personally organized ten trade unions in Denver between March and September 1887. Whether or not this claim was accurate, in his confrontation with Terence Powderly in May, Haskell did emerge as the leading voice for trade union supporters both in the Denver Knights of Labor and in that organization nationally.[70]

The organizational structure of the Rocky Mountain Social League reflected its increasing trade union orientation. In 1886, it had been made up of individuals from a wide variety of occupations and had maintained a very loose organization. Although the League continued to be open to all who might join, by the end of 1887 most trade unions in Denver had semiofficial representation in the organization. Thus under Haskell's leadership, the League began to emerge as the "ideological" arm of the trade union movement—or, at least, of the radicals within it. This development represented a complete reversal of De Leon's theory of the party/trade union relationship, but it was one much attuned to the protosyndicalism of the Denver socialists.[71]

Haskell himself proved to be an indispensable figure to Denver's labor radicals. Following his departure from Denver to help found the Kaweah cooperative colony in the Sierra Nevada mountains in late 1887, both the *Labor Enquirer* and the Rocky Mountain Social League collapsed. The final chapter of the League's history, however, is worth telling, for it reveals its role in shaping the syndicalist strain in twentieth-century western labor radicalism.

Shortly before Haskell left Denver, the members of the Rocky Mountain Social League proposed a merger of their organization with the national Socialist Labor party. As a condition of unification, however, they demanded that the SLP make a number of crucial changes in its policies. First, the League demanded that the SLP drop the word "party" from its name, changing its name to the "Socialist League" or the "Socialist Association." These terms were suggestive of the loose and democratic structure emphasized by syndicalists, as well as of their rejection of electoral activity; both terms were to be commonly used among syndicalist organizations of the early twentieth century. Second, the league called on the SLP to declare against political action. Third, it demanded that the organization devote less funds to supporting the socialist movement in Germany and more to supporting propaganda in the American labor movement, a demand that probably stemmed from the fact that, unlike SLP members, League members were not on the whole German Americans, and so felt little of the sense of connection to Germany that the SLP maintained. Finally, the League argued for the admission of the "anti-political" Chicago anarchists to the new organization.[72]

The 1887 national convention of the SLP debated this proposal at length. While some delegates, such as the Chicago editor Paul Grottkau, supported "the union of all Socialistic elements," others expressed the fear that the Rocky Mountain Social League was "not free of Anarchism." Delegates finally appointed a committee to look into the character of the organization, and this committee, "in a spirit of fraternity," proposed that the SLP reject all of the League's demands and assert that its own platform and principles were "complete, comprehensive, and satisfactory." The convention unanimously adopted this resolution and the Rocky Mountain Social League permanently disbanded in early 1888. Nevertheless, there is evidence that the League's protosyndicalist perspective, revealed in this last gesture, continued to have an influence among rank-and-file activists in Denver's labor movement. This influence was reflected in the tremendous popularity of a book by Laurence Gronlund, *The Cooperative Commonwealth*. Though Denver labor radicals may not have articulated a full radical vision in which trade unionism occupied the central place, Gronlund did.[73]

A Danish immigrant to America, Gronlund published the first edition of his book in 1884. Like his contemporary, Henry George, he had the ability to make complex matters of political economy accessible to a broad audience and denounced capitalism in a language of morality that had considerable resonance. As a result, *The Cooperative Commonwealth* was widely read, with about sixty-thousand copies sold in the United States. But Gronlund diverged from George in two crucial respects. First, he was a socialist—in fact, for a while, a leading theorist of the Socialist Labor party—and a severe critic of George's single tax theory. The early chapters of his book constituted a popularization of Marx's *Capital*. Second, and here he parted ways with both George and Marx, Gronlund articulated an early version of a significant part of the syndicalist outlook.[74]

It was not that Gronlund opposed political action. Despite his criticisms of Henry George's economic theory, he backed the single taxer's campaign for mayor of New York in 1886 and worked with him in the United Labor party until the break between the socialists and single taxers in 1887. Though critical of the Populists' Omaha platform for ignoring the industrial wage earner, he nonetheless supported the Populists in the

1890s as the only "reform," "moral," and "American" party. After the 1894 election, he called for the formation of a new "Plebian" party that would better represent workers' interests in the political arena.[75]

It was in his conception of the postcapitalist society, the delineation of which occupied the main body of the *Cooperative Commonwealth*, that Gronlund staked out the syndicalist position. The workplace organization of the proletariat occupied the central place in that conception. "'Political' power, 'Politics,' 'Politicians' will be unknown terms under the New Order," he wrote. Instead, workers themselves, represented in syndicalist fashion by organizations of their trades, "will decide what the Administration of the Future is to be." For Gronlund, the very existence of trade unions, the "invaluable skeletons" of the future society, proved that socialism was well-suited to American life. "The central spirit of these unions is that of Socialism, to wit, that the interests of all workers are the same, that each must postpone his own advantage to the common good and each yield his individual prejudice and crochet to the collective judgement." It is easy to see why the *Cooperative Commonwealth* would have a powerful resonance among radical trade unionists.[76]

Gronlund had a large impact on Denver and Colorado labor radicals. In 1887, the Rocky Mountain Social League devoted part of one of its meetings to a discussion of the book, and in the early months of 1888, articles by Gronlund began to appear in the *Labor Enquirer*. Gronlund's work hit the peak of its influence in Denver in the early 1890s, when the popularity of Edward Bellamy's *Looking Backward* (itself strongly influenced by Gronlund) and the appearance of a new, more readable, edition of the book put its utopian socialist vision in the public eye. In the southern Colorado steel town of Pueblo, an English-born shoemaker, William Bradfield, gave a local publisher and real estate speculator named Julius A. Wayland a copy of the book. Wayland later recounted that upon seeing the word "socialism" in Gronlund's subtitle, "I was tempted to throw the book away." But once he read it, Wayland claimed, his life was changed for ever. "To be brief, he [Gronlund] 'landed' me good and hard. I saw a new light and found what I never knew existed. I saw what the increasing dullness meant and went into the financial study so thoroughly that the result was, I closed up my real estate business and devoted my whole energies to the work of trying to get my neighbors to see the truths I had learned."[77]

Wayland would go on to become one of the most influential socialist journalists in American history, his Girard, Kansas, weekly, *Appeal to Reason*, becoming the most important Socialist party newspaper of the early twentieth century. While in Colorado, where he resided until 1893, Wayland claimed to have distributed hundreds of copies of Gronlund's *Cooperative Commonwealth*. He also provided his own version of Gronlund's ideas in his columns in a Pueblo daily paper and in his own weekly newspaper, the *Coming Crisis*, which played an important role in the Populist campaign of 1892. Although a small local paper when he took it over, Wayland claimed to have nearly four thousand paid up subscribers by December 1892. Since the paper was geared toward urban working people, rather than farmers, and since Denver was the main center of the Colorado labor movement in 1892, it is likely that a good percentage of the readers of the *Coming Crisis* (described by Wayland as "as surely and radically a socialist paper" as the SLP's *People*) were Denver workers. Here they encountered Wayland's version of Gronlund's ideas on a weekly basis.[78]

Gronlund's popularity among Colorado workers undoubtedly had many sources. Much of his book's power came from his religious rhetoric (a trait he shared with Henry George) and his persuasive critique of the doctrine of individualism. But the book's syndicalist orientation could not be missed. This was the basis for Edward Bellamy's criticism of the work. Though Bellamy felt that he and Gronlund had much in common, there was one crucial difference between them: "the germ of the coming order Mr. Gronlund professes to see in the trades unions," he complained, "while the nationalists see it in the nation." Though this aspect of Gronlund's work may have disturbed Bellamy, it effectively expressed and systematized the views of Denver's labor radicals.[79]

Syndicalism was never more than a minority current in the Denver labor movement in these years. AFL president Samuel Gompers was probably correct when he praised Denver Trades Assembly leader Adam Menche in 1890 by suggesting that he possessed "advantages for organizing our fellow-workers in Colorado over our friends Buchanan or Haskell." Gompers noted that "both these worthy men were known to have theories which the people neither appreciated nor understood." But despite their minority status, Denver's radical workers were never isolated, but on the contrary were an integral part of the city's labor movement. Equally important, by the early 1890s they had established the foundations of the syndicalist ideology that would emerge full-blown in twentieth-century labor radicalism.[80]

5 Depression, Populists and Industrial Unionism, 1893–98

In May 1898, a convention of working people meeting in Salt Lake City formed a new labor organization called the Western Labor Union. The Western Federation of Miners, an industrial union of hard rock miners in the West that had grown rapidly since its inception in 1893, played the leading part in the founding of the WLU. Although not yet totally hostile to the American Federation of Labor, the WLU sought above all to build industrial unions among unskilled western workers, an objective far removed from the craft union orientation of the AFL. "Through the medium of the Western Labor Union," proclaimed the founding document of the new organization, "such rights as tradesmen now enjoy will be extended to the common laborer."[1]

The WLU, which would achieve prominence in Denver in the early twentieth century, maintained and modified the emerging syndicalist orientation of western labor radicals discussed in the preceding chapter. But its outlook differed in one crucial respect from theirs. Its leaders had come to believe that craft unionism, and a labor movement restricted to skilled craftsmen—no matter how radical they might be—was antiquated and divisive. The movement that a new generation of Denver labor radicals envisioned was of an entirely different order. It would rely on the energies of *both* skilled and unskilled workers organized together in industrial, not craft, unions. This was an important distinction. It led Bill Haywood, a leading figure in the Denver working-class movement after 1900 and a founding member of the IWW, to conclude that the IWW did not really advocate syndicalism at all. Its philosophy, he argued, should be called "industrialism."[2]

This distinctive emphasis first emerged in the deep depression that lasted from 1893 to 1897. Although the industrial union form had made an appearance in Denver as early as 1884 with the organization of the Union Pacific Employees Association and although brewery workers and streetcar workers had adopted an industrial type of organization in the late 1880s and early 1890s, the 1890s depression, which struck Denver with tremendous force, placed the question of industrial unionism at the forefront of the labor movement. There were two reasons for this. First, traditional craft unions were manifestly powerless to prevent wage cuts or layoffs in the face of the depression, let alone achieve the sweeping social transformation envisioned by labor radicals. Second, the depression ushered in a new period of militant activism among unskilled workers, partly a result of their politicization by the Populist movement, that led radical skilled workers to view them as important—indeed essential—allies in the struggle for social change.

Industrial Union Precedents

Industrial unions, seeking to organize workers on an industry-wide basis rather than on the basis of the specific crafts they may practice, first appeared in Denver following the Union Pacific shop workers' strike of 1884. The Union Pacific Employees Association (D.A. 82 of the Knights of Labor), which grew out of the strike, eventually extended its jurisdiction all along the Union Pacific lines in the West, though Denver's L.A. 3218 continued to be its largest local assembly. The District Assembly embraced all grades of railroad shop workers in "mixed" assemblies. Not only did machinists, boiler makers, blacksmiths, and carpenters join the Union Pacific Employees Association, but so also did helpers, car repairers, and wipers, the lowest paid workers in the shops.[3]

Nonetheless, the Union Pacific workers' organization did not represent a full-fledged expression of industrial unionism. First, D.A. 82 never managed to extend its jurisdiction beyond a single corporation. Second, the engineers, firemen, and conductors, who were crucial to the operation of any railroad, remained outside of its ranks, usually retaining their membership in the conservative railroad brotherhoods. Finally, and most importantly, the organization did not represent the predominantly nonwhite or recent immigrant track laborers and section men, who (though their numbers varied from summer to winter) probably represented the largest single category of Union Pacific workers. As one of its leaders stated, although D.A. 82 stood "for the promotion, conservation and unification of the interests of all the employees of the Union Pacific System not otherwise affiliated," it was composed "especially" of "those employees in and about the shops."[4]

The growth of the Knights of Labor in Denver in the mid-1880s had been accompanied by considerable interest in organizing the unskilled, a development that might conceivably have raised the question of industrial unionism. There is no evidence, however, that the leaders of the

Knights in Denver attached any particular importance to the distinction between craft and industrial organizational forms. Joseph Buchanan's 1886 plan for the amalgamation of national trade districts in the Knights of Labor, for example, was designed to provide greater unity of action within the American working-class movement. In their internal organization, however, these trade districts were simply traditional trade unions. The difference lay in their formal attachment to the order, not in their departure from the practices of craft unionism.[5]

In the later 1880s, the first tentative steps were taken toward the organization of industrial unions. The Brewery Workers Union, organized in Milwaukee in 1886, adopted an industrial form of organization in the following year. Although skilled German brewers continued to constitute the core of the union, from 1887 on it considered coopers, engineers, firemen, and teamsters who worked in and around breweries to be under its jurisdiction. "Solidarity, man for man from roof to cellar, all for each and each for all—this alone can secure our future," proclaimed the national secretary of the union in 1887. In November of that year, forty brewers in Denver formed a local of the Brewery Workers Union, embracing its industrial structure. By the end of 1888, nearly all of the employees of Denver's breweries, regardless of occupation, were members of the union.[6]

In the late 1880s, some railroad workers in Denver also began to advocate a broad industrial union of railroad employees that would encompass both shopmen and trainmen and embrace all of the nation's railroad systems. In response to the significant defeat that engineers and firemen had suffered during the Chicago, Burlington, and Quincy Railroad strike of 1888, Eugene V. Debs and several other brotherhood leaders established a centralized federation of the various national railroad brotherhoods. Calling itself the Supreme Council of the United Order of Railway Employees, the new organization was greeted with criticism from some Denver railroad workers. There was no opposition to the general principle of federation. Indeed, Knights of Labor on the Union Pacific had been putting forward plans for federation since 1885. In 1886, even a rebellious Denver lodge of the Brotherhood of Locomotive Firemen had pointed out that labor had suffered "due to the independent action of distinct organizations, attempting to adjust difficulties that involve the interests of many branches of the industry." The problem, as the Denverites saw it, was that the new organization did not go far enough. It excluded shop workers from its ranks, and it possessed an overly centralized structure. The Supreme Council was a federation of distinct organizations, rather than a true industrial union. "Federation must begin at the bottom, not at the top," argued Julius Corbin of the Union Pacific Employees Association in 1889. "Its foundation must rest among those on the engines, trains, tracks and in the yard, shops, roundhouses and offices. It is these that have trouble and grievances, and it is those who know what they are, much better than any supreme council thousands of miles away. They must fight the battles and must be the ones to try and prevent them."[7]

In 1891, the Supreme Council collapsed, primarily as a result of conflicts between switchmen and brakemen on the Chicago and Northwestern Railroad. Debs, along with several other former leaders of the Council, went on to organize the American Railway Union, the most famous American industrial union of the nineteenth century. Even before the collapse of the Supreme Council, Debs was apparently beginning to be influenced by the industrial union model advanced by the Union Pacific workers. In July 1890, he came to Denver to meet with Corbin, representatives of the rebel Denver firemen's lodge, and Knights of Labor railroad workers "from throughout the West." Here, according to the report in the *Union Pacific Employees Magazine*, "various proposed details of practical federation [were] thrashed out with profit to all." When the ARU was formed in the early part of 1893, it followed the model that had been outlined by Corbin and the Union Pacific workers.[8]

Not surprisingly, the Union Pacific workers hailed the birth of the new organization as a major step forward for labor. At D.A. 82's annual meeting in September 1893, "E.V. Debs' efforts to unite all railroad employees were commended as a move in the right direction." Corbin maintained that the ARU's presence freed the Knights of Labor's D.A. 82 from the "detail work of a trade organization" and allowed it to enter "the broader field of social reform." By November 1893, the ARU had thoroughly organized workers on the Union Pacific railroad, and D.A. 82 merged entirely with the new industrial union the following year.[9]

It was, in addition, a legal conflict involving the Union Pacific workers that gave the ARU its first great victory. In October 1893, the Union Pacific system, faced with an array of deep financial difficulties exacerbated by the depression beginning that year, went into receivership. The receivers declared a wage cut for all Union Pacific employees and petitioned the Federal District Court of Nebraska to have all previous work rules and agreements with unions put aside. They also sought to enjoin workers from striking. In the tradition of Judge David Brewer's decision in the Denver and Rio Grande strike, and reflecting the increasing use of the injunction in railroad disputes in these years, Judge Elmer S. Dundy decided in favor of the receivers in late January 1894. He held that receivers were not bound by any labor agreements entered into before receivership and declared their revised rules, regulations and schedules to be "prima facie reasonable and just," though they had been adopted without any consultation with workers. He also issued an extremely broad injunction, declaring it unlawful for any UP employees "to conspire, combine or confederate together, or with, by or through any labor or other organization or the officers of committees thereof, or with any other person or persons whomsoever, for the purpose or with the intention of inducing a strike" or "for the purpose of hindering, impeding, delaying, obstructing, embarrassing or injuring the said Receivers in and about the conduct of the business." In a single decision, Dundy sought to wipe out nearly nine years of gains made by the Union Pacific workers.[10]

But in April 1894, after a week-long hearing, Judge Henry Clay Caldwell of the Eighth Circuit Court overruled the decision, throwing out Dundy's injunction and leaving all the original wage schedules and labor agreements intact. Caldwell, who had served thirty years on the federal bench and who had a reputation among contemporaries for placing personal rights over property rights, declared that the "employment of sober, intelligent, experienced and capable men" was essential to the running of a railroad and that when a court assumed the management of a road, it would not "upon light or trivial grounds, dispense with their services or reduce their wages." All wage schedules, work rules, and labor agreements in existence when the receivers took over, especially if these were "the result of a mutual agreement between the company and the employees, which has been in force for years," would be presumed to be "reasonable and just." Caldwell called the receivers' attempt to make changes in wage schedules without conferring with the workers' representatives a "fundamental error," likening it to "first hanging a man, and trying him afterwards." He also dismissed the opinions of the receivers as "of little value," noting that a majority of them were not "practical railroad men." "Two of them are lawyers residing in New York, one a merchant residing in Chicago," Caldwell pointed out.

Finally, in reversing Dundy's broad injunction, Caldwell offered powerful language legitimizing workers' rights to combine for self-protection. While a corporation was "capital consisting of money and property," organized labor was "capital consisting of brains and muscle," he argued. "If it is lawful for the stockholders and officers of a corporation to associate and confer for the purpose of reducing the wages of its employees . . . it is equally lawful for organized labor to associate, consult and confer with a view to maintain or increase wages. . . . Men in all stations and pursuits in life have an undoubted right to join together for resisting oppression or for mutual assistance," Caldwell maintained, and when the receivers unilaterally adopted new wage schedules, they naturally aroused "resentment in the breast of every self-respecting, intelligent and independent man in the service."[11]

Caldwell's vision of the court, and by implication the state as a whole, as an arbiter between capital and labor, rather than as agent of repression, left little lasting mark on the law. In the realm of labor relations, the era of government by injunction was only beginning. But the alternative vision of the state that Caldwell offered on the eve of the Pullman strike could be adopted by other sympathetic governmental officials, and within months Colorado's governor Davis Waite would be employing such language in his handling of labor conflict in the state. In more immediate terms, the UP workers' legal victory put the American Railway Union—and with it the idea of industrial unionism—on the map.[12]

Depression

Thus, important precedents for the industrial union movement already existed in Denver by the early 1890s. Nonetheless, it was the so-called Panic of 1893 that brought the question of industrial unionism to the center of discussions in the city's labor movement. The financial panic of May 1893 had severe effects throughout the nation, for it brought in its wake a long period of business failures and extremely high unemployment. The effects in Colorado were even more devastating than in the nation at large. Silver prices on the world market were already declining, and when Great Britain closed the Indian Mints to silver coinage in June, the last major market for American silver was effectively shut. In four days in late June, the price of silver dropped from eighty cents to sixty-two cents an ounce. By the end of the month, every mine in the once prosperous Leadville district had closed down.[13]

Highly dependent on this key extractive industry, Colorado's entire economy felt the impact of silver's collapse. Newly built steel mills at Pueblo shut down in July and the volume of railroad traffic throughout the state plummeted. In the three days from 17 July to 19 July, twelve of Denver's banks went out of business. Although unemployment was naturally highest in the mining districts, an estimated fourteen thousand workers in Denver, representing perhaps a quarter of the city's work force, were thrown out of work in the summer of 1893. Meanwhile, approximately four thousand unemployed miners from throughout the state drifted into the capital city, seeking employment or relief.[14]

The depression revealed with stark clarity the limitations of craft unionism. Denver Typographical Union No. 49, the strongest labor organization in the city, received a demand from all of the major daily newspapers for an immediate reduction of wages. It accepted the reduction without a strike. Throughout the city, "panic wages" remained the rule over the next two years. There was some resistance. In February 1894, cigar makers at the three largest Denver factories were locked out after refusing a wage cut, and the issue was eventually compromised, with workers taking a cut of $1 per thousand cigars instead of the original $2. But this was about the best craftsmen could expect. In the face of rapidly rising unemployment, unions could do little to prevent reductions in pay.[15]

Craft unions were equally powerless in the face of massive layoffs. Unskilled workers were actually the hardest hit by the reductions in work forces: Denver's three smelters began shutting down their operations and laying off laborers shortly after the June collapse of silver prices and many domestic servants were soon thrown out of work as well. But skilled workers, particularly those in transportation and the building trades, experienced very high levels of unemployment as well. Contemporary observers mentioned carpenters, bricklayers, teamsters, railroad train and shop workers, and printers as among those affected by layoffs. Some skilled craftsmen, such as carpenters, cigar makers and printers, received limited unemployment benefits from their unions, and this distinguished their experience from that of the unskilled. But in general, the economic crisis of 1893 seemed to have had the effect—at least temporarily—of reducing the differences in the conditions of life between skilled and unskilled working people in Denver. "High paid men are practically no better off than low paid men," observed a Union Pacific shop worker. "All the hard work done in establishing a rule of wages goes for naught when the ones who agree to pay wages refuse or have not the means to give employment." [16]

If the city's trade union movement could do little to prevent unemployment, it could take action to help the unemployed. By July 1893, workers in Denver began demanding relief, and demonstrations of the unemployed soon became a regular occurance, one of them attracting over two thousand people. Speakers at these demonstrations demanded that the city provide work for the unemployed and that landlords reduce rents.[17]

Finally the Denver Trades Assembly took matters into its own hands, and decided to provide food and shelter for the large numbers of unemployed itself. Obtaining tents and furniture, selecting cooks and waiters from among the unemployed, and soliciting supplies from local merchants, the Trades Assembly established a "Camp Relief" in Denver's Riverfront Park on 28 July. For the next seven weeks, Camp Relief provided shelter and two meals a day to between one thousand and fifteen hundred men.[18]

The importance of the Trades Assembly's efforts should not be underestimated. The Denver labor movement was attempting to perform a function that had previously been left to private charity. Its relief efforts thus fell within the tradition of mutuality characteristic of the nineteenth-century trade union movement. But Camp Relief also represented a significant broadening of that tradition, for it was set up to serve not only the skilled craftsmen of the city, but a broad spectrum of working class people. "Almost all sorts and conditions of men were represented in the camp," observed a writer in *Harper's Weekly:*

One man was there who lost $1300 by the suspension of a bank in Aspen. One was a striking coal miner from Pittsburgh, Kansas. In one tent there were a furniture salesman, a drug clerk, a railway conductor, and the exproprieter of a barber shop. In another were half a dozen Frenchmen who had been bakers or cooks at the hotels. In still another were a company of Swedes who had worked in the Denver smelteries. There were miners from the mountain towns, foreign immigrants stranded for want of a job, a few bricklayers, here and there a farm hand, and quite a number of waiters and of railroad laborers.

Life at the camp, like the depression itself, tended to weaken the social division between the skilled and the unskilled.[19]

Two weeks before it established Camp Relief, the Denver Trades Assembly hosted Colorado's first "Labor Congress," which reflected a parallel trend toward united action of both skilled and unskilled workers. Ninety-eight delegates, representing "the producers of the state of Colorado," attended the Congress, which was a direct predecessor of the Colorado State Federation of Labor. Most of the delegates represented Denver trade unions, with fully seven representing the Denver Trades Assembly itself. But the constituency of the Labor Congress was significantly broader than one of skilled craftsmen. Eight delegates, for example, came from the coal mining communities of the state that were being organized by the Knights of Labor and six delegates represented various local farmer's alliances.[20]

While focusing on issues of immediate concern to workers, the Labor Congress also put forward a broad program of political reform. Along with a call for woman's suffrage, it adopted in its entirety the Ocala platform of the Populist party, which included demands for the government control of railroads and telegraph companies, banking reform, and the direct election of U.S. senators. At the same time, the Congress registered the distrust of politicians that had become a characteristic of the Denver labor movement. As "a body of working men who have been repeatedly deceived by the vague promises of politicians," the Congress attempted to establish some procedure by which elected officials could be held more directly accountable to their working-class constituents. For their part, some ostensibly prolabor politicians expressed unhappiness with the Labor Congress' proceedings. Thomas Patterson, editor of the *Rocky Mountain News* who had fled the Democrats to become a leader of the silver wing of Colorado's Populist party, argued that the Congress should have limited itself to the silver issue. "The producers of the nation could march to victory on that simple issue," he maintained, "while they would be scattered to the winds for many years to come if they should try to accomplish at a blow all the Colorado labor platform calls for."[21]

Conditions worsened in late 1893 and the first half of 1894. The question of relief assumed less urgency as thousands of working people migrated out of Colorado. But the repeal of the Sherman Silver Purchase Act in the autumn of 1893 delivered another hard blow to Colorado's extractive economy. Wages remained at panic levels and layoffs continued, though at a somewhat slower pace. In this setting, a second Labor Congress, held in Denver in July 1894, emphasized again the broad reform measures of the first. Again farmers and Knights of Labor coal miners were represented and again the Congress expressed support for the full Populist program. The second Congress also had to come to grips with two new developments that were reshaping the relationship between labor and capital in Colorado in 1894. The first of these was the struggle of the American Railway Union in the Pullman strike. The second was the rise of a new and powerful nativist organization, the American Protective Association.[22]

On 29 June 1894, American Railway Union members all over Colorado walked off their jobs in sympathy with striking workers at the Pullman Company in Chicago. Justice Moses Hallet of the U.S. District Court in Denver immediately ordered the swearing in of deputy marshalls to protect railroad property in the state. On 4 July, the federal marshall at Denver issued broad instructions to his deputies, ordering them to prohibit any kind of gathering on or near company property. "I will engage only men who will fight," asserted the marshall in regard to his deputies. "I don't care whether they are horse thieves, hoboes or thugs, just so they will fight when it is necessary." During the very days in which the Labor Congress was being held in Denver, deputies were arresting strikers all over the state and transporting them to the capital city to face trial. The Congress declared that "legalized greed" was using the power of the federal government to crush the workers' movement and appointed a committee of three to coordinate aid to ARU members.[23]

Perhaps even more ominous than the government's suppression of the Pullman strike was the rise to prominence of the American Protective Association in Denver. Founded in a small Iowa railroad town in 1887, the APA became a mass nativist movement in the following decade, spreading rapidly through many parts of the nation in the wake of the Panic of 1893. An attack on Catholicism was the central theme of the organization's rhetoric, and Irish, Italians and eastern Europeans received hostile treatment in the organization's literature. Denver's anti-Catholics established their first council of the secret organization in May 1892.[24]

In the memory of one Denver resident, the city was "literally swept by religious bigotry" in the years from 1893 to 1895. By the summer of 1894, according to an ex-member, the APA had between eight and ten thousand members in Denver and "the classes of people that were members were a fair average of the people" of the city. Though its membership lists were secret, there is little doubt that the organization had significant support within the city's working class, and especially within the trade unions, "the chosen agencies through which to operate its plans," according to one observer. The first president of the Colorado organization was a Denver carpenter, his successor a railroad machinist, and there were charges that the organization built a particularly strong following in the Denver Typographical Union. Thus the APA had the effect—or at least the potential—of exacerbating ethnic and religious divisions among workers. As a Union Pacific shop worker put it, "religious frenzy has been brought in to divide men on real principles, and it would not be surprising if the enemies of the masses did not make a success of it, carrying off the meat and leaving the masses in the soup." Even the silver Populist Herb George, no friend of either the labor movement or of Catholics, came to regard the movement as an effort to throw "dust enough in the eyes of the people to get them fighting among themselves." [25]

The clearest expression of growing working-class support for the order could be seen in the Denver city and county elections in 1893. In November 1892, the Populists had swept Colorado and the Republican party, saddled with a national platform opposed to the free coinage of silver, suddenly appeared to have a dim political future in Denver. Nevertheless, Republicans won both April and November 1893 elections, partly, it appears, as a result of their alliance with the APA in some of Denver's working-class wards. [26]

Opposition to the organization soon developed. Thomas Malone, a Catholic priest and editor of the Colorado Catholic, took a strong stand against the APA and Tom Patterson, editor of the Rocky Mountain News, editorialized against the organization. In November 1893, the social gospel minister Myron Reed and several other leading Protestant clergymen organized the Society of Liberty and Loyalty, an association of anti-APA Protestants. In 1894, the Denver Labor Congress joined this emerging coalition against nativism. Especially fearful of the APA's potential to disrupt the labor movement and divide Colorado's working class, the Congress not only denounced the APA but established another organization, the Legion of Justice, to hold mass meetings defending immigrant workers against this resurgent nativism. [27]

In both their support for the American Railway Union and their fight against the APA, the skilled Denver workers who dominated the 1894 Labor Congress indicated their increasing orientation toward industrial unionism and the struggles of the unskilled. This is most clear in the case of the ARU endorsement, where the Coloradans' position clashed not only with that of the conservative railroad brotherhoods, but also with that of AFL president Samuel Gompers. While expressing general support for the Pullman strikers, Gompers worked effectively to suppress a general strike in sympathy with the ARU, in part because of its industrial and dual unionist character. The strong stand of the Colorado Labor Congress against the nativism of the APA was related to its support for the ARU's industrial unionism. While Gompers and other AFL leaders condemned the APA, its foremost national critic in the labor movement was the ARU's leader, Eugene Debs. Significantly, Debs combined an attack on the organization with a sharp criticism of the anti-immigration stance emerging in the leadership of American labor movement. While an array of prominent labor leaders, including both Gompers and Terence Powderly, argued for the restriction of immigration from southern and eastern Europe, by 1893 Debs had emerged as a leading critic of this stance. Since the new immigrants were concentrated in the unskilled sector of the work force, defending immigrants and building industrial unions went hand in hand for Debs. The 1894 Colorado Labor Congress echoed this view. In its support for the ARU and its strong condemnation of the APA, it pointed toward the assertion of a broad working-class solidarity that would soon take the shape of industrial unionism and the organization of unskilled, immigrant workers in the state.[28]

The State Federation of Labor

This trend reached its culmination in the policies of the Colorado State Federation of Labor, founded in Pueblo on May Day 1896. Although skilled craftsmen in Denver and Pueblo provided much of the leadership of the Federation throughout the late 1890s, Colorado's industrial unions—especially the ARU, the United Mine Workers, and the Western Federation of Miners—also occupied a central role. When the State Federation of Labor refused to join the AFL in 1897, it gave the "unnecessary expense" of membership as its cause. But the commitment of a good portion of its membership to the principles of industrial unionism may have contributed even more to this decision. The State Federation's industrial union orientation was signaled by the name of its weekly newspaper, the *Industrial Advocate*.[29]

Over the course of the later 1890s, the State Federation focused on a number of activities. It lobbied for prolabor legislation—above all, for the statutory eight-hour day for all workers—and, through use of the union label, it extended the Denver Trades Assembly's coordination of boycotts throughout the state. But first and foremost of its stated objects was "to devise means for the complete organization of labor in Colorado." In his testimony before the United States Industrial Commission in 1899, David C. Coates, a Pueblo typographer who was then president of the State Federation, emphasized that its efforts to unionize "all producers of wealth" meant specifically the unionization of the unskilled. Noting that most of Colorado's unskilled workers were foreign-born, drawn increasingly from southern and eastern Europe, Coates boasted that "recently we have organized a number of unions which probably 90 per cent of the membership is made up of foreign-speaking people."[30]

Several factors accounted for the Colorado State Federation of Labor's interest in organizing the foreign-born and unskilled. The single most important of these was the prominence of the Western Federation of Miners in its ranks. Founded in the wake of the disastrous Coeur d'Alene strike of 1892, the WFM gradually built a large membership of hard rock miners throughout the West. From the outset the WFM advocated a thoroughgoing industrial unionism and organized many of the unskilled workers who labored in the mountain mining towns. Although the WFM was not much of a force in Colorado when the State Federation of Labor was founded, it increased its following in the state rapidly in the years from 1896 to 1899. Its growing strength in the State Federation in these years provided an increasingly influential bloc in favor of organizing the unskilled generally.[31]

But even before the emergence of the WFM in Colorado, there were a number of important advocates of industrial unionism in the State Federation. These were individuals whose commitment to organizing the unskilled grew out of their socialist beliefs. While the link between socialism and industrial unionism was hardly a necessary one—neither Haskell nor Buchanan, for instance, had been advocates of industrial unionism—the two were increasingly drawn together in the 1890s. As noted previously, the Brewery Workers had explicitly connected Marxist theory with their industrial union practice as early as 1887. The conversion of America's most famous industrial unionist, Eugene Debs, to socialism in the mid-1890s furthered the connection.[32]

A new generation of Colorado socialists, mainly skilled craftsmen from Denver and Pueblo, came of political age in the 1890s, and they constituted an increasingly vocal and influential faction in the State Federation of Labor. David Coates, who headed the organization in the late 1890s, was an articulate socialist. Born in County Durham, England, in 1868, Coates came with his parents to America in 1881, living for a while in Pittsburgh before moving to Pueblo. Though he eventually learned the trade of compositor, Coates began his working life as a laborer in the Pueblo Steel Works, an experience that may have been decisive in orienting him toward the needs of the unskilled factory labor force. In the early twentieth century, Coates would go on to become a lieutenant governor of Colorado as well as a founder of the Industrial Workers of the World.[33]

An important ally of Coates was Roady Kenehan, secretary-treasurer of the International Horseshoers Union and a two-term president of the Denver Trades Assembly. Born in Dublin in the early 1860s, Kenehan was in many respects a political descendent of Denver's earlier Irish labor radical, Joe Murray. Though more religious—he was an active member of the Catholic Mutual Benevolent Association, for instance—Kenehan was clearly an heir to the radicalism of the Land League, printing many articles on the history of the Irish land struggle in the monthly journal he edited, the *Horseshoers' Magazine*. Kenehan also combined self-help and radicalism in a way reminiscent of Murray and the Knights: in the 1890s he was Denver's leading working-class temperance advocate. Finally, again like Murray, Kenehan's radical Irish nationalism shaded over into socialism. At the 1894 convention of the American Federation of Labor, held in Denver, Kenehan gave his support to the socialists' political program for labor.[34]

The debate over the political program dominated the Denver convention. At the previous AFL convention, the Chicago machinist and socialist, Thomas J. Morgan, had introduced a political program for consideration by the AFL. Though most of it consisted of long-established labor demands, two elements of it were new. The first, drawing on contemporary British workers' efforts at independent labor politics, was a call for the AFL to support third-party political action. The second was plank ten, which called for "the collective ownership by the people of all means of production and distribution." Between the 1893 and 1894 conventions, the AFL's new organ, the *Federationist*, had run a debate over the political program. Straw votes taken in a number of national unions indicated considerable rank-and-file support for it, despite the strong opposition of Gompers, John B. Lennon, Peter J. McGuire, and other AFL leaders.[35]

As the 1894 convention approached, Gompers expressed concern about the unpredictability of Denver's labor activists. "The fact that the convention will be held in Denver will be a great drawback," he wrote to McGuire in November. Although Gompers thought the city "a beautiful place" and a fine convention site "under ordinary circumstances," he was fearful that the financial difficulties of the national trade unions would force them to "select representatives living in Denver or adjacent to it, and thus [that] the convention may be dominated by local rather than National Union influences and environments." The Denver convention held in December was, in fact, one of the smallest AFL conventions of the nineteenth century, with only seventy-seven delegates in attendance. Five of these delegates were Denver residents.[36]

But Gompers' fears proved to be unfounded. With the exception of Kenehan, the Denver delegates backed him fully in his rejection of the political program. This may have reflected, in part, the influence of the one-time Denver resident Lennon, who still had many friends in the city's labor movement and who argued forcefully against the program. It may also have reflected the success of the anti-Morgan delegates in characterizing the program as fundamentally antagonistic to the goals of trade unionism.[37]

Whatever the cause, most of the Denver delegates rallied to Gompers' side. Yet the debate made it clear that there was a range of opinion among the Denverites who opposed plank ten and political action. John W. Bramwood, a leader of the Denver Typographical Union, admitted that "there are many members connected with the typographical union that can probably endorse Morgan's sentiments" and indicated that even he "was to a certain extent committed to going into politics"; but he argued that "what we should do is by all means in our power strengthen ourselves as a trade union organization before we take up any of these questions." Charles Greenhalgh, representing a local union of Denver core makers, took what was referred to at the convention as the "philosophical anarchist" position: pointing to the federal government's role in the suppression of the Pullman boycott, he declared that "control by the government is not control by the people and never can be for the government is the natural enemy of the people." Finally, there was Henry L. Cohen, recording and corresponding secretary for Denver Journeymen Tailors Union No. 3, Lennon's old local. Cohen had been a member of the Rocky Mountain Social League and a leader of the Colorado Union Labor party in the late 1880s. "I am not in trades unions pure and simple," he told the convention. "Socialism I have advocated for years and will still." But, perhaps reflecting the syndicalist ideas of the old Social League, Cohen opposed plank ten because it "supposed the State can carry everything." In a statement reminiscent of Joseph Buchanan's critique of the establishment of a federal bureau of labor statistics, Cohen argued that the Morgan supporters "are like the bad child who has burnt fingers and runs to its mother for help, and so they run to our grandmother, the government for every single thing, they run to her notwithstanding the fact that she never gave up any thing and the only thing they ever have achieved was through trades unionism."[38]

In the key vote of the convention, all three men, along with Denver plasterer's leader Andrew McCallin, voted for a substitute to plank ten, which called for the "abolition of the monopoly system of land holding and the substitution there for a title of occupancy and use only." But Roady Kenehan did not, despite the fact that the substitute had been designed partly to appeal to Irish American workers exactly like him, men and women with political roots in the Irish Land League or the single tax movement. When the socialist faction took its revenge on Gompers, defeating him in his bid for the presidency of the AFL, they repaid Kenehan by electing him as an AFL vice-president. In the early twentieth century, Kenehan would be a central figure in generating support for the industrial union movement within the Denver Trades Assembly, leading WFM president Ed Boyce to praise the horseshoer as a man "whose brain is as well developed as his brawny muscles, making him a giant in the cause of labor."[39]

At the first convention of the Colorado State Federation of Labor in 1896, socialists put forward their own version of Morgan's program. It indicted American capitalism as "the worst system of wage slavery in the history of the human race" and called for the election of Eugene Debs as president of the United States on a platform of free coinage of silver, direct legislation, and nationalization of all banks. As at the AFL convention two years earlier, the socialist program was defeated. But the outcome here was much closer, the socialist program losing by only five votes. And at the same convention, Otto F. Thum, a member of the Pueblo Typographical Union, was elected president of the State Federation. Thum "is a pronounced socialist, and known as such all over the state," commented his old friend, J. A. Wayland, in the *Appeal to Reason*. "This would seem to show that organized labor in Colorado has taken a few lessons in socialism and like as far as they have gone." A leader in the struggle to establish the initiative, referendum, and recall in Colorado, Thum was another key advocate of industrial unionism.[40]

Populism and the Militancy of the Unskilled

Both the miners in the WFM and the socialists among urban craftsmen, then, added their voices to the call for industrial unionism. But there was yet another force pushing the State Federation toward the industrial organization of the unskilled. This was the growing workplace militancy of Colorado's factory workers and laborers themselves. As in the 1930s, the activism of the unskilled dovetailed with the new initiatives on the part of radical craftsmen, creating a powerful dynamic toward organization.[41]

While the depression of the 1890s greatly weakened established trade unions of craftsmen, it simultaneously ushered in a wave of labor activism among Colorado's miners, factory operatives and laborers so sweeping that it eventually came to be known as "the revolt of labor." The trend first became apparent among coal miners in Colorado. In March, October, and November 1893, coal miners staged strikes at Rockvale, Creede and New Castle against wage cuts, layoffs, and attempts to increase hours. Their activism culminated in a June 1894 strike for increased pay at nearly all of the coal mines in the state, part of a national UMW strike. Although they eventually lost, the miners remained on strike until the fall, defying both management and the business cycle.[42]

More famous was the 1894 strike of hard rock miners at Cripple Creek. Because its mines produced gold, rather than silver, Cripple Creek was relatively unaffected by the collapse of silver prices in 1893. Seeking to take advantage of the high unemployment among hard rock miners generally, in January 1894 the mine owners here announced their intention to increase hours from eight to nine a day, without an increase of wages. The miners, newly-organized in the Western Federation of Miners, refused to accept this lengthening of the working day and went on strike in February. The Cripple Creek strike became the most violent in Colorado history to this date. Sheriff Bowers of El Paso County recruited an army of thirteen hundred deputies—many of them apparently APA members— to crush the strike and several pitched battles occurred. The conflict was resolved when Populist governor Davis Waite ordered in the state militia to protect the miners and then acted as their representative in negotiations with the mine owners. With this exceedingly rare example of state intervention on the side of labor, the strike was settled as a complete victory for the miners.[43]

Although mining strikes attracted the most attention during these years, unskilled workers in the city of Denver also participated in this wave of industrial actions. Especially dramatic was a strike of 200 workers —145 of them women—in May 1893 at the newly-built Overland Cotton Mills in Denver. Triggered by the company's effort to increase hours from sixty to sixty-five a week, the strike lasted thirty-six days and ended in a compromise, with management agreeing to advance wages 4.5 percent to compensate for the extra time. This was the first recorded strike of women workers in Colorado's history.[44]

Factory workers were not the only unskilled Denver workers to go on strike. In August 1893—at the very height of the silver panic—one hundred ditch diggers (many of them Italian immigrants) went on strike against the effort of a local contractor, J. B. Hindry, to pay wages of $1.20 a day rather than the $2.00 promised by the Board of Public Works. This strike also ended in a compromise, but only after police were called out to disperse a crowd of 400 unemployed workers who rallied in the strikers' support. In November of this year, sixty-two employees of the Consolidated Electric Company in the city joined this upsurge of Denver's unskilled and previously nonunionized workers in a strike against a 15 percent wage reduction. Though Denver was without lights for a brief time, the company hired new workers and broke the strike within three days.[45]

Though the growing militancy of Denver's laborers and operatives produced few clear-cut victories, it did lead to the emergence of unions in industries previously lacking them. With the gradual improvement of economic conditions in 1895, this trend accelerated. By the time of the first convention of the State Federation of Labor in 1896, a whole new group of unions had emerged in Denver. Cooks, waiters, stage hands, teamsters, and street railway workers all had representatives at the convention, along with railroad workers in what was left of the Knights of Labor and the ARU. Even the newsboys of Denver had organized a union—with a full 166 members—and sent two delegates to the convention, where they were welcomed with "hearty sympathy" and a pledge of "co-operation and assistance in furthering their cause." There were important limits to the State Federation's welcome however: an effort by several workers to draft resolutions "to oppose the drawing of Color Line in Labor Unions" came to naught. Nevertheless, the industrial stirring of Denver's unskilled—a "new unionism" comparable to that which had emerged in Britain in the wake of the famous 1889 dock strike—was beginning to change the character of the Denver labor movement.[46]

As was the case with Britain's "new unionism"—and, indeed, with most labor movements of the unskilled—a political ideology underlay the struggles of Denver's factory workers and laborers. Significantly, however, this ideology did not come from Denver's skilled craftsmen. The racially exclusive and patriarchal stance of these men, combined with their traditional distrust of the unskilled, gave them little influence among the new activists, many of whom were women and recent immigrants. Even radicals in the trade union movement, with their more sweeping internationalist and protosyndicalst ideas, could provide little ideological guidance to the city's dressmakers, day laborers and factory operatives. Indeed, the very linking of syndicalism and craft unionism that had taken shape in the years between 1887 and 1892 rendered the radicals within the labor movement *less* capable of responding to the needs of the unskilled, for the practice of workers' control which lay at the heart of syndicalism seemed impossible for them to attain. The motivating ideology of the unskilled workers movement came from an entirely different source. It was a product of Colorado's diverse and multi-faceted Populist movement and of the inspiration provided by Governor Davis Waite himself.[47]

Colorado's Populist party represented an uneasy coalition of distinct groups. Farmers, miners, and defecting silver Democrats vied for control of the organization. The resulting tensions, in part, accounted for the Denver labor movement's unwillingness to provide much support for the party. While identifying with the radical wing of the national Populist movement and supporting the radical Omaha platform, Denver's skilled craftsmen were particularly distrustful of the silver politicians who wielded so much power within the Colorado party. But the movement's relationship with unskilled workers was markedly different. Many of them embraced the movement and its leaders with unbounded enthusiasm. The Populist movement politicized many unskilled workers and, indirectly, provided an ideological basis for their industrial militancy. Thus the Populists inadvertently accomplished what the established labor movement had been unable or unwilling to do.[48]

An important source of Populist strength was its style of organization. Although the Union Labor party in 1887 and 1888 had attempted to build support among unskilled workers through its platform, the ULP leadership and candidates were drawn almost entirely from the organized labor movement in Denver. This greatly hindered its ability to build a broadly based working-class political movement. The Populist organization in Denver, however, operated on an entirely different model, the model of the political machine. Edward Keating, the seventeen-year-old son of Irish immigrants and a precinct captain in Denver's heavily immigrant Fifth Ward, later recalled that he had "tramped from house to house . . . spreading the gospel of Populism" as the election of 1892 approached. "I told them how to register and explained they couldn't vote unless they were registered." Keating also kept a book in which he recorded the names of those in the precinct who supported the party and on election day picked two "good men and true" to watch the count at the polls. This sort of careful precinct-level organizing had never been practiced by the Denver labor movement, which, as we have seen, was more and more focused on shop floor battles and suspicious of political action. It produced results. In 1892, Keating's precinct, long dominated by the Republican party, went for the Populists by a margin of nearly two to one. Young Keating meanwhile emerged as a kind of Populist "boss" in the city.[49]

The liberal strain in American Catholicism provided a second basis of Populist strength among Denver's unskilled workers. The key figure here was Father Thomas H. Malone, who was—like Kenehan—another heir to the radicalism of the Land League era. In his speeches to workers, and in his weekly newspaper, the *Colorado Catholic*, Malone attempted to transmit his version of working-class republicanism to both Irish and Italian Catholics in the city, representing a large proportion of unskilled workers. His newspaper, with a circulation of over eight thousand, reached far deeper into Denver's working-class community than the labor movement had ever done, and Malone's eventual endorsement of the Populist party was recognized as a crucial basis of its strength in the city. Significantly,

Malone also supported "the rights of workmen to the full product of their labor and to dictate through combination how and when they should labor." The complete unionization of the working class was necessary, he believed, "to protect the laboring man from the greed and heartless aggressiveness of capital."[50]

Thus, the ward- and precinct-level political organizing of men like Keating and the updated Irish radicalism of Malone contributed to the politicization of Denver's unskilled workers. Indirectly this paved the way for their increasing industrial militancy: the fundamental rights of producers could be asserted at the workplace as well as at the ballot box. Another, and perhaps even more important, key to this fusing of political and industrial struggles was Davis Waite himself. Both the fiery speeches and the bold actions of the governor served to legitimize and inspire the upsurge of the unskilled. Before being elected governor in 1892, Waite had been the editor of a reform newspaper in Aspen and a member of the Knights of Labor. Although some Denver trade unionists were struck by "the liberal and progressive ideas" on "the labor problem" he expressed in his first speech to the Colorado legislature in January 1893, Waite's initial position seemed exceedingly moderate. The hardships caused by the Panic of 1893, however, altered his stance dramatically. Declaring that Colorado now stood "upon the brink of industrial slavery," the governor called the legislature into special session in January 1894. Here, he presented a sweeping program of reform that included the eight-hour day, an overhaul of the state banking system, the introduction of the initiative and referendum, and a complicated scheme for selling Colorado's silver to Mexico.[51]

The program was defeated almost in its entirety by a combination of Republican strength and Populist disunity in the legislature. Nevertheless, Waite left a lasting influence on working-class thought and action in Colorado. In the course of his short political career, the governor emerged as Colorado's most important advocate of workers' attempts to defend themselves against capital. Waite's previously discussed decision to send in the milita to protect the Cripple Creek miners was emblematic of this stance. While he did not provide the same kind of assistance to coal miners in the strike of April–July 1894, he did send Colorado's attorney general to the coal fields in an attempt to mediate the dispute. He also refused the frantic request of the Las Animas county sheriff for troops to be used against the strikers.[52]

In addition, Waite defended the right of Coxey's Army of unemployed workers to cross Colorado en route to the nation's capital in the spring of 1894, turning down demands from the receivers of the Union Pacific Railroad that the state provide it protection from "a large number of men demanding by force and violence to be carried eastward." Because of its large number of unemployed workers, Denver became a major recruiting center for Coxey's Commonwealers, leading the city's more conservative newspapers to raise the specter of a "revolution of tramps." Colorado's Republican Senator Edward O. Wolcott spoke for conservatives when he launched an attack on the Commonwealers from the floor of the Senate, labeling their leaders as "either insane, or cranks or vicious" and proposing that it was time "to cultivate more of a regard for the perpetuity of Republican institutions [and to] stand together against this socialism and Populism and paternalism which is running riot in this country." Wolcott's remarks angered many working people in Colorado, including both the Denver Trades Assembly (who had gone on record in support of Coxey's movement) and the remaining Knights of Labor in the city, who argued that the senator "does not express the sentiments of the majority of our citizens but the desires of the monopolies he represents."[53]

Waite took exactly the same position in a speech to a Denver mass meeting in support of the Commonwealers. "How resigned is this hireling of the corporations," he said of Wolcott, "that the trusts, the banking and other monopolies should retain the benefit of all the franchises and usurious profits they have robbed from the people by iniquitous legislation. This is in the natural course of events a dispensation of an all-wise Providence; but to seek redress in legislation from the loss of prosperity, the depressed wages of labor and diminished values of commodities and of real estate; why this is anarchy and lunancy." Waite, in sum, aimed to stand for the rights of the oppressed. "Their cause is just and they should be aided instead of hindered," he said of the Coxeyites.[54]

Finally, Waite emerged as a forceful spokesperson for Colorado's American Railway Union members in their struggle against the court-ordered injunction. "The most dangerous anarchy in the State of Colorado," the governor wrote in an angry letter to U.S. District Judge Moses Hallet, came not from the striking railroad workers, but rather from "the United States court at Denver, which has allowed the U.S. Marshall to enlist a private army to suppress alleged state troubles, of which neither the County or State authorities had any notice . . . and is Waging actual war in Colorado without any declaration thereof."[55]

In these words and actions, Waite defended the rights of workers already engaged in struggle. As an orator, he also directly contributed to the working-class explosion of the mid-1890s. Faced with increasing opposition to his program in the state legislature, Waite began to argue that the ballot might not be enough to remedy the plight of the masses. In his most famous speech, delivered in Denver during the depression-wracked summer of 1893, Waite brought the language of class conflict close to home, denouncing not only the national Democratic and Republican leaders, Cleveland and Harrison, but also "their supporters on Wall street or in Denver" who "dare assume to drive into poverty and exile a half million of American freemen." Waite proclaimed that if legislative action failed, "then we need another revolution—another appeal to arms and the God of hosts." Waite hoped this second American revolution would be a nonviolent one. But, he concluded, "if the money power shall attempt to sustain its usurpation by the 'strong hand,' we will meet that issue when it is forced upon us, for it is better, infinitely better that blood should flow to the horses' bridles than our national liberties should be destroyed."[56]

The speech predictably created outrage among Colorado's defenders of the status quo, who thereafter referred to the governor as "Bloody Bridles" Waite. His speeches and actions brought down the wrath of conservatives across the state. U.S. Justice Hallet denounced the administration as one composed of "imbeciles and anarchists." From the APA to the large-scale mining and financial interests represented by the Business Men's League, Colorado conservatives acted in unity in a desperate and finally effective effort to defeat the governor's bid for reelection in 1894.[57]

But Waite's effect on workers was entirely different. The governor was virtually worshipped. Immediately after the speech, the Aspen Trades Assembly, dominated by WFM delegates, praised the governor for his "strong, noble and patriotic utterances" and characterized his critics as "upholders of plutocracy." The Assembly resolved "that Davis H. Waite will live in the hearts of the toiling millions and his memory be a thing of sweetness, light and hope long after the memories of his Shylock traducers have sunk in the mire and filth, the darkness and obscurity of merited oblivion." The *Union Pacific Employees Magazine* enthusiastically reprinted the entire speech, noting that it would be "of interest to many who have got all their information regarding it from the mouthings of the press of the money power."[58]

The views of rank-and-file working people in Denver are harder to gauge. Significantly, Keating's immigrant and working-class precinct in the Fifth Ward went for Waite again in 1894, although by a considerably smaller margin than in 1892. In the city as a whole, Waite received 12,470 votes, only 31 percent of the vote, though this does not necessarily mean (as the embittered ex-governor charged) that Denver's workers had failed to support him. In Colorado City, a town seventy miles south of Denver, populated in large part by immigrant smelter workers, Waite won in 1894. The problem in Denver may well have been simply that there were not enough industrial workers to provide him with the margin of victory.[59]

Certainly, observers believed that there had been a swelling up of working-class support for the governor. "The people whom you have served so faithfully love you just as much as when they believed you would be elected," wrote a Denver journalist to Waite after his defeat in 1894. "You have accomplished what no other governor of our state ever has—enshrined yourself in the hearts of the people." Waite's "bloody bridles" speech, in particular, dominated by the religious and republican cadences so important in the language of American radicalism, inspired and legitimized the growing industrial militancy of unskilled workers in Denver and throughout Colorado.[60]

The New Unionism

By the end of 1896, economic conditions in Denver were beginning to improve. The nation as a whole was emerging from the depression, and Colorado's recovery was aided by an increase in the production of gold at Cripple Creek. Wages had not been restored to their pre-1893 levels but employment, according to the Colorado Bureau of Labor Statistics, was gradually and steadily improving, thus increasing workers' bargaining power. Not surprisingly, the Denver labor movement began to make advances after 1896.[61]

But it was not the same labor movement. The depression, the mobilization of the unskilled, and the emergence of new industrial unions had changed it in important ways. This was most clearly apparent in the growing activism among the employees of Denver's three large smelters. The largest group of industrial laborers in the city, overwhelmingly unskilled and predominantly foreign-born, smelter workers seemed the least able to organize effective unions. There had been a short strike over the need for more helpers at the Grant smelter in 1884 but it had ended in total defeat. Joseph Buchanan's comment on the strike reveals the pessimism with which even a socialist skilled worker regarded the smelter workers' efforts. "The men were without organization, and have consequently lost," Buchanan reported to readers of *John Swinton's Paper*. As if by way of further explanation, he added that "a great many men who cannot speak English are employed at this smelter."[62]

In April 1888, about fifty men (mainly Hungarians and Poles) struck the Holden smelter, protesting the dismissal of a fellow worker, but according to a sympathetic railroad shop worker, "it was not done by organized men or by order of a union and resulted in nothing favorable to the men, unless it is to teach them that organization is absolutely necessary to give even hope of success." Just what the smelter workers were up against was illustrated by a third smelter strike the following year, when laborers at the Globe smelter walked out. Three of the strike leaders were arrested by authorities in Globeville, which had not yet been incorporated by Denver. When the wives of the arrested men went to Dennis Sheedy, the president and general manager of the Globe, to plead for their husbands' release, he agreed to help them, but only on the condition that they leave town. Shortly thereafter, the Irish-born Sheedy began replacing the largely Irish work force with Italians, whom he thought to be more docile.[63]

Yet by the end of the 1890s, the smelter workers had successfully organized. Their first union, established in 1896, collapsed a short time later. But in 1899 the smeltermen revived their organization. By July of that year a leader of the Denver Smeltermens Union estimated that of eleven hundred smelter workers in the city, only thirty remained outside the union. In the opening years of the twentieth century, the union, dominated by unskilled foreign-born immigrants, would be one of the most militant in the city.[64]

Another important union was the Denver local of the United Garment Workers, an industrial union composed of a variety of workers in the men's clothing industry founded in New York in 1891. The Denver local had emerged from a strike at the Underhill overalls factory in April 1896. Eighty women at the factory went on strike against a new company demand that they turn in each garment for inspection, an added labor for which they would receive no extra pay. The owner attempted to fill the places of the strikers and continue operations. But falling unemployment in the city and the solidarity of the working women prevented him from doing so. The company gave in after three days and the UGW local was formed.[65]

The local grew steadily over the next few years, moving beyond its original base in the overalls factory to include smaller sweat shops turning out shirts, pants, duck coats, vests, and aprons. Its leaders, Anna Ensminger, Mrs. F. J. Ramsey, and Mrs. M. F. Wheeler, became active and influential figures in both the Denver Trades Assembly and the State Federation of Labor, developing close ties with David Coates, Otto Thum, and other socialists in the Colorado labor movement. Their growing status within the State Federation was recognized in 1898, when Wheeler was elected by acclamation as second vice-president of that organization. In 1897, the Denver garment workers broke decisively with the "pure-and-simple" tradition in the American labor movement when they declared that the discussion of politics would be allowed at their local meetings. In light of the connection between political mobilization and industrial unionism sketched above, this should not be surprising. "We will do our part in the work of political reform," declared the UGW in a resolution delivered to the Denver Trades Assembly.[66]

The new unions of the laborers and factory workers were admitted to the Trades Assembly, which endorsed their boycotts and provided financial assistance during their strikes. But perhaps more significant was the growing mutual support between *rank-and-file* skilled and unskilled workers in the city. When skilled plasterers struck for higher wages in

May 1897, newly unionized building laborers went out with them. When semiskilled bookbinders' helpers, the so-called bindery women, went on strike in September of that year, all of the printers, pressmen, and other skilled workers in the affected shops went out in sympathy. The sympathy strike was called by Denver's new Allied Printing Trades Council. While not an industrial union, the council served a similar function by coordinating action among all workers in Denver's printing industries. "It is commonly said that working people will not stand together," noted Willis Hall, a Denver typographer and the editor of the State Federation of Labor's weekly organ, the *Industrial Advocate*. "If anything was needed to prove otherwise, the action of the members of the Allied Printing Trades in the strike of the Bindery Girls' Union would be sufficient. . . . Here were seven unions standing as one individual for a just demand." A new kind of solidarity was emerging in the Denver working-class movement, one that increasingly crossed lines of skill, ethnicity, and gender.[67]

When the leaders of the Western Federation of Miners organized the Western Labor Union in May 1898, they received enthusiastic support from many in the Denver labor movement. Fearful about the new organization's challenge to the AFL, John B. Lennon, now treasurer of the AFL and a close ally of Gompers, sent a long plea for loyalty to the organized workers of the city. Although he claimed to have lost none of his "interest or identity with the welfare of the union people in the Rocky Mountain region," Lennon argued forcefully against anything resembling "dual unionism." But despite his warnings, the WLU's effort to form industrial unions and organize the unskilled in the West struck a powerful chord among Denver's working people. The new federation "should meet with a full response from the labor organizations in this state," Hall predicted in the *Industrial Advocate*. "We want western men to direct western labor movements."[68]

The State Federation of Labor was divided over the new organization. Though it accepted an invitation to send two delegates to the convention that founded the WLU, the convention also resolved that the sending of the delegation "shall not be construed to mean that the [State Labor] Federation will affiliate with a Western Federation if such is formed." Sentiment in the State Federation seemed about equally divided between the WLU and the AFL. The new industrial unions favored the former, while many of the craft unions retained their loyalty to Gompers, Lennon, and the AFL. But as the examples of Coates, Hall, Thum, and Kenehan illustrate, the industrial unionism of the WLU also had important supporters within the ranks of the skilled craftsmen of Denver and Pueblo.[69]

Most importantly, when the Western Labor Union was formed in 1898, it took into full account the recent upsurge in organization among the unskilled workers of the West, including Denver. The WLU, as envisioned by its founders, was to be made up of unskilled as well as skilled workers, in large cities as well as isolated mining camps. The industrial unions of the Brewery Workers, the ARU, and the WFM had all contributed to the new direction in the western working-class movement, as had the socialists among the craftsmen. But the new direction was also a product of the wave of industrial militancy among western unskilled workers themselves, and this was especially noticeable in Denver. In fact, Denver would be the major urban stronghold of the WLU throughout its short but eventful history.

6 The Emergence of Western Working-Class Radicalism, 1899–1905

In January 1905, twenty-seven labor activists, four of them Denver residents, issued a document entitled the "Manifesto of Industrial Unionists," which called for a convention to be held in Chicago the following June. The June convention gave birth to the Industrial Workers of the World, an organization that would occupy a central place in the history of American labor radicalism. The manifesto itself was the most fully realized statement of American syndicalist thinking to date. The new organization, it proclaimed, "will build up within itself the structure of an Industrial Democracy—a Workers' Co-operative Republic—which must finally burst the shell of capitalist government, and be the agency by which the working people will operate the industries, and appropriate the products to themselves."[1]

The causes of the IWW's emergence at this moment are well known. Although it had grown rapidly in the first few years of the twentieth century, the Western Labor Union (renamed the American Labor Union in 1902) faced extinction by the end of 1904. Labor radicals needed a new and broader organization to take its place. The crisis of the ALU had resulted from the so-called Colorado labor wars of 1903–4. Backed up by various local citizens' alliances and the full military power of the state under Governor James H. Peabody, mine owners across Colorado took part in an eighteen-month struggle to destroy the Western Federation of Miners and its allies in the American Labor Union. Cripple Creek and Telluride, in particular, became the scenes of bloody armed battles, mass arrests, and the mass deportations of union miners. This struggle badly weakened the WFM and the ALU and led directly to the formation of the Industrial Workers of the World. Scars left by the violence of these years underlined its founders' belief in "the class struggle," that "irrepressible conflict between the capitalist class and the working class."[2]

While the events of 1903–4 are crucial to an understanding of the timing of the IWW's emergence, the ideology of the new organization had been taking form over a much longer period of time. Previous chapters have traced the origins and development of various strands of twentieth-century western working-class radicalism as they found expression in the labor movement of Denver. In the last two decades of the nineteenth century, internationalism, syndicalism, industrial unionism, and the commitment to building a movement culture all made an appearance in the city's labor movement. The early years of the twentieth century brought all of these ideological strands to the fore again. More importantly, it was in the years from 1899 to 1903 that these distinct strands of working-class ideology became fused in a synthesis that became known as revolutionary industrial unionism. The emergence of this synthesis is the subject of this chapter.

A number of developments in turn-of-the-century Denver contributed to the shaping of this synthesis. The increasingly divisive character of AFL-style craft unionism in the face of both the industrial mergers of 1899–1903 and the growing power of Denver's organized antiunion employers hastened the move toward industrial unionism. The failure of the state legislature to enact an eight-hour day law in 1903, after it had been approved overwhelmingly by Colorado's voters, furthered the syndicalist tendency. At the same time, the success of some groups of unskilled workers in winning some degree of shop floor control of production by 1902 made that tendency seem more appropriate to their needs than it had earlier. The increasingly conscious manipulation of ethnic and racial divisions by Denver employers forced labor radicals at last to embrace a much broader internationalist perspective than they had ever before. Finally, the efforts of the city's employers to win support for their anti-union crusade within the middle and working classes of the city forced the radical labor movement to wage a broad cultural struggle of its own.

Three points require some emphasis. First, in moving toward revolutionary industrial unionism, Denver's labor radicals were not building from scratch; rather, they drew upon and elaborated ideas and strategies generated by the previous twenty years of Denver's labor history. Second, although the labor wars of 1903–4 may have *triggered* the formation of the IWW, the ideological synthesis it would uphold had been worked out in the American Labor Union's leadership by the summer of 1903—that is, immediately before the bloody struggles of the miners that ensued. Finally, radicalism never dominated the labor movement in these years but rather emerged as a powerful minority current within it.

Industrial Unionism

The great merger movement that swept American industry in the years from 1899 to 1903 occupied an important place in the thinking of the men and women who founded the IWW. They believed that the unification of capital represented by the rise of the new trusts needed to be countered by an equally unified organization of the entire working class. Of all of Colorado's industries, it was that of smelting and refining that was most affected by the turn-of-the-century merger movement.[3]

On 4 April 1899, a New Jersey charter was obtained for a new corporation, the American Smelting and Refining Company. The formation of ASARCO marked the unification of a number of smaller smelting firms throughout the West; at the moment of its birth, it controlled approximately two-thirds of the nation's smelting and refining capacity. Its only significant competition came from the Meyer Guggenheim smelting holdings and from a handful of independent firms that remained outside its control. From this point on, two of Denver's three smelters, the Grant and the Globe, were part of the ASARCO empire. Ex-Governor James B. Grant, who had previously owned the Omaha and Grant Smelting Company, became director of operations for the new corporation, with his headquarters at Denver. Although the owners of Denver's Argo smelter took part in merger talks with ASARCO, these eventually collapsed. The emergence of ASARCO, referred to by hostile contemporaries as the "smelter trust," set the stage for the first big strike of smelter workers in Denver's history, in the summer of 1899.[4]

The working life of the smeltermen was perhaps harsher than that of any other occupational group in the city. Although outdoor laborers around the smelters worked an eight-hour day, the furnace men inside worked twelve hours a day, seven days a week. During the Panic of 1893, their wages had been reduced by 10 percent and, despite the rapid increase in the cost of living in the closing years of the decade, they were still working at 1893 wages in 1899.[5]

Smelter workers suffered more than long hours and low wages. Extremely high levels of lead dust in the smelters caused numerous cases of lead poisoning and forced many men to take off six or seven days each month without pay. Though excruciatingly painful, lead poisoning was a reversible condition. But this fact often led men to return to work too soon after being "leaded" and then to experience a recurrence of the problem. Lead poisoning, in addition, contributed to gastritis, kidney disease, and cirrhosis of the liver. At the Argo smelter, men often tied damp rags or burlap sacks around their mouths and noses to keep out the dust. But this was insufficient to protect them from lead poisoning or from exposure to arsenic oxides, sulfur dioxide, and a variety of other toxic dusts and fumes. "There is scarcely an employment in the west that is more destructive to the lives of those engaged in it than the lead smelting industry of Colorado," argued one writer in a turn-of-the-century labor newspaper. "A man goes quick while making dividends for the smelting trust."[6]

Two developments in the late 1890s, though, gave Denver's smelter workers some hope of improving their conditions. The first was the progress of unionization in the industry. Though efforts to organize the smeltermen had met with no success in the 1880s and mid-1890s, in the last years of that decade the Western Federation of Miners began to make serious efforts to bring smeltermen throughout the West into their union. Led by three long-time smelter workers, Max Maelich, Joe Mehelic, and E. J. Smith, workers at Denver's Globe and Grant smelters organized a local union of the WFM, Mill and Smelter Workers Local No. 93, in May 1899 and within five weeks had built a membership of eleven hundred.[7]

The second development was the Colorado legislature's passage of an eight-hour day bill for miners and those working in mining-related industries. Since most miners were already working eight hours a day, the new law applied mainly to the smeltermen. Passed shortly before the formation of ASARCO, the measure was signed into law by Governor Charles S. Thomas and became law on 15 June 1899. ASARCO attorneys, however, immediately challenged the constitutionality of the law in the Colorado courts. Underlying the company's opposition to the specific legislation was a refusal to grant any form of recognition to the demands of a union among smelter workers—and particularly the WFM.[8]

ASARCO's determination on this matter set the stage for the 1899 smelter strike, which began in the San Juan mining region of Colorado two weeks before the eight-hour law was due to take effect. On 1 June, ASARCO posted notices at its plants throughout the region announcing a change from day-based to hourly-based pay. While the company declared that it would not require men to work beyond the legal eight hours daily, they would have to continue at twelve-hour shifts to maintain their current wage. That afternoon a committee from the smelter workers union notified ASARCO that they would go on strike the following day if the notices were not removed. ASARCO remained implacable, and on 2 June, 150 men at the smelter in Durango walked off the job.[9]

At this point, director of operations Grant began making efforts to forestall what could clearly turn into a statewide strike of smeltermen. He offered to increase wages by 10 percent, thus restoring the pay scale of 1892, but refused to give in on the question of hours. Discussions between workers and managers at Durango, Pueblo, and Denver over the next two weeks produced no compromise. When the eight-hour law went into effect on 15 June, workers at all three locations went on strike.[10]

The events of the following weeks illustrated the company's determination to maintain the twelve-hour day and to refuse union recognition. Every effort at compromise on these issues proved a failure due to ASARCO's intransigence. Grant rejected an offer by the State Federation of Labor to mediate the dispute, arguing that it knew nothing of conditions in the smelting industry. A citizens' committee appointed by Governor Thomas to resolve the strike met several times but accomplished nothing. Grant now offered a wage increase of 20 percent to the men, but would go no further. Finally the State Board of Arbitration was called in. Its three members, appointed by the governor, called for the parties to submit the dispute to binding arbitration. But while the smelter workers agreed to this, ASARCO refused.[11]

Although the strike affected all of ASARCO's smelters in Colorado, it involved only this single corporation. The owners of the independent Argo smelter in Denver worked out a compromise with their workers before the 15 June deadline, as did the managers of the Guggenheim smelter in Pueblo. Both compromise formulas involved at least tacit recognition of the WFM as the legitimate representative of the smelter workers. Grant, however, remained firm in his refusal to deal with the union. The company's position on this issue had been worked out at its headquarters in New York. ASARCO's president, Edward W. Nash, was quoted as saying that he would rather see the company go under than recognize an organization like the WFM.[12]

The economic consolidation of Colorado smelting thus produced a combativeness and unity of purpose on the business side when it came to dealings with workers. By contrast, in their own ranks, Colorado's smelter workers found only disunity and conflict. In late June, workers at the ASARCO plant in Leadville returned to work on the basis of Grant's offer of a 10 percent wage increase. Three weeks later, the Colorado Supreme Court ruled the eight-hour day law unconstitutional, just as Grant had predicted it would, and the strike began to collapse all over the state. By early August, ASARCO's smelters at Durango, Pueblo, and in the Arkansas Valley were back in operation.[13]

The Denver smelter workers continued their strike alone. Greatly strengthened by the Supreme Court's ruling and by the collapse of the strike in other areas of Colorado, however, ASARCO refused to move beyond its earlier offers. Finally on 17 August, with their financial resources nearly depleted, Denver Mill and Smelter Workers No. 93 declared the strike over, and the men returned to work on the company's terms. The only positive development to come out of the strike was the public attention given to smelter workers' testimony before the State Board of Arbitration. Focusing on health and safety conditions in the Denver smelters and on the extremely low standard of living of the immigrant workers, such testimony helped build some concern within the wider working-class community (and to some extent within the city's middle class) for their plight. As the WFM's monthly magazine noted, "making these things known will do much to help the smeltermen's cause the next time they come before the public, as come they must."[14]

As the leaders of the WFM predicted, the 1899 strike was only the opening round in what would be a long battle of the city's smelter workers for shorter hours and union recognition. The 1903 strike of Denver's smeltermen, as we shall see, was much more serious, threatening at points to become a full-blown struggle between the city's organized workers and its business class, organized in the Citizens Alliance. Though less dramatic than this later conflict, the 1899 strike was extremely significant for what it revealed about the changing character of industrial conflict in the early twentieth century.

Most obvious was the role of the state Supreme Court in undoing the eight-hour legislation of the Colorado General Assembly. This action fell into a broad national pattern of court rulings hostile to organized labor, a pattern not fully reversed until the 1930s. The workers of Colorado, however, had a tool to counteract the power of the courts, the legal mechanism of the initiative. By Colorado law, the state constitution could be amended by popular initiative to allow for an eight-hour law. The passage of such an amendment was immediately taken up by the Colorado labor movement, and in 1902 success crowned its efforts when the state's voters passed an eight-hour initiative by a margin of nearly two to one.[15]

Equally important was the disunity of the workers in the face of the determination of the powerful American Smelting and Refining Company. "The smelter strike in Colorado last summer marked a new epoch in the labor movement," noted a writer in the the WFM's *Miners Magazine* in April 1900. "It was the first time that organized labor gave battle to organized capital in the form of a trust." The outcome of the battle revealed the weakness of any union that did not include all of the West's smelter workers in a single, disciplined industrial union. William D. Haywood, the newly elected secretary-treasurer of the WFM, who moved to Denver in 1901 when the union's headquarters were transferred there, made the organization of the city's smelter workers his highest priority. This had been a desirable goal in earlier years, but the rise of ASARCO now rendered it essential.[16]

If the disunity of unskilled industrial workers in the face of the large corporation presented a serious problem for the labor movement, it was overshadowed by an even more destructive conflict: that between workers committed to the radical industrial unionism of the Western Labor Union and those who remained loyal to the AFL. In the opening years of the new century, conflict between the WLU and AFL assumed major proportions in a number of western communities. In no locality was the conflict more bitter than in Denver.[17]

Across the nation, the unions affiliated with the AFL increased their membership dramatically in the years of prosperity and high employment from 1898 to 1903. The membership of some AFL national unions increased by as much as 300 percent in these years. Such staggering growth could be seen in Denver. Local No. 55 of the United Brotherhood of Carpenters and Joiners, for example, which had barely four hundred members in November 1898, claimed over twelve hundred in May 1903. By the latter date, the Colorado Bureau of Labor Statistics estimated that there were approximately seventeen thousand union members in Denver.[18]

But growth was not confined to the AFL craft unions. In western communities where the WLU had managed to establish a foothold, it also grew rapidly. Denver was one such community. After the transfer of Western Federation of Miners headquarters to the city in 1900, and especially after the opening of a WLU office there in May 1901, the WLU began a period of astonishing growth. Of the seventy-one new charters the WLU issued to unions between May 1901 and February 1902, seventeen were to organizations in Denver. The WLU's initial base in Denver lay with the eleven hundred workers at the Globe and Grant smelters, who held membership in the WLU through the Western Federation of Miners. But the WLU in the city was far from a mere paper organization or a front for the miners union. Rather it represented a diverse array of urban workers— many, though not all, of them unskilled—organized mainly in industrial organizations.[19]

Leading the WLU contingent in Denver, for example, was the powerful Butchers Protective Union, which claimed nearly fifteen hundred members in 1902. A model industrial union, it included both skilled butchers and unskilled meatpackers who worked at the newly built Swift and Company packing plant in Denver. Other groups of workers organized under the WLU's banner as well: grocery clerks, laundry workers, cooks and waiters, hack drivers, and mattress makers. Until October 1901, these new WLU unions were regularly admitted to the Denver Trades Assembly.[20]

The rapid growth of the Western Labor Union in Denver and other western cities led to increasing concern on the part of Gompers and other AFL leaders. As early as 1899, Gompers made a speaking tour of the West in an effort to cement the loyalty of the region's workers to the AFL. There was, of course, little hope of bringing the western hard rock miners back into the fold, but AFL leaders desperately hoped to keep urban workers like those in Denver from being lost to the WLU.

The Denver Trades Assembly became a central arena of AFL strategy. In October 1901, the Trades Assembly decided by a very narrow margin of thirty-nine to thirty-seven to refuse admittance to any new local unions that were not affiliated with the international unions of their crafts. Since the AFL internationals already prohibited affiliation of locals connected to the WLU, this decision in effect kept any new Denver WLU locals from joining the Trades Assembly. The WFM's organ, the *Miners Magazine*, charged that the Trades Assembly's action demonstrated "the increasing virulence" of the "rule or ruin policy of the paid agents" of the AFL, and it is clear that the AFL national leadership provided guidance and support for the Denverites' action. But it had widespread support within a number of Denver craft unions. At a meeting of Denver Typographical Union No. 49 the following month, for example, the long-time local labor leader, W. H. Montgomery, argued forcefully that the printers' delegates to the Trades Assembly should "vote at all times for the maintenance of the supremacy of organizations having a national head." The union backed his position by passing a motion declaring that its delegates should "be instructed to vote for American Federation of Labor."[21]

Bitter conflict over the issue raged in the Trades Assembly for the next few months. As the WLU continued to add members in Denver, sentiment in the Trades Assembly gradually shifted in its favor. Socialists among Denver's craft unionists, particularly horseshoer Roady Kenehan and printer David Coates led the fight, but a two-thirds vote was now necessary to change the assembly's ruling. On 9 March 1902, at a heated meeting of the Trades Assembly, lasting nearly eight hours, the WLU supporters lost the call on the admission of new unions by a single vote, thirty-one to sixty. But then they shifted their approach. A majority (all that was needed) voted to return their charter to the AFL and to seek the affiliation of the entire Trades Assembly with the Western Labor Union.[22]

This action triggered what the *Miners Magazine* called "a war to the knife." Later that month, delegates representing twenty local unions withdrew from the Trades Assembly and formed a new central body, the "Incorporated Trades Assembly (A.F. of L.)." According to W. H. Montgomery, who played a critical role in the formation of the new body, "every step taken by the legal Trade Assembly has been endorsed by the executive council of the A.F. of L." Max Morris, leader of the Denver clerks who was also a vice-president of the AFL, and J. D. Pierce, an AFL general organizer who had been in Denver for the previous six months, helped coordinate the actions of the dissidents but, again, the number of trade unions involved indicates that local support for their position was widespread. Among the unions participating in the new body were the Granite Cutters, the Machinists, the Plumbers, the Cigar Makers, the Printers, the Book Binders, the Job Pressman, the Retail Clerks, the Leather Workers, the Bindery Women, the Bartenders, the Egg Candlers, the allied Metal Mechanics, the Tailors, the Waiters, and the Engineers. It could legitimately claim, as Montgomery put it, to represent "the old-time trades-union organizations, the people who have built up the movement in this vicinity for the past 25 years."[23]

No trade union was unanimous in its views however; rather, conflict took place within unions just as much as it did between them. The Denver Typographical Union provides a particularly stark example of this. Some printers were angry at their own president, Harvey Garman, who, in his role as president of the State Federation of Labor, "has recognized the W.L.U. faction as the bone fide Trades Assembly, accepted the per capita tax from them, and has practically ignored the legal Trades Assembly." Garman, they believed, "had forgotten everything fair and honorable in a mad desire for personal advancement." At a meeting of the printers, W. H. Montgomery stated that because the printer David Coates owed his primary allegiance to the WLU, not the ITU, he should be expelled. Coates's reply, according to the union minutes, "became personal" and "Mr. Montgomery objected strongly to the terms applied to him by Mr. Coates." At another member's request, "Mr. Coates apologized and, in turn, 'Monty' followed suit." The vote taken to "accept and concur in" Montgomery's report on the new Trades Assembly, however, indicates the extent of the division remaining in this union. While forty-eight voted to back Montgomery's position, nineteen voted against.[24]

Action in the courts ensued over the question of which organization represented the legitimate trades assembly. A decision was finally handed down in favor of the WLU supporters. But this represented only one aspect of the struggle between the WLU and the AFL in Denver. Beginning in early 1902, AFL organizer Pierce began to form rival unions among Denver workers in trades dominated by the WLU. He was especially effective in building organizations among strikebreakers in industries where WLU affiliates were engaged in strikes. Such organizations, accurately labeled "scab unions" by the Western Labor Union, were formed by Pierce at George J. Kindel's mattress factory, the Rocky Mountain Paper Mill, and several other concerns. But such a strategy, while producing results in the short run, could not but hurt the AFL's prestige among Denver's organized workers in the long run. Even Lennon, now national treasurer of the AFL and a Gompers supporter, expressed dismay over Pierce's strategy. He predicted that Pierce's scab unions would have the effect of driving all of Denver's craft unions into the WLU Trades Assembly and called on Gompers to dismiss the organizer.[25]

This increasingly bitter conflict within Denver's labor movement set the stage for the actions taken at the convention of the Western Labor Union held in the city in May 1902. Before the convention, Gompers began calling for unity between the two organizations and, at least according to one delegate, "a majority of the members of the WLU convention came to Denver with the determination to bring about reconciliation between the AF of L and the WLU." During the convention, however, a strike of building laborers was in progress and the delegates saw Pierce's strategy of organizing strikebreakers at firsthand. "With the contemptible fight in Denver and the more contemptible farce at conciliation, it turned the stomach of mostly all who before had an appetite for peace." Rather than seeking reconciliation with the AFL, the convention changed the WLU's name to the American Labor Union and declared its intention to seek members throughout the nation. It was now a full-fledged rival labor federation.[26]

From this point until April of the following year, momentum in the Denver labor movement lay with the American Labor Union. Just as Lennon had predicted, several AFL unions—including Gompers' own Cigar Makers—left the Incorporated Assembly and rejoined the original Denver Trades and Labor Assembly. After a talk by Coates on the AFL's "dual and scab unions in Denver," followed by two months of investigation and deliberation, even the Denver Typographical Union withdrew from the assembly it had helped found, giving "the unsettled condition of the labor situation in this city" as its reason. Meanwhile, blacksmiths working in the shops of the antiunion Colorado and Southern Railroad in Denver organized an ALU local and won union recognition after a strike in March 1903. After a year-long boycott supported by many Denver working people, even mattress workers at George Kindel's factory won their demand for union recognition. Kindel was certainly "a hard fighter," noted the new *American Labor Union Journal* after the victory in February 1903, but he "is regarded as a sensible man and must appreciate that nothing is gained from trouble."[27]

The ALU's assessment of Kindel, however, was badly off the mark. In April 1903, only two months after his concessions to his workers, Kindel took a leading role in founding the Denver Citizens Alliance, an organization committed to the total destruction of radical unionism in the city. Within several weeks, the Alliance built a membership of over one thousand Denver residents. Also in April, James C. Craig, a leader of the Denver Citizens Alliance, met with antilabor figures in other cities to coordinate nationwide resistance to unionism, setting in motion a trend that culminated in the creation of the powerful Citizens Industrial Association, an organization that would stand at the center of the national open shop drive, later in the year. As early as May, the Denver Citizens Alliance was ready for its first round with organized labor.[28]

On 9 May, the Hurlburt Grocery Company, a Citizens Alliance affiliate whose workers were organized in the ALU, discharged two of its team drivers. No reason was given for the dismissal but the fact that the two men were ALU activists and that the ALU was on the eve of its 1903 convention in Denver revealed the company's intentions clearly enough. The ALU proclaimed a "life and death struggle in Denver" and immediately began to call out its members in a sympathy strike. By 20 May, forty-two hundred men and women were on strike and the business of the city was, according to one observer, "at a standstill." Butchers, cooks, waiters, bakers, brewery workers, and mattress workers went out, while nearly every other labor organization in the city went into emergency meetings to determine an appropriate response. Then, on 21 May, the Hurlburt Company and the Citizens Alliance agreed to recognize the right of workers to join the ALU and to rehire employees. The near-general strike ended and workers returned to their jobs. But from the first, Denver employers acted in violation of their agreement and, further, began to blacklist all workers who had participated in the sympathy strike. What had seemed a victory turned out to be a defeat.[29]

Although Denver's labor activists did not understand it at the time, the short strike of May 1903 became a turning point in the history of Denver's working-class movement as a whole. The new element was the Citizens Alliance. Building a close relationship with Republican Governor James Peabody, the Denver organization played a major role in the defeat of the second big strike of Denver smelter workers in the summer of 1903. The alliance also produced a crop of imitators in Telluride, Cripple Creek, and several other Colorado mining towns, which became important antiunion forces in the bloody strikes of 1904. James Craig, the president of the Denver Citizens Alliance, toured the country, explaining the principles of his organization to business people as far away as Chicago and New York.[30]

But another problem became apparent in the Denver strike: the absence of a thorough working-class solidarity that could have checked the rise of the Citizens Alliance. Especially notable was the unwillingness of the city's major craft unions to participate in the general strike. On 19 May, Local No. 188 of the Iron Molders Union responded to a request to join the strike by instructing their corresponding secretary to write to national headquarters "for instructions." Denver molders could have easily predicted the nature of instructions they would receive, for their national president, Martin Fox, had been a prominent figure in the National Civic Federation since 1900. As such, he gave vigorous support to that body's effort to suppress sympathy strikes, to replace traditional expressions of working-class solidarity with binding national trade agreements and the arbitration of disputes. By the time the Denver iron molders received a reply stating that they "had nothing to gain in going out on a sympathetic strike," the issue had become moot.[31]

The situation in the printers union was more complicated, for here there was considerable support for the ALU and for participation in the sympathy strike. The final decision of the union not to go out was shaped in large part by the intervention of the national leadership of the union, and particularly by John W. Bramwood. Bramwood had served as president of the Denver Typographical Union in the mid-1890s, and had been an important supporter of Gompers's antisocialist position at the 1894 Denver convention of the AFL. He had been elected secretary-treasurer of the International Typographical Union in 1896 (a position he would hold for the next twelve years) and had moved to Indianapolis in that year. But, like John B. Lennon, he still wielded considerable influence among Denver workers. At a special meeting of the Denver Typographical Union on Sunday, 17 May, while a general strike committee waited outside in the hall, debate raged about what course to take. According to the union minutes, the matter was settled when an official read a telegram from Bramwood "virtually forbidding us to go out on a sympathetic strike. He said we must abide by our contracts with publishers." Rather than strike, the printers decided to appoint a committee to confer with the general strike committee and various employers "as to the best means of settling the present difficulty."[32]

As was the case with the 1899 smelter strike, the May 1903 conflict led to the emergence of ideas that became part of the overall thinking of working-class radicals in the West. Its principal lesson was the same as that of 1899: in the face of a unified front of employers, workers required complete solidarity. But such solidarity could not be provided by AFL-style craft unions that placed so much emphasis on the autonomy of their respective crafts and increasingly opposed the use of the sympathy strike.

The statistics of the May strike revealed the extent of the problem. While there were nearly fifteen thousand Denver trade unionists in 1903, only forty-two hundred participated in the strike. "Here was the first contest fought between the [Citizens] Alliance on the one side and the workers on the other," wrote Allan Ricker, a labor radical, in early 1904, attempting to understand this first round in what had by then become the Colorado labor wars. "Had the union men stood together, the alliance would have been annihilated, but now comes the test of the two policies of the eastern and western labor movements. The unionists of the western movement stood together, but the members of the AF of L, true to the tactics of Gompers, dillied, dallied, resolved, expressed sympathy, and being a divided agency against a united one, the strike was lost." In a glance at the on-going struggle of miners at Cripple Creek, Ricker ended his analysis on a somber note: "The Citizens Alliance, flushed with its first victory, now prepares to crush the western movement."[33]

Thus, the criticism of the AFL's craft unionism and the advocacy of a broad industrial unionism of skilled and unskilled workers was firmly planted in the western labor movement by the early part of 1904. Industrial unionism had deep roots in Denver, going back to the experiments of the 1890s depression. However, the new developments in turn-of-the-century Denver, particularly the rise of ASARCO, the emergence of the Citizens Alliance, the antiunion behavior of J. D. Pierce and the AFL, and the failure of old-line craft unions to stand by other workers in the city, placed the commitment to a unified industrial union movement at the very center of the thinking of radical western labor activists.

Syndicalism

New developments also brought the syndicalist tendency in the Denver labor movement back into prominence. Most important of these developments was the failure to achieve the eight-hour day for smelter workers through legal means. Following the defeat of the 1899 smelter strike and the Supreme Court ruling that an eight-hour law was unconstitutional, the Colorado labor movement threw a great deal of effort into an initiative that would amend the state constitution to allow for such a law. Smelter workers' testimony before the State Board of Arbitration had done much to create public sympathy for such an amendment. By the time of the November 1900 elections, public support for an eight-hour law was so strong that all three large political parties, the Democrats, the Republicans, and the Populists, put the call for an amendment in their platforms. Although the eight-hour amendment would not appear on the state ballot until November 1902, its passage seemed inevitable.[34]

And so it was. The State Federation of Labor worked hard for the amendment throughout 1902 and again all three political parties backed it. In November 1902, Colorado's voters approved the measure by an overwhelming vote of 72,980 to 26,266. The problem, though, was that the amendment passed by the voters did not actually enact the eight-hour day. It merely *allowed* the state legislature to pass such a law. In the same election, the Republicans gained control of the legislature and the vigorously antilabor Republican, James Peabody, was elected governor. The American Smelting and Refining Company now went into action with a massive lobbying effort in the legislature to defeat the law. They were successful. Despite the ostensible support of the Republican party for an eight-hour bill, the state legislature adjourned its session in June 1903 without even considering it. "Rarely," wrote the journalist Ray Stannard

Baker, "has there been in this country a more brazen, conscienceless defeat of the will of the people, plainly expressed, not only at the ballot, but by the pledges of both parties."[35]

On the night of 3 July 1903, the members of Mill and Smeltermen's Union No. 93 held a meeting at the Elyria town hall in Denver to decide upon a course of action. Bill Haywood and Charles H. Moyer, president of the WFM, were present at the meeting and counseled against rash action. But the 300 smelter workers at the meeting voted overwhelmingly for an immediate strike. Shortly before midnight, the 300 men entered the Grant smelter and persuaded the 125 workers there to leave their jobs. Then the crowd moved on to the Globe smelter, broke down the gates, and brought out the men working there, about 150 in number. Several foremen and an engineer at the Globe smelter resisted the action, and some violence occurred. But the fires at both smelters were extinguished and massive picketing of the smelters began the next day.[36]

ASARCO's position in this conflict was far stronger than it had been in 1899. For one thing, it now had the full resources of the Denver Citizens Alliance at its disposal. Through the alliance's offices, ASARCO received the most sweeping injunction ever issued in Colorado. Judge Dixon in Denver prohibited the WFM, Local No. 93, the ALU, the Denver Trades Assembly, and the State Federation of Labor from interfering in any way with the operation of the Globe or Grant smelters. His injunction even prohibited these organizations from publishing materials designed to encourage men to strike. City authorities also lent their support to the corporation. After consulting with the Citizens Alliance, Denver's mayor and chief of police decided to send in ninety-two special deputies along with a number of regular police officers to insure the protection of strikebreakers that ASARCO began recruiting from as far away as Missouri.[37]

The strike lasted into the fall of 1903 and was never officially called off. Nevertheless, the great political resources of the corporation guaranteed its victory. By September the Globe smelter was back in operation with a force of imported strikebreakers. The Grant smelter, considered by ASARCO executives to be out of date, never reopened. "Since the fourth of July, 1903, no smoke has curled from its top," wrote Bill Haywood in the 1920s. "It stands, let me dedicate it, a monument to the eight-hour day."[38]

Though unsuccessful, the 1903 strike of the Denver smelter workers foreshadowed a central tenet of the ideology of the IWW: the belief that the political process had been so corrupted by the influence of large corporations that workers had to turn to direct action at the point of production to win their objectives. With the failure of the Colorado legislature to carry out the will of the voters, the smelter workers resorted to a kind of legislation by strike. Their ultimate failure, revealing the close links between ASARCO, the Citizens Alliance, and the political authorities of the city, only reinforced the syndicalist tendency in the Denver labor movement.

Another strategy was open to Denver workers. The Socialist party, organized in Denver in 1901, also stressed the corruption of the political process; but rather than advocating direct action at the workplace, the Socialists called for the building of a working-class political movement that would *transform* the state. Many of Denver's labor radicals were attracted to this vision. Both Haywood and the WFM's first president, Ed Boyce, joined the Denver branch of the SP in 1901. And the Western Labor Union convention in Denver in 1902, when it changed its name to the American Labor Union, also fully endorsed the Colorado Socialist party ticket in that year.[39]

A full alliance between the Socialist party and the ALU, however, was precluded by the response of Socialist leaders across the nation to the action taken in Denver in 1902. While praising the explicit identification of the western working-class movement with socialism, they leveled a barrage of criticism at the dual unionism embodied in the ALU's attack on the American Federation of Labor. Trade unionists in the party, led by the typographer Max Hayes, believed that whatever the failings of the AFL, the struggle for socialism had to go on within that organization; it could not simply be dismissed as the westerners had done. Some important figures in the party did dissent from this view, most notably Eugene Debs, who wrote an important defense of the the ALU in the *International Socialist Review*, the organ of the party's left wing. Nevertheless, the predominant stance of the party's leadership toward the ALU remained one of pronounced hostility.[40]

The failure of the political socialists to support the ALU, like the failure of the political process itself on the question of the eight-hour day, furthered the syndicalist tendency among Denver's labor radicals. This is to focus only on the "negative" side of the syndicalist vision, however, the rejection of political action and political parties. There was also a "positive" side of syndicalism: the belief that through action at the point of production, workers could begin to exercise real power in society. This theme also made an appearance in the Denver labor movement, particularly in the period between mid-1902 and May 1903.

Until the early twentieth century, workers' control seemed impossible for unskilled workers to achieve. But in cases where unskilled or semiskilled workers were able to build strong unions, some kind of order could be brought to bear in even the most difficult circumstances. The case of the beer drivers, organized by the ALU in Denver, provides a good example. Before the emergence of the ALU union among the drivers, these workers often dreaded the coming of winter. With the cold weather, the consumption of beer fell, with resulting layoffs and hard times for the drivers. By an agreement the drivers managed to impose on their employers in 1902, however, they were laid off during the winter months in rotation, one week at a time. This new system, instead of causing economic hardship, gave the men "a chance to go out hunting and kill mountain lions or other game, or if he chooses he can take a good rest. It is just what a fellow needs if he has worked hard all summer," noted one driver in praise of the new lay-off policy.[41]

At the peak of the ALU's power in Denver in 1902–3, the written working agreement, along with the boycott and the liberal use of the ALU label on the products of "fair" employers, provided a key to the growing control that unskilled and semiskilled workers were able to exert over the conditions of their labor. The very real power that they came to exercise, as much as the failure of previous political strategies, fueled the movement toward a fully developed syndicalist ideology.[42]

The first formal statement of this ideology appeared in the columns of the *American Labor Union Journal* in September 1903, in a long article by William E. Trautmann, the editor of the Brewery Workers' journal in Chicago. Combining reflections on his experience in the American labor movement with his broad knowledge of intellectual currents in the European working-class movement, Trautmann put forward the fundamental syndicalist idea that the labor union of the capitalist present contained within it the seed of a socialist future. "Who can judge how to regulate the required production of utilities in the various lines of industry better than those directly employed in a given industry?" Trautmann wrote. "Industrial organizations are the forerunners of the society established on socialist foundations."[43]

Coming after the failure of the legislative eight-hour day, the "betrayal" of the ALU by the Socialist party, and the small but very real steps toward workers' control by the ALU's Denver locals, Trautmann's statement naturally resonated within Denver's working-class movement. Bill Haywood and David Coates immediately took up and expounded the idea among their fellow labor radicals in the city. Coates, the Colorado printer who was now residing in Chicago as president of the ALU, expressed the syndicalist view clearly when he contrasted the political party and industrial union on the eve of the IWW's first convention in 1905:

A political party can never fight the every day battles of the workers with the master class; the workers organized as a class into a great labor union can. A political party can never wrest control of the industries from the exploiting master class, give them over to the workers and protect the workers in possession of them. Industrial unionism, as marked out in the Chicago manifesto can and will do that very thing, and will also have prepared them to assume posses-sion of their own and administer the Co-operative Commonwealth.[44]

Although it grew out of the experience of Denver working people, syndicalism remained a minority—if powerful—current within the city's labor movement. The dominant current was shaped by trade unionists who were actively engaged in politics. Almost without exception in these years, they focused their efforts on the Democrats.

The years following Colorado's Populist interlude saw the gradual rise of the Democratic party. First in fusion with Populists and Silver Repub-licans and, after 1902, on their own, the Democrats finally demonstrated that they could win elections at the state level and in Denver. Though Davis Waite had lost to a little-known Republican, Albert McIntyre, in 1894, Colorado Democrats, benefiting tremendously from the new pro-silver national leadership of William Jennings Bryan, won the state gov-ernorship in 1896 and held it until the inauguration of James Peabody in January 1903. Throughout these years, but especially as the ranks of organized labor expanded at the turn of the century, the party reached out to the Denver labor movement. Labor hit the peak of its influence in party circles in 1900, when the Democrats—mainly to block a move toward independent political action in the State Federation of Labor—placed Coates, who was then president of the Federation, on its winning ticket as candidate for lieutenant governor.[45]

Labor had another ally in Thomas Patterson, publisher of the *Rocky Mountain News*, who returned to the Democratic party in 1900 to become one of its most important state leaders. Though far from a radical, Patter-son had by now established a fairly consistent prolabor stance. When he was elected to the United States Senate in 1900, even the WFM's Ed Boyce declared it a victory for "the common people."[46]

At the municipal level, as well, a new breed of Democrats—some-times labeled "urban liberals" by historians—began to emerge, many of them with roots in the Populist party or other reform movements. In 1896, Edward Keating and a group of other ex-Populists organized a re-form Democratic organization in Denver's Fifth Ward, managing to oust a long-time party boss, and winning for themselves the title of the "Fifth Ward Savages." The Savages eventually became a powerful political orga-nization in their own right, attracting many ambitious politicians with little interest in social reform. But the intellectual leader and orator of the group remained John McGauran, a single-tax enthusiast and Irish nationalist who gave the Savages their official name: the "Fifth Ward Henry George Club."[47]

The advent of urban liberalism within Denver's Democratic party could have a direct payoff for the city's organized workers. Among those boosted to political office by the Savages was a young Irish American proofreader named John Mullins, elected a justice of the peace despite some opposition from established Democratic leaders. Though he worked in the arena of machine politics and was hardly a radical, Mullins was an important friend of labor. In the 1903 smelter strike, when other Denver judges were handing out sweeping injunctions against striking smelter workers, Judge Mullins broke ranks by granting an equally sweeping injunction against the Denver Citizens Alliance.[48]

Finally, though, it was the violently antilabor administration of James Peabody that cemented the turn to the Democrats. While labor radicals may have believed that the Peabody regime conclusively demonstrated the futility of using political action against a powerful capitalist government, most Denver labor activists absorbed a quite different message: Peabody had to be defeated. In 1904, the city's trade unionists—on the whole—rallied behind the candidacy of the old-time Democrat, Alva Adams, in order to defeat the most antilabor chief executive anyone could remember. For most, there was no going back.[49]

Internationalism

Syndicalism and industrial unionism were the most prominent tenets of the ideology of the Industrial Workers of the World. But a commitment to working-class internationalism and a condemnation of racism also figured prominently in its outlook. "There are organizations that are affiliated . . . with the A.F. of L., which in their constitution and by-laws prohibit the initiation of or conferring of the obligation on foreigners," noted Bill Haywood in his opening address to the IWW's founding convention. "What we want to establish at this time is a labor organization that will open wide its doors to every man that earns his livelihood either by his brain or his muscle." The commitment to internationalism was embodied in the very name of the new organization, with its emphasis on workers *of the world.*[50]

Although the internationalist emphasis had deep roots in the Denver labor movement, going back to the struggles over the meaning of Irish nationalism in the early 1880s, it had ebbed and flowed over the next twenty years. A number of the trade unions that grew so rapidly in the late 1880s and early 1890s, for example, excluded blacks and immigrants. All opposed Chinese immigration. Although partially counteracted by the fight against the American Protective Association in the mid-1890s, racism and nativism continued to play a large role in the labor movement, and among labor radicals as well. Anti-Chinese sentiments ran high throughout the period, even though Denver's Chinese population continuously declined through the last two decades of the century.[51]

The changing character of class relations at the turn of the century, however, forced a rethinking of this issue by many within the working-class movement. This chapter has already noted the growing aggressiveness and unity of Denver employers and the rise of the large-scale corporation. Among the strategies for defeating labor organizations that emerged in this period was one that would continue to be of central importance in the twentieth century: the manipulation of racial and ethnic divisions with the working class. As a response to this increasingly conscious employers' strategy, the leaders of the ALU reasserted the labor movement's internationalist tradition and extended that tradition to embrace the Chinese.

Colorado coal operators had been employing nonwhite strike breakers in an effort to divide workers along racial lines since the 1880s. Garfield County operators continued these efforts in 1895, when they hired forty-five African American miners from Pueblo to break a strike over wage cuts. ASARCO experimented with the employment of black workers at its smelters in Denver in the late 1890s in an effort to reduce wages, but this proved to be unsuccessful. In the 1903 Denver smelter strike, the recruitment of strikebreakers became an essential part of ASARCO's strategy. They first brought in a train of sixty-two men from Joplin, Missouri, but upon learning that a strike was in progress, all but twenty of them refused to work. After this failure, the company brought in another fifty or sixty men, this time Chicanos from New Mexico.[52]

This emerging strategy on the part of Denver employers forced labor radicals in the city to reconsider a central tenet of their previous outlook, the demand for Chinese exclusion. Chinese strikebreakers were virtually unheard of in this era, but radicals understood that a break with the traditional hostility toward the Chinese would constitute a powerful symbol of international working-class solidarity. The Western Federation of Miners took the lead. In May 1903, Haywood announced that the WFM would thereafter attempt to organize Chinese and Japanese laborers in and around the mines. This was a tremendously important new departure in the history of American labor.[53]

At its convention the same month, the ALU followed the lead of the WFM. Before the convention, the editors of the *American Labor Union Journal* began advocating the admission of those they called "Mongolians" into the organization. Their continued exclusion, they argued, "will not help the workers but only injure them by splitting their ranks." The *Journal* also argued for an end to the labor movement's longstanding support for Chinese and Japanese exclusion laws.[54]

Many ALU members opposed this new departure and fought the issue at the 1903 convention, but in the end the advocates of inclusion carried the day. As a result, the ALU rewrote its constitution to include the statement that "no working man or woman shall be excluded from membership in local unions because of creed or color." The new emphasis proved to be of great importance to the Denver smelter workers in their struggle with ASARCO three months later. When the Mexican American workers arrived to take the places of the strikers in the city, the strikers convinced a number of them to desert the company and return to their homes.[55]

Chicanos throughout the Southwest had established a powerful tradition of labor militancy by the early twentieth century. In the late 1880s and early 1890s, the *Gorras Blancas*, or White Caps, of San Miguel County, New Mexico, had not only defended communal lands against the intrusion of large land companies by cutting fences and destroying property, but had also worked jointly with the Knights of Labor in the region to improve wages and protect workers from exploitation. Their leader, Juan José Herrera, was also a district organizer for the Knights who had been influenced in part by Joseph Buchanan's labor radicalism while living in Colorado in the mid-1880s. Many of these Chicano Knights and White Caps supported New Mexico's important and prolabor People's party in the 1890s as well.[56]

At the opening of the twentieth century, Chicano working people in New Mexico and southern Colorado organized *mutualistas*, mutual aid societies, which not only provided insurance programs, but also fought discrimination and sometimes supported unionization. Though Mexican Americans sometimes took jobs as strikebreakers, on other occasions they played active roles in leading and supporting strikes. In the important hard rock mining strike at Telluride, Colorado, in 1901, for instance, Chicanos could be found among the ranks of both strikers and strikebreakers. In 1902, labor organizing also took root among Chicano workers in the Arizona copper mining region, where Abraham Salcido was sentenced to prison for his role as a labor organizer.[57]

This tradition of labor militancy may well have shaped the decision of Chicano smelter workers to leave Denver once they realized that they were to be employed as strikebreakers. Nevertheless, such an outcome would have been highly unlikely in the absence of a commitment to international and interracial organizing on the part of the WFM and the ALU. The ALU's internationalism, like its commitments to syndicalism and industrial unionism, had become an important force by the summer of 1903.

Racism, of course, did not disappear among rank-and-file members of the ALU simply because official policy shifted. WFM locals throughout the West remained notoriously ethnocentric. Moreover, even the commitment of the WFM's leaders to ethnic tolerance remained partial. In October 1907, for example, the *Miners Magazine* took issue with the slogan, "workers of the world unite," arguing that "the vast percentage of the [WFM] membership will feel a reluctance in remaining idle and silent, while corporate giants . . . are endeavoring to innundate their land with the slaves from Asia." On the other hand, the internationalist position staked out by the ALU in 1903 did not disappear, but rather became a linchpin of the ideology of its successor, the IWW.[58]

The Cultural Struggle

Like the internationalist current, the struggle to build social and cultural institutions for workers had deep roots in the Denver labor movement, stretching back to the Knights of Labor in the mid-1880s. When the Western Labor Union began to grow in the city in the early years of the twentieth century, its local unions adopted many features of this struggle. For example, a number of them expressed dissatisfaction with low membership participation in union affairs and followed the practice of craft unions like the printers in fining members for not attending union meetings. Other ALU locals, whose members did not have sufficient financial resources to employ this strategy, began the practice of printing the names of members with poor attendance records in the columns of the *ALU Journal*, in an effort to embarrass them into more frequent attendance.[59]

Other locals turned to a more effective and longer-term strategy: they sought to build an entire social life around the institution of the local unions, a project built on the tradition established by the Knights of Labor twenty years earlier. In 1902, for example, the powerful Butchers Protective Union announced a ball to be held on Thanksgiving Eve "which promises to be an extra choice cut in that line." ALU locals held such social events with great frequency in the months before the employers' offensive of May 1903.[60]

As was the case with the Knights, much of the purpose behind these social events was to meet the needs of working people for recreation and companionship. This was one function of the Denver labor movement. But the distinctive character of the employers' offensive in the early twentieth century also seemed to make the struggle to establish a movement culture essential to the very survival of the labor movement. Though dominated by local employers who used it to combat unionism in their industries, the Denver Citizens Alliance was in several respects quite different from earlier employers' associations in the city. First, unlike such associations, the Citizens Alliance opened its membership to the middle class as a whole (and theoretically to working people also) as well as to employers. Its very name implied a struggle, not between workers and employers, but between "citizens" and the "lawless element." Such a formula indicated a pronounced concern with public opinion and with building popular support for its antiunion position within the middle class and to some extent within the working class.[61]

The leaders of the Citizens Alliance were well placed to do this, for two of its three founding members had had experience in broad popular movements in the city. Herb George, one of the founders of the alliance, had originally achieved political prominence as a leader of Colorado's Populist movement in the 1890s. Although identified with its silver wing, rather than its more radical, Waite-led antimonopoly wing, George nevertheless used his paper, *George's Weekly*, to try to speak for the "producing classes" as a whole. George Kindel, though never a Populist, built something of a popular movement in Denver in support of a more favorable railroad rate structure. This movement also drew on the hostility of workers toward railroads and other monopolies and furthered Kindel's reputation as a friend of the city's working people and small businessmen.[62]

But the most important new development of the employers' offensive of 1903, which signaled the war for popular opinion, was the support given the Citizens Alliance by the hierarchy of Denver's Catholic church. On 31 May 1903, immediately after the conclusion of the near-general strike in the city, Bishop Nicholas C. Matz launched the first of a series of highly publicized attacks on "anarchists" in the WFM and the ALU. From this point on, his sermons focused on a defense of the morality of private property and capitalism. In a city where 44 percent of all church members were Catholics, the bishop was a figure of potentially great influence.[63]

The actual success of these efforts remains somewhat in doubt. Despite its name and the background of its leaders, the Citizens Alliance drew few working-class citizens to its ranks. Matz's sermons probably had more influence. One historian has concluded that in the struggle for "the hearts and minds of Colorado's workingmen," the bishop was extremely effective, and that a number of Catholic workers dropped their membership in the WFM and the ALU as a result of his intervention. But the results of the 1904 Colorado election provide a basis for questioning this conclusion. The campaign was a clear referendum on the antilabor policies of Governor Peabody, who was running for reelection with the support of both the Citizens Alliance and Bishop Matz. The governor went down to defeat. Moreover, as James Wright has shown, the anti-Peabody vote came from counties marked by variables indicating union labor, foreign-born population, and—most importantly—Catholics. "Perhaps religious appeals were meaningless in a campaign in which there were no religious issues at stake," Wright concludes.[64]

Nevertheless, the employers' new strategy of trying to build broad public support for their antiunion position created considerable concern among the leaders of the ALU and the WFM in Denver. They responded by stepping up the drive to create a cultural world for workers within the labor movement, a cultural world that would hold up its own brand of anticapitalist morality in opposition to Matz and the Citizens Alliance. In particular they called for the study of socialist philosophy and political economy at local union meetings; to facilitate such study, the *American Labor Union Journal* began running a column entitled "Lessons in Social Economy." Covering topics such as the history of slavery, the origins of capitalism, and the relationship between science and religion, the column was designed for use in local union meetings. "The labor union," Bill Haywood declared in May 1905, "is a lyceum for the study of political economy." Denver Knights of Labor had made the same point twenty years earlier, but the question had now taken on considerably greater urgency.[65]

Thus, by the summer of 1903, all of the key features of the IWW's ideology had been brought together by the ALU's activists in Denver. None of these features—syndicalism, industrial unionism, internationalism, or the struggle to build a movement culture—were new. All of these ideological and organizational currents had appeared at one point or another in the course of the growth and development of Denver's labor movement. What was new was the synthesis of all of these currents by the city's working-class radicals in a coherent and internally consistent worldview.

These radicals had not carried the city's labor movement as a whole with them. Labor's dominant figures remained committed to a relatively narrow craft unionism and to cooperation with the Democratic party. But by 1903 radicalism had emerged as a powerful minority force in the city's working-class movement. Equally important, its key emphases would be taken over directly by the Industrial Workers of the World.

Epilogue: The IWW in Denver

Following the publication of the "Manifesto of Industrial Unionists" in January 1905, a flurry of activity took place in the ranks of Denver's labor movement. "The call is meeting with a magnificent reception,"
declared one Denver labor activist in April, and in the following month
ALU members in the city met to select delegates to the June convention
that would give birth to the Industrial Workers of the World. Seven Denver residents attended the IWW's founding convention and four of them,
Bill Haywood, Emma Langdon, Luella Twining, and M. E. White, took
on leadership roles.[1]

Plagued by bitter factionalism and repression, the IWW had some
trouble establishing itself in Denver. Repression was especially significant
in a city where the antilabor Pinkerton Detective Agency was headed by
James McParland, the man who had achieved fame for his role in the
arrest and execution of the Molly Maguires in the 1870s. On 17 February 1906, McParland and the Denver police arrested Haywood, Charles
Moyer and George A. Pettibone for the murder of Frank Steunenberg, a
former governor of Idaho, and the three men were immediately extra-
dited to that state to stand trial. Although they were acquitted in July
1907, the arrests and trial caused considerable damage to the IWW in
Denver. Funds that might otherwise have gone into organizing were used
to pay legal costs and an image of violence attached itself to the new
labor organization.[2]

Nonetheless, the IWW gradually established a presence in Denver.
In early 1913, local Wobblies waged a long and successful free speech
fight in the city, filling the jails for months and finally forcing Denver authorities to allow them the freedom to speak on street corners. "Since the
settlement of the free-speech fight, extensive agitation has been carried
on with splendid results," wrote the secretary of Denver Local No. 26 to

IWW headquarters in June 1913. By the following year, a second IWW local, No. 133, was operating in the city.[3]

In 1916, Denver was the site of one of the most significant organizing efforts in the IWW's history. In this year, Jane Street, a Denver domestic worker, founded IWW Local No. 113, the Domestic Workers Industrial Union. Though the union never enrolled many domestic workers, it set up a women's employment agency and a boarding house—institutions that had been pioneered by the Knights of Labor's Hope Assembly in the 1880s—in an effort to put Denver's "shark" employment agencies out of business. Attacked by employers, employment agencies, and the YMCA, and undermined also by the hostility of many of Denver's male Wobblies, Local No. 113 eventually went under. But for a period of time, as Street wrote a fellow organizer in Tulsa, the union "got results." "We actually have the *power* to do things. We have raised wages, shortened hours, bettered conditions in hundreds of places."[4]

Like earlier radicals, the IWW remained a minority force in the Denver labor movement as a whole. Printer W.H. Montgomery, Max Morris, a leader of the Denver Retail Clerks and a close ally of Gompers, and other AFL-oriented labor leaders regained full control of the Denver Trades Assembly by 1909. Such leaders not only practiced a narrow version of craft unionism, but also cemented the alliance of the city's labor movement with Colorado's Democratic party. In the process, Morris catapulted himself to a position as a Democratic representative in the Colorado legislature while Montgomery ended up as state commissioner of labor.[5]

They were aided in their efforts by a new group of sympathetic Democratic politicians at the local and state level. "Boss" Robert Speer, the most important of these politicians, was the Democratic mayor of Denver from 1904 to 1912 and from 1916 to 1918. While taking generous contributions from public service corporations and liquor and gambling interests, he also provided much needed services to Denver's working-class residents. He built playgrounds and swimming pools in working-class districts, made contributions to charity organizations, and maintained a close relationship with the Democratic party-oriented figures in the city's labor movement.[6]

But Speer was not the only new figure in local politics. Equally important were his opponents, the various progressive reformers who captured much attention in Denver in the first decade of the twentieth century. Edward Costigan, Judge Ben Lindsey, who had established the first juvenile court in the nation, and George Creel, who would go on to become head of the Office of Public Information under Woodrow Wilson, led the progressive insurgency. Their efforts reached a culmination in the administration of Colorado's Democratic governor, John Shafroth, from 1909 to 1913. Shafroth helped to enact an impressive body of labor legislation, including a child labor law and a factory inspection law, and began to build support for final passage of an eight-hour day law in mining and smelting. No less a figure than Roady Kenehan was drawn to Shafroth's orbit, serving as state auditor in his administration. Mainstream politics could clearly bring results.[7]

By 1912, in fact, Colorado was seen by many within the American labor movement as the state with the most fully realized trade union–Democratic party alliance in the nation. This book has revealed the deep roots of this alliance, which came to dominate Denver in a way that effectively kept labor radicals in a minority position. It has also indicated why Colorado was the nursery of so many prominent labor-oriented progressives and New Dealers in the twentieth century. Such individuals drew on the legacy of Democratic party activism pioneered by Denver's trade union leaders in the 1880s and 1890s.[8]

But labor radicals, like those in the IWW, also drew on the legacy of Denver's nineteenth-century craft union and labor reform movements, though in different ways. As this book has shown, Denver's history in the closing decades of the nineteenth century provides important keys to an understanding of the IWW's ideology. This ideology embodied four principal components: syndicalism, industrial unionism, working-class internationalism, and a belief in the importance of building a movement culture to strengthen working-class consciousness. All of these various strands emerged in Denver's working-class movement in the years from 1880 to 1898 and were brought into a synthesis by the American Labor Union at the turn of the century.

Internationalism emerged in the early 1880s as a result of a struggle between the Denver labor movement and city's Land League branch over the meaning of Irish nationalism. It provided a basis for the interethnic solidarity upheld by the Knights of Labor in the mid-1880s. Although eclipsed by the decline of the Knights in the later years of the decade, it resurfaced in the struggle against the American Protective Association in the 1890s. The ALU extended internationalism to include Asian immigrants in the early twentieth century.

The attempt to build a movement culture was one of the hallmarks of the Denver Knights of Labor in the mid-1880s and was most clearly expressed in their opposition to the saloon. While discarding prohibitionism, leaders of the city's labor movement continued to believe that the creation of autonomous working-class institutions was central to building solidarity. With the ideological struggle against the Citizens Alliance in the early years of the twentieth century, the WFM and the ALU gave this project considerable emphasis.

Syndicalism, the most well known feature of the IWW's outlook, emerged in the trade union upsurge of the late 1880s and early 1890s.

Originating as a vague distrust of politics and a belief in the power of shop floor struggles to bring about sweeping social change, syndicalist ideas were formalized by the Rocky Mountain Social League, a small but significant radical organization in the 1880s. Though not an important force in the depression of the 1890s, a syndicalist outlook emerged again in Denver's radical working-class movement by 1903.

Industrial unionism was mainly a product of the depression of the 1890s, a crisis that revealed the limits of craft unionism and ushered in a wave of militancy among Denver's unskilled laborers and factory operatives. Their militancy was profoundly affected by the radical wing of the Populist party, but in the early twentieth century it was harnessed to the syndicalism of the WLU, the ALU, and finally the IWW.

By itself, Denver's history cannot provide all the keys to the IWW's ideological origins. More research is still needed on western mining communities, though this research should be focused on the gradual evolution of working-class politics and culture rather than on the violent industrial conflicts that have traditionally dominated accounts. In light of the fact that much of the Wobblies' history was played out in eastern cities like Paterson and Lawrence, further study of these communities would also add much to our understanding of the origins of the IWW's ideology.[9]

Nevertheless, Denver's history does illuminate the links that existed between the world of nineteenth-century craft unionism and labor reform and the world of twentieth-century working-class radicalism. Key concerns of the earlier movement had been updated and broadened, not discarded. The "reverence" the labor radical Emma Langdon expressed for the old printer, Charles Semper, made some sense after all.

Notes

Abbreviations

AFL	American Federation of Labor
ALUJ	*American Labor Union Journal*
APA	American Protective Association
AQ	*American Quarterly*
ASARCO	American Smelting and Refining Company
CBLS	Colorado Bureau of Labor Statistics
CHS	Colorado Historical Society
CM	*Colorado Magazine*
CSA	Colorado State Archives
CSFL	Colorado State Federation of Labor
DCD	*Denver City Directory*
DPL	Denver Public Library, Western History Department
DR	*Denver Republican*
DT	*Denver Tribune*
DTR	*Denver Tribune-Republican*
DTU	Denver Typographical Union
IMJ	*Iron Molders Journal*
ISR	*International Socialist Review*
IW	*Irish World*
IWA	International Workingmens Association
IWW	Industrial Workers of the World
JAH	*Journal of American History*
JKL	*Journal of the Knights of Labor*
JSH	*Journal of Social History*
JSP	*John Swinton's Paper*
JUL	*Journal of United Labor*
KOL	Knights of Labor
LE	*Labor Enquirer*
LH	*Labor History*
MM	*Miners Magazine*
MVHR	*Mississippi Valley Historical Review*

PHR	*Pacific Historical Review*
RMN	*Rocky Mountain News*
SLP	Socialist Labor party
UBCJA	United Brotherhood of Carpenters and Joiners of America
UP	Union Pacific Railroad
UPEM	*Union Pacific Employees Magazine*
WCTU	Woman's Christian Temperance Union
WHC	Western Historical Collections, University of Colorado
WHQ	*Western Historical Quarterly*

Introduction

1. David Brody, *Workers in Industrial America: Essays on the Twentieth Century Struggle* (New York, 1980), pp. 32–39.

2. Emma F. Langdon, *Labor's Greatest Conflicts* (Denver, 1908), pp. 135–39.

3. For a particularly clear statement of this point of view, see Richard Jules Oestreicher, *Solidarity and Fragmentation: Working People and Class Consciousness in Detroit, 1875–1900* (Urbana, Ill., 1986), pp. xviii–xix. For the the view that the IWW was shaped mainly by "the general characteristics of the frontier," see John R. Commons, et al., *History of Labor in the United States* (New York, 1918–35), 4:169–247. Although far more thorough and persuasive, Melvyn Dubofsky's analysis of the IWW's origins in his full history of the organization also neglects the role of nineteenth-century labor traditions, emphasizing instead the rapid proletarianization of hard-rock miners in the late nineteenth-century West. See "The Origins of Western Working Class Radicalism, 1890–1905," *LH* 7 (Spring 1966): 131–54; and *We Shall Be All: A History of the Industrial Workers of the World* (1969; reprint ed., Urbana, Ill., 1988), pp. 19–87. For recent historiographical discussions of the IWW, see Joseph R. Conlin, "Introduction," to *At the Point of Production: The Local History of the I.W.W.*, ed. Joseph R. Conlin (Westport, Conn., 1981), pp. 3–24, and Dubofsky, *We Shall Be All*, pp. 541–44. For thoughtful assessments of continuities and discontinuities in the labor movements of these eras, see David Montgomery, "Labor and the Republic in Industrial America, 1860–1920," *Le Mouvement Social*, no. 111 (1980), pp. 201–15; and Leon Fink, *Workingmen's Democracy: The Knights of Labor and American Politics* (Urbana, Ill., 1983), pp. 178–233.

4. IWW, *Proceedings of the First Convention, 1905*, p. 5.

5. For a helpful discussion of the IWW's syndicalism and the more widespread "syndicalist mood" in the American working-class movement that it expressed, see Bruce Nelson, *Workers on the Waterfront: Seamen,*

Longshoremen, and Unionism in the 1930s (Urbana, Ill., 1988), pp. 6–10. For a survey and analysis of early twentieth-century syndicalism in a number of nations, see Marcel van der Linden and Wayne Thorpe, eds., *Revolutionary Syndicalism: An International Perspective* (Aldershot, Eng., 1990), pp. 1–24.

6. John Reed, *The Education of John Reed: Selected Writings*, ed. John Stuart (1955; reprint ed., New York, 1972), p. 217; Lawrence Goodwyn, *Democratic Promise: The Populist Movement in America* (New York, 1976), pp. 525–55. Salvatore Salerno discusses the movement culture of the IWW in his *Red November, Black November: Culture and Community in the Industrial Workers of the World* (Albany, N.Y., 1989), but this aspect of the organization is most thoroughly documented in Joyce L. Kornbluh, ed., *Rebel Voices: An I.W.W. Anthology*, (Ann Arbor, Mich., 1964).

7. For a forceful critique of deterministic interpretations of the IWW's origins, see William Preston, "Shall This Be All? U.S. Historians Versus William D. Haywood, et al.," *LH* 12 (Summer 1971): 435–53.

Chapter 1: Denver in the Later Nineteenth Century

1. William M. Thayer, *Marvels of the New West: A Vivid Portrayal of the Stupendous Marvels in the Vast Wonderland West of the Missouri River* (Norwich, Conn., 1890), p. 355.

2. Frank Fossett, *Colorado: Its Gold and Silver Mines, Farms and Stock Ranges, and Health and Pleasure Resorts* (New York, 1879), p. 33. For other travelers' observations on Denver, see Robert G. Athearn, *Westward the Briton* (Lincoln, Neb., 1953), pp. 43–47.

3. *LE*, 27 Jan. 1883.

4. My categorization of cities follows Sam Bass Warner, Jr., *The Urban Wilderness: History of the American City* (New York, 1972), pp. 84–98. For late nineteenth-century class formation in large cities, see Martin Shefter, "Trade Unions and Political Machines: The Organization and Disorganization of the American Working Class in the Late Nineteenth Century," in *Working-Class Formation: Nineteenth-Century Patterns in Western Europe and the United States*, ed. Ira Katznelson and Aristide R. Zolberg (Princeton, N.J., 1986), pp. 197–276.

5. A great deal of the so-called new labor history has been focused on such places. For a pioneering attempt to conceptualize the distinction between the complex metropolis and the small industrial city, see Herbert G. Gutman, "The Workers' Search for Power," reprinted in his *Power and Culture: Essays on the American Working Class* (New York, 1987), pp. 70–92. For Troy and Cohoes, see Daniel J. Walkowitz, *Worker City Company Town: Iron and Cotton-Worker Protest in Troy and Cohoes, New York 1855–84* (Urbana, Ill., 1978).

6. Carl Abbott, "Frontiers and Sections: Cities and Regions in American Growth," *AQ* 37 (Bibliography 1985): 406, 409–10. For the core/periphery distinction as used here, see David Ward, *Cities and Immigrants: Geography of Change in Nineteenth Century America* (New York, 1971), pp. 11–49.

7. Recent accounts of Denver's history include Carl Abbott, "Boom State and Boom City: Stages in Denver's Growth," *CM* 50 (Summer 1973): 207–30; Gunther Barth, *Instant Cities: Urbanization and the Rise of San Francisco and Denver* (New York, 1975); Lyle W. Dorsett, *The Queen City: A History of Denver* (Boulder, Col., 1977); and Stephen J. Leonard and Thomas J. Noel, *Denver: Mining Camp to Metropolis* (Niwot, Col., 1990).

8. Horace Greeley, *An Overland Journey from New York to San Francisco in the Summer of 1859* (1860; reprint ed., New York, 1964), pp. 103–5; Abbott, "Boom State and Boom City," pp. 208–11; *Denver and Auraria: The Commercial Emporium of the Pike's Peak Gold Regions In 1859* (n.p., n.d.), pp. 11–12; Thomas J. Noel, *The City and the Saloon: Denver, 1858–1916* (Lincoln, Neb., 1982), pp. 8–9.

9. Rodman Wilson Paul, *Mining Frontiers of the Far West, 1848–1880* (New York, 1963), pp. 114–21; Jerome C. Smiley, *History of Denver, with Outlines of the Earlier History of the Rocky Mountain Country* (Denver, 1901), p. 441; Abbott, "Boom State and Boom City," 212–13, Glenn Chesney Quiett, *They Built the West: An Epic of Rails and Cities* (New York, 1934), p. 156.

10. Quiett, *They Built the West*, pp. 155–61; Thomas J. Noel, "All Hail the Denver Pacific: Denver's First Railroad," *CM* 50 (Spring 1973): 91–116.

11. D. W. Meinig, "American Wests: Preface to a Geographical Interpretation," *Annals of the Association of American Geographers* 62 (June 1972): 165–66; Abbott, "Boom State and Boom City," pp. 213–15; Clyde Lyndon King, *The History of the Government of Denver* (Denver, 1911), pp. 45–46, 70; *History of the City of Denver, Arapahoe County, and the State of Colorado* (Chicago, 1880), pp. 221–27, 230; *DCD, 1871*, p. 260; Isabella L. Bird, *A Lady's Life in the Rocky Mountains* (1879; reprint ed., Norman, Okla., 1960), p. 138.

12. Paul, *Mining Frontiers*, pp. 126–27; King, *History of the Government of Denver*, pp. 66–71; Charles S. Thomas, Manuscript Autobiography, p. 51, CHS; Highlands Park Estate, "Report of the Trustees for 1875," in Willam A. Bell Papers, CHS; *History of the City of Denver*, pp. 228–33; Eugene Frank Rider, "The Denver Police Department: An Administrative, Organizational, and Operational History, 1858–1905" (Ph.D. diss., University of Denver, 1971), pp. 154–56.

13. Paul, *Mining Frontiers*, pp. 126–27. The Dun credit reports are in the R.G. Dun & Co. Collection, "Colorado," vols. 1 and 2, and "West-

ern Territories," vol. 1, Baker Library, Harvard University. Although the Dun records are extremely useful for information on specific individuals, they are not complete. Thus, proportional statements like this one must be taken as suggestive rather than definitive. For a discussion, see Margaret Walsh, *The Manufacturing Frontier: Pioneer Industry in Antebellum Wisconsin, 1830–1860* (Madison, Wis., 1972), pp. 230–32.

14. Fred R. Niehaus, *Development of Banking in Colorado* (Denver, 1942), pp. 15–25; Nolie Mumey, *Clark, Gruber and Company, 1860–1865: A Pioneer Denver Mint* (Denver, 1950), pp. 3–5; DCD, 1866, pp. 106–8; Denver Board of Trade, *Report*, 1877, pp. 14–21; Dorsett, *Queen City*, pp. 14–21. On the importance of banking in western urban growth, see Oliver Knight, "Toward an Understanding of the Western Town," *WHQ* 4 (Jan. 1973): 27–42. For the theory of "inital advantage," see Allan Pred, "Industrialization, Initial Advantage, and American Metropolitan Growth," *Geographical Review* 55 (Apr. 1965): 158–85.

15. Robert Athearn, *Rebel of the Rockies: The Denver and Rio Western Railroad* (New Haven, Conn., 1962), pp. 1–27; Howard Roberts Lamar, *The Far Southwest, 1846–1912: A Territorial History* (New Haven, Conn., 1966), pp. 277–84; Meinig, "American Wests," p. 166; Colin B. Goodykoontz, "Some Controversial Questions before the Colorado Constitutional Convention of 1876," *CM* 17 (Jan. 1940): 10–13.

16. Gunther Barth, "Metropolitanism and Urban Elites in the Far West," in *The Age of Industrialism in America*, ed. Frederick Cople Jaher (New York, 1968), pp. 175–76; Lamar, *The Far Southwest*, p. 301. On the commercial orientation of urban elites across the West, see Earl Pomeroy, "The Urban Frontier of the Far West," in *The Frontier Challenge: Responses to the Trans-Mississippi West*, ed. John G. Clark (Lawrence, Kans., 1971), pp. 13–14.

17. Smiley, *History of Denver* pp. 872–78; Lawrence H. Larsen, *The Urban West at the End of the Frontier* (Lawrence, Kans., 1978), pp. 38–39; *Colorado Condensed: Industrial Information for Capitalists and Immigrants* (Denver, 1883), p. 68; James E. Fell, Jr., *Ores to Metals: The Rocky Mountain Smelting Industry* (Lincoln, Neb., 1979), p. 28; Ellsworth C. Mittick, "A History of Mining Machinery Manufacture in Colorado," *CM* 24 (Nov. 1947): 225–30. For a good discussion of the character of frontier manufacturing, see Walsh, *The Manufacturing Frontier*, pp. v–xi, 21–20. Smiley estimates the value of industrial production in 1871 as $800,000.

18. Paul, *Mining Frontiers*, pp. 127–29.

19. Abbott, "Boom State and Boom City," pp. 216–17; Robert G. Dunbar, "History of Agriculture," in *Colorado and Its People: A Narrative and Topical History of the Centennial State*, ed. LeRoy R. Hafen (New York, 1948), 2:120–57; King, *History of the Government of Denver*, pp. 94–95.

20. *History of the City of Denver*, p. 239; Thomas, Manuscript Auto-

biography, pp. 78–79; Abbott, "Boom State and Boom City," pp. 213, 217–22.

21. Abbott, "Boom State and Boom City," pp. 216–17; Smiley, *History of Denver*, pp. 844–46, 886–88; *Denver by Pen and Picture* (Denver, 1898), p. 10; Niehaus, *Development of Banking*, pp. 35–42.

22. Barth, "Metropolitanism and Urban Elites," p. 176; *RMN*, 1 Jan. 1884; Dorsett, *Queen City*, p. 62. For a classic analysis of urban growth emphasizing the shifting perspective of urban elites toward industrialization, see Bayrd Still, "Patterns of Mid-Nineteenth Century Urbanization in the Middle West," *MVHR* 28 (Sept. 1941): 187–206.

23. U. S., Census Office, *Tenth Census*, 2:398; *Twelfth Census*, 1900, vol. 8, pt. 2, pp. 70–73; "Colorado as Seen by a Visitor of 1880: Diary of Rezin H. Constant," *CM* 12 (May 1935): 108.

24. Allan R. Pred, *The Spatial Dynamics of U.S. Urban-Industrial Growth, 1800–1914: Interpretive and Theoretical Essays* (Cambridge, Mass., 1966), pp. 16–25, 118. The 1885 figures are calculated from Enumerators' Schedules for Arapahoe County, "Colorado State Manufacturing Census, 1885."

25. U. S. Industrial Commission, *Report, 1901*, 4:251–64; King, *History of the Government of Denver*, pp. 96–97; Leonard and Noel, *Denver*, pp. 118–19.

26. Smiley, *History of Denver*, pp. 551–56; Fell, *Ores to Metals*, pp. 135–65; Denver Chamber of Commerce and Board of Trade, *Seventh Annual Report, 1889*, p. 33; *Ninth Annual Report, 1891*, p. 134; U. S. Immigration Commission, *Report, 1911*, pt. 25, vol. 3, p. 163; Stephen J. Leonard, "Denver's Foreign Born Immigrants, 1859–1900" (Ph.D. diss., Claremont Graduate School and University Center, 1971), p. 149.

27. Paul, *Mining Frontiers*, p. 126; Mittick, "History of Mining Machinery Manufacture," pp. 230–36; U. S., Census Office, *Twelfth Census, 1900*, vol. 8, pt. 2, pp. 70–71; Julian Ralph, *Our Great West: Study of the Present Conditions and Future Possibilities of the New Commonwealths and Capitals of the United States* (New York, 1893), p. 328.

28. Smiley, *History of Denver*, p. 884; *Colorado Condensed*, pp. 61–68; Herbert O. Brayer, *William Blackmore: Early Financing of the Denver-Rio Grande Railway and Ancillary Land Companies, 1871–1878* (Denver, 1949), 2:18–19; U. S., Census Office, *Twelfth Census, 1900*, vol. 8, pt. 2, pp. 70–71.

29. Denver Chamber of Commerce and Board of Trade, *Ninth Annual Report, 1891*, pp. 35–36, 93; Minutes of Denver Chamber of Commerce and Board of Trade, 14 Dec. 1903, in Denver Chamber of Commerce Records, DPL; Smiley, *History of Denver*, pp. 651, 884; *ALUJ*, 18 Dec. 1902; *Polly Pry*, 12 Dec. 1903, p. 7.

30. Fell, *Ores to Metals*, pp. 28, 40, 71–72, 220–25. For further discussion, see chapter 6 in this volume.

31. In the early 1880s, Gould had a controlling interest in the Denver, South Park and Pacific, the Colorado Central, and the Denver and Rio Grande. See Noel, "All Hail the Denver Pacific," p. 109; Robert G. Athearn, *Union Pacific Country* (Chicago, 1971), p. 109; King, *History of the Government of Denver*, pp. 98–99; Dorsett, *Queen City*, pp. 60–61; Allen duPont Breck, *William Gray Evans, 1855–1924: Portrait of a Western Executive* (Denver, 1964).

32. Ellsworth C. Mittick, "A History of Mining Machinery Manufacture in Colorado," *CM* 25 (Jan. 1948): 34–39; C. W. Hurd, "J. K. Mullen, Milling Magnate of Colorado," *CM* 29 (Apr. 1952): 104–18; Noel, *The City and the Saloon*, pp. 79–80; Smiley, *History of Denver* pp. 885–86; Leon W. Fuller, "Colorado's Revolt Against Capitalism," *MVHR* 21 (Dec. 1934): 347.

33. Calculated from U.S., Census Office, *Tenth Census, 1880,* 1:875; *Eleventh Census, 1890,* vol. 1, pt. 2, p. 660; *Twelfth Census, 1900,* vol. 1, pt. 2, pp. 558–61. For an important analysis of class structure and class relations in Denver during the 1860s and early 1870s, see Richard Hogan, *Class and Community in Frontier Colorado* (Lawrence, Kans., 1990), pp. 19–48.

34. Abbott, "Boom State and Boom City," pp. 213–16; Sandra Dallas, *Cherry Creek Gothic: Victorian Architecture in Denver* (Norman, Okla., 1971), pp. 24–28, 39; Thomas L. Karnes, *William Gilpin: Western Nationalist* (Austin, Tex., 1970), pp. 332–33; Louis L. Simonin, *The Rocky Mountain West in 1867*, trans. Wilson Clough (Lincoln, Neb., 1966), p. 38.

35. Abbott, "Boom State and Boom City," pp. 218–19; Barth, "Metropolitanism and Urban Elites," pp. 172–73; Dorsett, *Queen City*, pp. 61, 68–71; Duane A. Smith, *Horace Tabor: His Life and the Legend* (Boulder, Col., 1973), pp. 79–108, 149–67; Dallas, *Cherry Creek Gothic*, pp. 48–52. For a collective profile of these new men of wealth, see Richard H. Peterson, *The Bonanza Kings: The Social Origins and Business Behavior of Western Mining Entrepreneurs, 1870–1900* (Lincoln, Neb., 1977).

36. Dorsett, *Queen City*, p. 80; Noel, *The City and the Saloon*, pp. 67–78; William Allen West and Don Etter, *Curtis Park: A Denver Neighborhood* (Boulder, Col., 1980), pp. 3–21; Ruth E. Wiberg, *Rediscovering Northwest Denver: Its History, Its People, Its Landmarks* (Denver, 1976).

37. Noel, *The City and the Saloon*, p. 68; Don D. Etter, *Auraria: Where Denver Began* (Boulder, Col., 1972).

38. Noel, *The City and the Saloon*, pp. 16, 68–70; Fossett, *Colorado*, p. 242; *Colorado Condensed*, p. 68; Bernard Rosen, "Social Welfare in the History of Denver" (Ph.D. diss., University of Colorado, 1976), pp. 173–74.

39. Emily French, *Emily: The Diary of a Hard-Worked Woman*, ed. Janet Lecompte (Lincoln, Neb., 1987), p. 52. For a good discussion of the

complex issues surrounding class segregation, see Stuart M. Blumin, "The Hypothesis of Middle-Class Formation in Nineteenth-Century America: A Critique and Some Proposals," *American Historical Review* 90 (Apr. 1985): 332–34.

40. CBLS, *Third Biennial Report, 1891–92*, p. 117; Robert W. DeForest and Lawrence Veiller, eds., *The Tenement House Problem* (New York, 1903), 1:152; U.S., Census Office, *Twelfth Census, 1900*, vol. 1, p. clxxxvi. For recent assessments of housing conditions in late nineteenth-century American cities, see Jules Tygiel, "Housing in Late Nineteenth-Century American Cities: Suggestions for Research," *Historical Methods* 12 (Spring 1979): 84–97; and Martin J. Daunton, "Cities of Homes and Cities of Tenements: British and American Comparisons, 1870–1914," *Journal of Urban History* 14 (May 1988): 283–319.

41. Larry Betz, *Globeville: Part of Colorado's History* (n.p., 1972), pp. 14–17, 22; Leonard and Noel, *Denver*, p. 65.

42. U.S., Census Office, *Eleventh Census, 1890*, vol. 1, pt. 2, pp. 660–61; Joyce D. Goodfriend, "The Struggle for Survival: Widows in Denver, 1880–1912," in *Widows and Widowhood in the American Southwest, 1848–1939*, ed. Arlene Scadron (Urbana, Ill., 1988), pp. 166–94; W. H. Bergtold, "Denver Fifty Years Ago," *CM* 8 (Mar. 1931): 68–69; French, *Emily*, p. 7; Mrs. Anna Haydon Fader Haskell, Diary, 5 July 1888, Haskell Family Papers, Bancroft Library, University of California, Berkeley. For a fine discussion of working-class women's unpaid labor, see S. J. Kleinberg, *The Shadow of the Mills: Working-Class Families in Pittsburgh, 1870–1907* (Pittsburgh, 1989), pp. 84–93, 209–18.

43. Calculated from U.S., Census Office, *Eleventh Census, 1890*, vol. 1, pt. 2, pp. 660–61. Late nineteenth-century Denver is often thought of as a city with an overwhelmingly white, native-born population. It is true that only about one-quarter of Denver's *total population* was foreign-born in the last two decades of the nineteenth century. But if we focus our attention on *manual workers*, rather than on the total population, and if we group nonwhites and those born of immigrant parents with the foreign-born, Denver's apparent ethnic and racial homogeneity suddenly disappears. See Meinig, "American Wests," p. 166, and Gutman, *Power and Culture*, pp. 380–94.

44. Leonard, "Denver's Foreign Born," p. 238.

45. Sarah Deutsch, *No Separate Refuge: Culture, Class and Gender on an Anglo-Hispanic Frontier in the American Southwest, 1880–1940* (New York, 1987), pp. 30–32, 88–89, 127–61; Lawrence A. Cardoso, *Mexican Emigration to the United States, 1897–1931* (Tucson, Az., 1980), pp. 18–37; *RMN* 4 Aug. 1881.

46. Lionel Dean Lyles, "An Historical-Urban Geographical Analysis

of Black Neighborhood Development in Denver, 1860–1970" (Ph.D. diss., University of Colorado, 1974), pp. 43–67; George H. Wayne, "Negro Migration and Colonization in Colorado, 1870–1930," *Journal of the West*, 15 (Jan. 1976): 102–20.

47. James R. Harvey, "Negroes in Colorado," *CM* 26 (July 1949): 165–76; Smith, *Horace Tabor*, pp. 262–63.

48. Gerald E. Rudolph, "The Chinese in Colorado, 1869–1911" (M.A. thesis, University of Denver, 1964), pp. 91–106; Fumio Ozawa, "Japanese in Colorado," in *Japanese American Who's Who* (Denver, 1959), pp. 56–64.

49. Rudolph, "Chinese in Colorado," pp. 91–97; Lyles, "Black Neighborhood Development," pp. 68–108.

50. Abbott, "Boom State and Boom City," p. 219; Daniel Doeppers, "The Globeville Neighborhood in Denver," *Geographical Review* 57 (Oct. 1967): 506–11; Stephen J. Leonard, "The Irish, English, and Germans in Denver, 1860–1890," *CM* 54 (Spring 1977): 151. The absence of European immigrant neighborhoods in Denver was characteristic of a number of medium-sized cities of this era. See Sam B. Warner and Colin B. Burke, "Cultural Change and the Ghetto," *Journal of Contemporary History* 4 (Oct. 1969): 603–15; Kathleen Neils Conzen, "Immigrants, Immigrant Neighborhoods, and Ethnic Identity," *JAH* 66 (Dec. 1979): 603–15; and Howard P. Chudacoff, "A New Look at Ethnic Neighborhoods: Residential Dispersion and the Concept of Visibility in a Medium-Sized City," *JAH* 60 (June 1973): 76–93.

51. Robert M. Tank, "Mobility and Occupational Structure on the Late Nineteenth-Century Urban Frontier: The Case of Denver, Colorado," *PHR* 47 (May 1978): 211–14; Athearn, *Denver and Rio Grande*, p. 102; Sidney Heitman, ed., *Germans from Russia in Colorado* (Ann Arbor, Mich., 1978), pp. 74, 84; Dorsett, *Queen City*, p. xi.

Chapter 2: Irish Nationalism and the Ideological Origins of the Knights of Labor, 1878–83

1. CBLS, *First Biennial Report, 1887–88*, p. 80; John B. Lennon, letter to *JSP*, 14 Sept. 1884; Commons, *History of Labor*, 2:367–68.

2. "Colorado Labor Union Story," *RMN*, 19 Apr. 1959; Harold V. Knight, *Working in Colorado: A Brief History of the Colorado Labor Movement* (Boulder, Col., 1971), pp. 11–13; LeRoy R. Hafen, "Supplies and Market Prices in Pioneer Denver," *CM* 4 (Aug. 1927): 136–42; John L. Dailey Diary, 21, 23, 24, 26, 27 Apr. 1860, in John L. Daily Papers, DPL.

3. "Colorado Union Story"; Knight, *Working in Colorado*, p. 11; Smiley, *History of Denver*, p. 426; Minutes of DTU No. 49, Feb. 1865, in DTU No. 49 Records, WHC. For wartime inflation and trade unionism

in other areas of the country, see David Montgomery, *Beyond Equality: Labor and the Radical Republicans, 1862–1872* (New York, 1967), pp. 96–101, 142–44.

4. Dailey Diary, 21 Apr., 7, 18 June, 3, 14 July 1860; Robert L. Perkin, *The First Hundred Years: An Informal History of the Rocky Mountain News* (New York, 1959), pp. 197–98. For examples of similar work habits among other groups of craftsmen in the nineteenth century, see Herbert G. Gutman, *Work, Culture and Society in Industrializing America: Essays in American Working Class and Social History* (New York, 1976), pp. 32–39.

5. Minutes of DTU No. 49, July, Dec. 1864.

6. Ibid., Jan., Feb., 20 Aug. 1865, 3 Aug. 1866, 9 May 1869.

7. *History of the City of Denver*, p. 228; *RMN*, 17 Jan. 1873, 6 July 1876; Howard R. Lamar, "Colorado: The Centennial State in the Bicentennial Year," *CM* 53 (Spring 1976): 119.

8. *RMN*, 2, 4 June 1863, 7 Feb. 1866; CBLS, *First Biennial Report, 1887–88*, pp. 76–79, 104–5; Reed C. Richardson, *The Locomotive Engineer, 1863–1963* (Ann Arbor, Mich., 1963), pp. 186–89.

9. CBLS, *First Biennial Report, 1887–88*, pp. 88–89, 103, 118–19, 124–25; Charles J. Stowell, *Studies in Trade Unionism in the Custom Tailoring Trade* (Bloomington, Ill., 1913), pp. 57–60, 93–94; *RMN*, 8 July 1882.

10. *JSP*, 11 Nov. 1883; CBLS, *First Biennial Report, 1887–88*, pp. 73, 76–77, 79–80; Elizabeth Jameson, *Building Colorado: The United Brotherhood of Carpenters and Joiners of America in the Centennial State* (Denver, 1984), pp. 10–11; *IMJ*, 10 June 1880, p. 10. On the high rates of geographic mobility among iron molders, see Frank T. Stockton, *The International Molders Union of North America* (Baltimore, 1922), pp. 94–95.

11. The best discussion of the value system of the "autonomous craftsman" in this era is David Montgomery, *The Fall of the House of Labor: The Workplace, the State, and American Labor Activism, 1865–1925* (New York, 1987), pp. 9–57.

12. Joseph R. Buchanan, *The Story of a Labor Agitator* (New York, 1903), p. 41; *IMJ*, 1 Aug. 1887, p. 2; James E. Cebula, *The Glory and Despair of Challenge and Change: A History of the Molders Union* (Cincinnati, 1976), p. 30; CBLS, *First Biennial Report 1887–88*, p. 89; Stowell, *Studies in Trade Unionism*, pp. 91, 115–16. Though the struggle against piecework was central to the formation of the national carpenters union in these years, the issue does not appear to have played much of a role in the organizing of Denver carpenters. See Robert A. Christie, *Empire in Wood: A History of the Carpenters' Union* (Ithaca, N.Y., 1956), pp. 19–45, and Jameson, *Building Colorado*, pp. 3–23, 134–47.

13. CBLS, *First Biennial Report, 1887–88*, pp. 70–71, 73–74; *Second Biennial Report, 1889–90*, pp. 27–30; Buchanan, *Labor Agitator*, p. 41. On apprenticeship rules and the restriction of foremen's rights among Den-

ver printers, see Minutes of DTU No. 49, 7 July 1884, 11 Mar. 1885. For the ideological contest between acquisitive individualism and mutualism in late nineteenth-century working-class life, see Montgomery, *Fall of the House of Labor*, pp. 1–8, and his *Workers' Control in America: Studies in the History of Work, Technology, and Labor Struggles* (New York, 1979), pp. 9–31.

14. Buchanan, *Labor Agitator*, pp. 42–43; Minutes of DTU No. 49, 7 July 1884.

15. CBLS, *First Biennial Report, 1887–88*, pp. 90–91; *DR*, 7 Aug. 1882; *RMN*, 13 Nov. 1882, 1 Sept. 1890.

16. Minutes of DTU No. 49, 7 July 1884; *JSP*, 20 Apr. 1884. On the importance of the boycott throughout the nation in this era, see Michael A. Gordon, "The Labor Boycott in New York City, 1880–1886," *LH* 16 (Spring 1975): 184–229.

17. CBLS, *First Biennial Report, 1887–88*, pp. 90–92; *LE*, 16 Dec. 1883.

18. Gene Ronald Marlatt, "Joseph R. Buchanan: Spokesman for Labor during the Populist and Progressive Eras" (Ph.D. diss., University of Colorado, 1975), pp. 4–20, 131–35. See also Daniel Walker Howe, *The Political Culture of the American Whigs* (Chicago, 1979). Howe's reinterpretation of the Whigs helps illuminate the relationship between Buchanan's Whig political upbringing and his subsequent labor radicalism. It would be interesting to know whether other labor leaders of the 1870s and 1880s came from Whig families but, unfortunately, the political outlook of labor leaders' *parents* is not addressed in Warren Van Tine, *The Making of the Labor Bureaucrat: Union Leadership in the United States, 1870–1920* (Amherst, Mass., 1973) or in Gary M. Fink, ed., *Biographical Dictionary of American Labor* 2d ed. (Westport, Conn., 1984).

19. Marlatt, "Buchanan," pp. 21–54; Buchanan, *Labor Agitator*, pp. 5–49. See also Paul T. Bechtol, Jr., "The 1880 Labor Dispute in Leadville," *CM* 47 (Fall 1970): 313–25; and Charles Merrill Hough, "Leadville, Colorado, 1878 to 1898: A Study in Unionism" (M.A. thesis, University of Colorado, 1958), pp. 44–60.

20. Marlatt, "Buchanan," pp. 136–39; Buchanan, *Labor Agitator*, p. 47; *LE*, 10 May 1884. For Campbell and Kellogg, see Montgomery, *Beyond Equality*, pp. 425–47; Chester McArthur Destler, *American Radicalism, 1865–1901* (New Haven, Conn., 1946), pp. 50–77; and Robert P. Sharkey, *Money, Class, and Party: An Economic Study of Civil War and Reconstruction* (Baltimore, 1959), pp. 187–92. Montgomery distinguishes between a labor theory of wealth and a labor theory of value. The latter, playing a key role in both Ricardian and Marxist economic theory, was rejected by the Greenback theorists.

21. Marlatt, "Buchanan," p. 136; *LE*, 30 Dec., 4 Aug. 1883. For George, see Stephen J. Ross, "Political Economy for the Masses: Henry

George," *Democracy* 2 (July 1982): 125–34, and John L. Thomas, *Alternative America: Henry George, Edward Bellamy, Henry Demarest Lloyd and the Adversary Tradition* (Cambridge, Mass., 1983).

22. *LE*, 16 Dec. 1882; Montgomery, *Beyond Equality*, pp. 426–30. Buchanan did not refuse "to accept the permanence of an industrial society" any more than did other leaders of the Knights or the National Labor Union before them. Gerald N. Grob's influential interpretation of the Knights, which argues this point, is an inadequate guide to the character of their thought. See Grob, *Workers and Utopia: A Study of Ideological Conflict in the American Labor Movement 1865–1900* (Evanston, Ill., 1961), pp. 58–59. For a far more persuasive interpretation of how Knights' leaders' used the past to "capture alternative images of human possibility," see Fink, *Workingmen's Democracy*, pp. 3–17.

23. CBLS, *First Biennial Report, 1887–88*, pp. 70–71, 73–74, 76–77; Leonard, "Denver's Foreign Born," pp. 150–51. For the pioneering role played by the ASC and ASE in the development of the American labor movement, see Rowland Tappan Berthoff, *British Immigrants in Industrial America, 1790–1950* (Cambridge, Mass., 1953), pp. 88–91, and Clifton K. Yearley, Jr., *Britons in American Labor: A History of the Influence of the United Kingdom Immigrants on American Labor, 1820–1914* (Baltimore, 1957), pp. 186–91.

24. Minutes of DTU No. 49, 3 Nov. 1869; Eugene H. Berwanger, "Reconstruction on the Frontier: The Equal Rights Struggle in Colorado, 1865–1867," *PHR* 44 (Aug. 1975): 315–16, 325–26, 328; Philip S. Foner, *Organized Labor and the Black Worker, 1619–1973* (New York, 1974), pp. 43–44; Philip S. Foner, ed., *The Life and Writings of Frederick Douglass* (New York, 1955), 4:219. For powerful analyses of the role of racism in nineteenth-century white working-class life, see David R. Roediger, *The Wages of Whiteness: Race and the Making of the American Working Class* (New York, 1991); and Alexander Saxton, *The Rise and Fall of the White Republic: Class Politics and Mass Culture in Nineteenth-Century America* (New York, 1990).

25. Roy T. Wortman, "Denver's Anti-Chinese Riot, 1880," *CM* 42 (Fall 1965): 275–91. See also Patricia K. Ourada, "The Chinese in Colorado," *CM* 29 (Oct. 1952): 273–84, and Rudolph, "The Chinese in Colorado," pp. 107–21.

26. Wortman, "Denver's Anti-Chinese Riot," pp. 285, 287

27. CBLS, *Second Biennial Report, 1889–90*, pp. 50, 57; *LE*, 16 Dec. 1882, 10, 31 Mar., 16 June, 14 July 1883; Buchanan, *Labor Agitator*, pp. 66–67, 275–78. Though mobilization of anti-Chinese sentiments played an important role in the efforts of Colorado's Democratic party to build working-class support, it never served as a central organizing tool for Denver's labor movement, as it did in California. For that state, see

Gwendolyn Mink, *Old Labor and New Immigrants in American Political Development: Union, Party, and State, 1875–1920* (Ithaca, N.Y., 1986), pp. 71–112; and Alexander Saxton, *The Indispensable Enemy: Labor and the Anti-Chinese Movement in California* (Berkeley, Calif., 1971).

28. Philip S. Foner, *Women and the American Labor Movement: From Colonial Times to the Eve of World War I* (New York, 1979), pp. 148–50; Helen L. Sumner, *Equal Suffrage: The Results of an Investigation in Colorado Made for the Collegiate Equal Suffrage League of New York State* (New York, 1909), pp. 173–74; Minutes of DTU No. 49, 4 Oct. 1885; *IMJ*, Mar. 1885, p. 8; Stockton, *International Molders Union*, pp. 61–63; CBLS, *First Biennial Report, 1887–88*, pp. 88–89, 338. For the best discussion of the contradictory outlook of male trade unionists in the second half of the nineteenth century, see Alice Kessler-Harris, *Out to Work: A History of Wage-Earning Women in the United States* (New York, 1982), pp. 75–107.

29. *UPEM*, May 1886, p. 106; *RMN*, 13 Nov. 1882; *JUL*, 15 May 1881, Nov., Dec. 1882; *DCD, 1881, 1882*. For references to engineers and firemen as "labor aristocrats," see *UPEM*, Jan. 1886, p. 21, June 1886, p. 130. Section men, who maintained track, and wipers, who cleaned excess oil and grit from engines, represented two of the largest categories of railroad employees.

30. *UPEM*, Jan. 1886, p. 1.

31. For recent discussions of voluntary organizations that are especially sensitive to issues of class and ideology, see Walkowitz, *Worker City, Company Town*, pp. 156–70, and Brian Greenberg, *Worker and Community: Response to Industrialization in a Nineteenth-Century American City, Albany, New York, 1850–1884* (Albany, N.Y., 1985), pp. 89–101.

32. Leonard, "Irish, English, and Germans," pp. 131–32; *DCD, 1866, 1874*.

33. Tank, "Mobility and Occupational Structure," pp. 189–216; Denver *Turnverein, Souvenir des Denver Turnvereins* (Denver, 1890), pp. 101–2; *DCD, 1873*.

34. Harmon Mothershead, "Negro Rights in Colorado," *CM* 40 (July 1963): 213; Forbes Parkhill, *Mister Barney Ford: A Portrait in Bistre* (Denver, 1963), p. 142.

35. Eugene Berwanger, *The West and Reconstruction* (Urbana, Ill., 1981), pp. 144–48, 155–56; Eugene H. Berwanger, "William J. Hardin: Colorado Spokesman for Racial Justice" *CM* 52 (Winter 1975), 61.

36. Leonard, "Denver's Foreign Born," pp. 117–46, 151; *LE*, 17 Mar. 1883; *DCD, 1873*, p. 46.

37. Leonard, "Irish, English, and Germans," pp. 150–51; W. R. Hentschel, *The German Element in the Development of Colorado* (Denver, 1930), pp. 19–21. For evidence on the close relationship between Scottish and Welsh social clubs and the anti-Catholic organization, the Patriotic

Order of the Sons of America, see *Report of a Lecture by a Dynamite Fiend and How It Strikes the Average American Citizen* (Denver, 1884), pp. 11–13. See also Montgomery, *Beyond Equality*, pp. 42–43.

38. James Edward Wright, *The Politics of Populism: Dissent in Colorado* (New Haven, Conn., 1974), pp. 80–83; Paul Kleppner, "Voters and Parties in the Western States, 1876–1900," *WHQ* 14 (Jan. 1983): 49–68; Donald Wayne Hensel, "A History of the Colorado Constitution in the Nineteenth Century" (Ph.D. diss., University of Colorado, 1957), pp. 189–95; Billie Barnes Jensen, "The Woman Suffrage Movement in Colorado" (M.A. thesis, University of Colorado, 1959), pp. 44–45.

39. *Colorado Antelope*, Dec. 1879, Jan. 1880. For Churchill's role in the suffrage movement, see Carolyn Stefanco, "Networking on the Frontier: The Colorado Women's Suffrage Movement, 1876–1893," in *The Women's West*, ed. Susan Armitage and Elizabeth Jameson (Norman, Okla., 1987), pp. 265–76; and Caroline Nichols Churchill, *Active Footsteps* (Colorado Springs, Colo., 1909).

40. Eric Foner, *Politics and Ideology in the Age of the Civil War* (New York, 1980), p. 151.

41. Eric Foner, *Politics and Ideology*, pp. 154–55; Paul Bew, *Land and the National Question in Ireland, 1858–82* (Dublin, 1978), pp. 46–73; Samuel Clark, *Social Origins of the Irish Land War* (Princeton, N.J., 1979). For an excellent discussion of late nineteenth-century Irish nationalism, see Kerby A. Miller, *Emigrants and Exiles: Ireland and the Irish Exodus to North America* (New York, 1985), pp. 436–47.

42. Eric Foner, *Politics and Ideology*, p. 156; Thomas N. Brown, *Irish-American Nationalism, 1870–1890* (Philadelphia, 1966), pp. 85–115; Michael Davitt, *The Fall of Feudalism in Ireland or the Story of the Land League Revolution* (London, 1904), p. 252; T. W. Moody, *Davitt and Irish Revolution, 1846–82* (New York, 1981), pp. 358, 382–415.

43. Brown, *Irish-American Nationalism*, p. 108; Eric Foner, *Politics and Ideology*, pp. 158–60, 168–79; Michael Allen Gordon, "Studies in Irish and Irish-American Thought and Behavior in Gilded Age New York City" (Ph.D. diss., University of Rochester, 1977), pp. 431–38.

44. *RMN*, 11 July 1865, 25 Apr. 1866, 6 July 1868, 5 July 1869; Leonard, "Denver's Foreign Born," pp. 92–94; Sheldon Zwieg, "The Fenian Movement in Colorado" (Paper, 1951), WHC; "The Fenian Brotherhood: Colorado," *Éire-Ireland* 4 (Summer 1969): 717; William D'Arcy, *The Fenian Movement in the United States* (Washington, D.C., 1947).

45. *RMN*, 12 July 1865; Montgomery, *Beyond Equality*, pp. 127–34.

46. *RMN*, 15 Feb., 6, 7 July 1876, 19 Feb. 1883; *IW*, 12 July 1879; *DCD*, 1879–1884; Brown, *Irish-American Nationalism*, pp. 64–73. Of the sixteen workers among the Bull Whackers, six were skilled craftsmen and ten

were laborers. Nearly half (twenty-five) of the group were not traceable in the city directories, though it is likely that many of these were manual workers as well.

47. *LE*, 7 July 1883; *RMN*, 12 July 1882.

48. *RMN*, 12 Jan., 9 June 1882, 12 Mar. 1883; Leonard, "Denver's Foreign Born," pp. 143–45, 163. On the Land League's efforts to reduce sectarian tensions in Ireland, see Bew, *Land and the National Question*, pp. 217–18.

49. F. Sheehy-Skeffington, *Michael Davitt: Revolutionary, Agitator and Labor Leader* (London, 1908), pp. 114–16; *RMN*, 1 Apr., 4 Dec. 1881; *IW*, 16 July 1881; Joseph Lee, *The Modernisation of Irish Society, 1848–1918* (Dublin, 1973), pp. 93–94; Margaret Ward, *Unmanageable Revolutionaries: Women and Irish Nationalism* (London, 1983), pp. 4–39. The Ladies Land League was a far more significant organization among Irish American women than Hasia Diner's *Erin's Daughters in America: Irish Immigrant Women in the Nineteenth Century* (Baltimore, 1983), p. 128, suggests.

50. *RMN*, 15 Feb. 1876; Leonard, "Irish, English, and Germans," pp. 143–44.

51. *RMN*, 12 June 1882. Joseph Lee argues that the Land League brought about a sharp decline in the deference commanded by the church hierarchy in Ireland. See *The Modernisation of Irish Society*, pp. 89–92.

52. 1870 statistics compiled from U.S., Census Office, "1870 Manuscript Census, Arapahoe County, Colorado Territory," pp. 11–21. See also Leonard, "Denver's Foreign Born," pp. 97–104. 1890 statistics calculated from U.S., Census Office, *Eleventh Census, 1890*, vol. 1, pt. 2, pp. 660–61. It is now widely recognized that the Irish American middle class was considerably larger in western and mid-western cities than in those of the East. See, for example, Jo Ellen Vinyard, *The Irish on the Urban Frontier: Detroit, 1850–1880* (New York, 1976) and R. A. Burchell, *The San Francisco Irish, 1848–1880* (Berkeley, Calif., 1980). The Denver evidence is consistent with their findings.

53. *RMN*, 22 May 1882; *DCD,1879–84*; Miller, *Emigrants and Exiles*, pp. 545–47; Victor A. Walsh, "'A Fanatic Heart': The Cause of Irish-American Nationalism in Pittsburgh during the Gilded Age," *JSH* 15 (Winter 1981): 196–97.

54. *Rocky Mountain Celt*, 19 July 1884; *RMN*, 19 Feb. 1883; Leonard, "Denver's Foreign Born," p. 153; Brown, *Irish-American Nationalism*, p. 46; Miller, *Emigrants and Exiles*, pp. 544–48.

55. *RMN*, 9 June 1882, 19 Feb. 1883; Leonard, "Denver's Foreign Born," p. 154.

56. Hurd, "J.K. Mullen," pp. 104–18; Minutes of UBCJA Local No. 55,

28 Feb., 28 Mar. 1899, WHC; *LE*, 24 Mar. 1883; Leonard, "Denver's Foreign Born," pp. 121, 142, 168; Wright, *Politics of Populism*, p. 24; Hough, "Leadville," pp. 2–35.

57. William O'Brien and Desmond Ryan, eds., *Devoy's Post Bag, 1871–1928* (Dublin, 1953), 2:233–35; Miller, *Emigrants and Exiles*, pp. 540–41; Brown, *Irish-American Nationalism*, pp. 162–64; Henry M. Hunt, *The Crime of the Century; or, The Assassination of Dr. Patrick Henry Cronin* (Chicago, 1889), pp. 64–67; *LE*, 1 Sept. 1883; *Rocky Mountain Celt*, 19 July 1884.

58. *RMN*, 4, 11 Nov. 1881; Leonard, "Denver's Foreign Born," pp. 164–65.

59. *LE*, 11 Aug. 1883. For further discussion of the organization of women in the Knights, see chapter 3 in this volume.

60. Gutman, *Work, Culture and Society*, p. 89; *LE*, 1 Sept. 1883.

61. Henry J. Browne, *The Catholic Church and the Knights of Labor* (Washington, D.C., 1949), pp. 232–33.

62. *LE*, 3 Nov. 1883; Thomas, *Alternative America*, pp. 175–81. See also Walsh, " 'A Fanatic Heart,' " pp. 197–99.

63. *LE*, 4 Aug., 1 Sept. 1883.

64. Ibid., 24 Mar. 1883.

65. Buchanan, *Labor Agitator*, pp. 50–60; *LE*, 3 Nov., 15 Dec. 1883.

66. James MacCarthey, *Political Portraits by Fitz-Mac* (Colorado Spring, Colo., 1888), pp. 201–4; Montgomery, *Beyond Equality*, pp. 38–40.

67. Horace Greeley quoted in Robert S. Fogarty, "American Communes, 1865–1914," *Journal of American Studies* 9 (Aug. 1975): 149; David Boyd, *A History: Greeley and the Union Colony of Colorado* (Greeley, Colo., 1890), pp. 232, 263, 274, 322–23, 376, 394, 403, 406–9. See also James F. Willard, ed., *The Union Colony at Greeley, Colorado, 1869–1871* (Boulder, Colo., 1918); Dolores Haden, *Seven American Utopias: The Architecture of Communitarian Socialism, 1790–1975* (Cambridge, Mass., 1976), pp. 260–87; and Hogan, *Class and Community*, pp. 79–117.

68. Richard Welty, "The Greenback Party in Colorado," *CM* 28 (Oct. 1951): 310–11; Leah M. Bird, "The History of Third Parties in Colorado" (M.A. thesis, University of Denver, 1942), p. 30; *JUL*, 15 July 1881; *LE*, 10 Nov. 1883.

69. MacCarthey, *Political Portraits*, p. 201.

70. *LE*, 15 Dec. 1883; *RMN*, 10 Dec. 1883; *IW*, 5 Jan. 1884.

71. Buchanan, *Labor Agitator*, pp. 70–100; Jonathan Ezra Garlock, "A Structural Analysis of the Knights of Labor: A Prolegomenon to the History of the Producing Classes" (Ph.D. diss., University of Rochester, 1974), p. 255; CBLS, *First Biennial Report, 1887–88*, p. 80; Leonard, "Denver's Foreign Born," pp. 148–50, 160.

72. Thomas, *Alternative America*, p. 176.

Chapter 3: The Knights of Labor and the Fight against the Saloon, 1884–86

1. *RMN*, 23, 31 Oct. 1886; Wright, *Politics of Populism*, pp. 108–9. The best study of the political upsurge led by the Knights is Fink, *Workingmen's Democracy*.

2. For perspectives on working-class temperance in the nineteenth century, see Brian Harrison, *Drink and the Victorians: The Temperance Question in England, 1815–1872* (London, 1971) and James S. Roberts, *Drink, Temperance and the Working Class in Nineteenth-Century Germany* (London, 1984). For antisaloon and antidrink sentiments among the Knights of Labor, see Samuel Walker, "Terence V. Powderly, the Knights of Labor, and the Temperance Issue," *Societas* 5 (Autumn 1975): 279–93, and Francis G. Couvares, *The Remaking of Pittsburgh: Class and Culture in an Industrializing City, 1877–1919* (Albany, 1984), pp. 51–61. For a fine study of working-class leisure in late nineteenth-century America, see Roy Rosenzweig, *Eight Hours for What We Will: Workers and Leisure in an Industrial City, 1870–1920* (New York, 1983).

3. KOL, *Proceedings of the Fourth General Assembly, 1880*, p. 213; *Proceedings of the Fifth General Assembly, 1881*, p. 342; *Proceedings of the Sixth General Assembly, 1882*, p. 389; *Proceedings of the Seventh General Assembly, 1883*, pp. 401, 547, 551; *Proceedings of the Eighth General Assembly, 1884*, pp. 822, 825. Coal miners in Erie, Colorado, had organized the first Local Assembly of the Knights in the state, in July 1878. See CBLS, *First Biennial Report, 1887–88*, p. 80.

4. Buchanan, *Labor Agitator*, pp. 47–50.

5. Athearn, *Union Pacific Country*, pp. 341–42; Maury Klein, *Union Pacific: Birth of A Railroad, 1862–1893* (Garden City, N.Y., 1987), pp. 453–54; *LE*, 10 May 1884; CBLS, *First Biennial Report, 1887–88*, pp. 120–21, 126–27.

6. Buchanan, *Labor Agitator*, pp. 70–77; *LE*, 3 May 1884; *RMN*, 5 May 1884; *DT*, 3 May 1884; KOL (Colorado), "District Assembly No. 82 Circular, 30 July 1887," pp. 1–2, in Terence V. Powderly Papers (microfilm); Marlatt, "Buchanan," pp. 74–77; Gregory Alexander Bence, "The Knights of Labor in Colorado" (M.A. thesis, University of Northern Colorado, 1974), pp. 66–67; Klein, *Union Pacific*, pp. 453–54.

7. Buchanan, *Labor Agitator*, p. 73; *DT*, 3 May 1884; Marlatt, "Buchanan," p. 76; Bence, "Knights of Labor," p. 68. The workers' disciplined behavior resembled that of railroad strikers of the early 1870s analyzed by Herbert G. Gutman. See *Work, Culture, and Society*, pp. 299–305.

8. Klein, *Union Pacific*, pp. 453–54.

9. Buchanan, *Labor Agitator*, pp. 77–78; *LE*, 10, 17 May 1884.

10. *UPEM*, Jan. 1887, pp. 4–5.

11. *JSP*, 3, 17 Aug. 1884; *LE*, 24 May, 9 Aug. 1884; Marlatt, "Buchanan," pp. 79–80, 87; Shelton Stromquist, *A Generation of Boomers: The Pattern of Railroad Labor Conflict In Nineteenth-Century America* (Urbana, Ill., 1987), pp. 66–72.

12. Buchanan, *Labor Agitator*, pp. 77–78; Stromquist, *Generation of Boomers*, pp. 61–62, 68.

13. *LE*, 10, 17 May, 5 July, 16 Aug. 1884; *JSP*, 24 Aug. 1884; Buchanan, *Labor Agitator*, pp. 79–81; Marlatt, "Buchanan," pp. 80–82.

14. Buchanan, *Labor Agitator*, pp. 81–99; *LE*, 16 Aug. 1884; *JSP*, 24 Aug. 1884; Stromquist, *Generation of Boomers*, pp. 30–33, 66–69. For further discussion of the Union Pacific Employees Association and of struggles in Denver over workers' control, see chapter 4 in this volume.

15. KOL, *Proceedings of the Eighth General Assembly, 1884*, pp. 559, 747–48; "Addresses of the District and Local Assemblies," in KOL Records, Bancroft Library; *JUL*, 10 June, 10 Aug., 10 Oct., 10 Dec. 1884, 10 Apr., 10 May 1885; Garlock, "A Structural Analysis of the Knights of Labor," p. 255; Buchanan, *Labor Agitator*, pp. 104–6; Marlatt, "Buchanan," p. 87.

16. CBLS, *First Biennial Report, 1887–88*, pp. 101–2, 120–21; Stowell, *Studies in Trade Unionism*, pp. 63–67. In this year, Lennon was elected third vice-president of the national union. In 1887, he was elected general secretary and editor of the official journal and shortly thereafter he moved to New York, the headquarters of the national union.

17. Buchanan, *Labor Agitator*, pp. 47–48, 63; Minutes of DTU No. 49, 4 Jan. 1885.

18. *LE*, 28 Feb. 1885; *RMN*, 23 Feb. 1885; *DTR*, 21, 23 Feb. 1885; Marlatt, "Buchanan," p. 108; Buchanan, *Labor Agitator*, pp. 134, 137–40.

19. Buchanan, *Labor Agitator*, pp. 140–41.

20. CBLS, *First Biennial Report, 1887–88*, pp. 118–23.

21. Ibid., pp. 118–23.

22. Ibid., pp. 143–44; Athearn, *Denver and Rio Grande*, pp. 152–53; Buchanan, *Labor Agitator*, pp. 193–94.

23. *JUL*, 25 Aug., 10 Sept. 1885; Buchanan, *Labor Agitator*, pp. 174–90; CBLS, *First Biennial Report, 1887–88*, pp. 146–67.

24. James Henry to Terence V. Powderly, 30 Aug. 1886, Powderly Papers. See also *JSP*, 25 July 1886, and Stromquist, *Generation of Boomers*, pp. 190–91.

25. Terence V. Powderly, *Thirty Years of Labor, 1859–1889* (New York, 1890), p. 311.

26. CBLS, *First Biennial Report, 1887–1888*, p. 67.

27. *LE*, 2 Oct. 1886, quoted in Wright, *Politics of Populism*, p. 25.

28. *LE*, 28 Feb. 1885. The fullest discussion of the ambiguities of the Knights' labor republicanism is Fink, *Workingmen's Democracy*. But see also Richard Oestreicher, "Terence Powderly, The Knights of Labor,

and Artisanal Republicanism," in *Labor Leaders in America*, ed. Melvyn Dubofsky and Warren Van Tine (Urbana, Ill., 1986), pp. 30–61.

29. Buchanan, *Labor Agitator*, pp. 139–40.

30. Ibid., pp. 48, 137–39; Bence, "Knights of Labor," p. 57; Joseph R. Buchanan to Terence V. Powderly, 27 June 1885, Powderly Papers. For the role of Protestantism in the Gilded Age labor movement generally, see Gutman, *Work, Culture, and Society*, pp. 79–117.

31. *The National Cyclopedia of American Biography* (New York, 1922), 18:392–93; Howard H. Quint, *The Forging of American Socialism: Origins of the Modern Movement* (Indianapolis, 1953), p. 285; Buchanan, *Labor Agitator*, p. 48.

32. Buchanan, *Labor Agitator*, pp. 57–59. For the later history of Denver's clerks, see chapter 4.

33. U.S., Census Office, *Tenth Census, 1880*, 1:875; *Eleventh Census, 1890*, vol. 1, pt. 2, p. 660. See also Joyce D. Goodfriend and Dona K. Flory, "Women in Colorado before the First World War," *CM* 53 (Summer 1976): 219–28.

34. CBLS, *First Biennial Report, 1887–88*, pp. 317–18, 325–28, 336–62; *Third Biennial Report, 1891–92*, pp. 8–10, 23–24. For wages and working conditions of domestic workers nationally, see David M. Katzman, *Seven Days a Week: Women and Domestic Service in Industrializing America* (Urbana, Ill., 1981), pp. 3–43, 95–145, 303–14.

35. *JSP*, 27 July 1884, 12 Sept., 17 Oct. 1886; Buchanan, *Labor Agitator*, pp. 198–99; *LE*, 30 Jan. 1886.

36. Buchanan, *Labor Agitator*, pp. 53, 135–37; Minutes of DTU No. 49, 15 Feb. 1885; *JUL*, 7 Apr. 1888. For a fine study of women in the Knights of Labor and of the role of domesticity in their ideology, see Susan Levine, *Labor's True Woman: Carpet Weavers, Industrialization, and Labor Reform in the Gilded Age* (Philadelphia, 1984).

37. *LE*, 30 Aug. 1884; Craig Storti, *Incident at Bitter Creek: The Story of the Rock Springs Chinese Massacre* (Ames, Iowa, 1991), pp. 130–31, 145–58; Klein, *Union Pacific*, pp. 482–88; J. N. Corbin to Terence V. Powderly, 1 Nov. 1885, Thomas Neasham to Powderly, 1 Nov. 1885, John Mushett to Powderly, 2, 3 Nov. 1885, Powderly Papers.

38. Melton A. McLaurin, *The Knights of Labor in the South* (Westport, Conn., 1978), pp. 131–48; CBLS, *First Biennial Report, 1887–88*, pp. 139–40; *LE*, 28 Feb. 1885.

39. *MM*, 20 June 1912, quoted in James H. Timberlake, *Prohibition and the Progressive Movement, 1900–1912* (Cambridge, Mass., 1966), p. 94. The following account of Denver saloons relies heavily on Noel, *The City and the Saloon*. For other recent treatments that emphasize the centrality of the saloon in late nineteenth- and early twentieth-century working-class life, see Rosenzweig, *Eight Hours for What We Will*; Perry R. Duis,

The Saloon: Public Drinking in Chicago and Boston, 1880–1920 (Urbana, Ill., 1983); and Elliott West, The Saloon on the Rocky Mountain Mining Frontier (Lincoln, Neb., 1979).

40. Fossett, Colorado, p. 35; Noel, The City and the Saloon, pp. 68–70; Rider, "The Denver Police Department," pp. 176–77.

41. Noel, The City and the Saloon, pp. 53–56; LE, 7 Apr. 1883.

42. History of the City of Denver, p. 291. For working-class housing, see chapter 1. On the exclusion of saloons from Denver's middle-class suburbs, see Noel, The City and the Saloon, pp. 67–78. On the urban saloon as the locus of a working-class "male ethic," see Jon M. Kingsdale, "The 'Poor Man's Club': Social Functions of the Urban Working-Class Saloon," AQ 25 (Oct. 1973): 472–89.

43. Louisa Ward Arps, Denver in Slices (Denver, 1959), pp. 101, 107, 174–75, 210–23. See also Foster Rhea Dulles, A History of American Recreation: America Learns to Play (New York, 1965), pp. 185–91, 221–23.

44. History of City of Denver, p. 291; William Elliott West, "Dry Crusade: The Prohibition Movement in Colorado" (Ph.D. diss., University of Colorado, 1971), pp. 33–35; Noel, The City and the Saloon, pp. 38, 75, 116.

45. West, "Dry Crusade," pp. 104–51; C. Howard Hopkins, History of the Y.M.C.A. in North America (New York, 1951), pp. 119, 227–28; Raymond Calkins, Substitutes for the Saloon (Boston, 1901), pp. 117–19; Robert G. Athearn, The Coloradans (Albuquerque, N.M., 1976), p. 150.

46. Colorado WCTU, Eleventh Annual Report, 1890, pp. 63–64; West, "Dry Crusade," pp. 144–47. See also Ruth Bordin, Woman and Temperance: The Quest for Power and Liberty, 1873–1900, (Philadelphia, 1981), pp. 104–8, which shows that although the WCTU's national leader, Frances Willard, managed to effect an alliance between her organization and the Knights of Labor in the later 1880s, most middle-class WCTU members continued to regard the Knights with alarm.

47. LE, 28 Apr. 1883; DCD, 1884–1886; Minutes of DTU No. 49, 7 May 1884.

48. LE, 18, 25 Aug. 1883; JSP, 18 Apr. 1886.

49. Of the leading middle- and upper-class clubs in Denver in the 1880s, only one admitted women. See Edward Ring, "Denver's Clubs of the Past," CM 9 (July 1942): 140–41.

50. LE, 28 July, 4 Aug. 1883; CBLS, First Biennial Report, 1887–88, p. 255. See also Levine, Labor's True Woman, for a discussion of these issues.

51. LE, 18 Sept. 1883; RMN, 1 May 1885.

52. LE, 31 Mar., 28 Apr. 1883; Buchanan, Labor Agitator, p. 170.

53. Vernon L. Lidtke, The Alternative Culture: Socialist Labor in Imperial Germany (New York, 1985), pp. 185–87; Rachel Wild Peterson, The

Long-Lost Rachel Wild; or, Seeking Diamonds in the Rough (Denver, 1905), pp. 192–93.

54. *JUL*, 19 Nov. 1887; *LE*, 26 Mar. 1887.

55. Buchanan, *Labor Agitator*, pp. 254–64; Saxton, *The Indispensable Enemy*, pp. 194–200; Bruce Dancis, "Social Mobility and Class Consciousness: San Francisco's International Workmen's Association in the 1880s," *JSH* 11 (Fall 1977): 75–98; *LE*, 26 Dec. 1885. Only six IWA membership cards for Denver residents can be found in the IWA Records, Bancroft Library. For a full discussion of socialism in Denver in these years, see chapter 4.

56. *LE*, 26 Dec. 1885, 2, 9 Jan. 1886; *DCD*, *1885*; Buchanan, *Labor Agitator*, pp. 135, 356.

57. *LE*, 1 May, 23 Oct. 1886.

58. Anna Haskell Diary, 17 July 1887.

59. *UPEM*, Mar. 1886, p. 46, Apr. 1886, p. 77.

60. Ibid., June 1886, p. 160; Minutes of DTU No. 49, 6 Nov. 1884.

61. *LE*, 16 Oct. 1886.

62. See West, "Dry Crusade," pp. 25–29, for a fine discussion of these developments.

63. West, "Dry Crusade," pp. 29–30; Timberlake, *Prohibition*, pp. 102–5.

64. *RMN*, 23, 31 Oct. 1886.

65. King, *History of the Government of Denver*, p. 105; Wright, *Politics of Populism*, pp. 69–70, 75.

66. Wright, *Politics of Populism*, pp. 71–72; *RMN*, 20 Aug. 1885, 31 Oct. 1886.

67. *LE*, 13, 20 Jan., 24 Mar. 1883; Bird, "The History of Third Parties," pp. 32–35.

68. *DTR*, 8 May 1885; *LE*, 28 Mar., 11 Apr. 1885; Buchanan, *Labor Agitator*, pp. 60–64.

69. For an excellent discussion of the bases of Republican strength in Colorado, see Wright, *Politics of Populism*, pp. 51–84.

70. *History of the City of Denver*, p. 651; Noel, *The City and the Saloon*, pp. 33–40.

71. Noel, *The City and the Saloon*, pp. 103, 107–8; Elliott West, "Dirty Tricks in Denver," *CM* 52 (Summer 1975): 225–43.

72. *LE*, 7 Apr. 1883, 2 Jan. 1886. For Murray's early career, see above, chapter 2.

73. *RMN*, 7 Oct., 1 Nov. 1886.

74. Marlatt, "Buchanan," pp. 177–78; John R. Commons, "John Brown Lennon," in *Dictionary of American Biography*, 11:170–71; Buchanan, *Labor Agitator*, pp. 170–73; *LE*, 2 Jan., 1 May 1886.

75. *DTR*, 26 Mar. 1886.

76. Stuart B. Kaufman and Peter J. Albert, eds., *The Samuel Gompers Papers*, (Urbana, Ill., 1986–), 3:622, 647–48. Lennon was speaking at the 1894 AFL convention in the debate over independent political action. For a discussion of this convention, see in this volume chapter 5.

77. R. G. Dill, *The Political Campaigns of Colorado* (Denver, 1895), pp. 111–13; *RMN*, 11 Oct. 1886; *LE*, 16 Oct. 1886.

78. *RMN*, 11 Oct. 1886.

79. Wright, *Politics of Populism*, p. 109.

Chapter 4: Trade Unionism and the Beginnings of Syndicalism, 1887–92

1. CBLS, *Third Biennial Report, 1891–92*, pp. 47–48, 116–18; *RMN*, 4, 5, 6 Sept. 1892.

2. Garlock, "A Structural Analysis of the Knights of Labor," p. 255; *Guide to the Local Assemblies of the Knight of Labor*, comp. Jonathan Garlock (Westport, Conn., 1982), p. 29; Bence, "Knights of Labor," pp. 120–50; Buchanan, *Labor Agitator*, p. 330.

3. Boyd, *A History*, p. 407; KOL, *Proceedings of the Twenty-Second General Assembly, 1898*, pp. 19–20.

4. For many years, American labor historians held that the shifting fortunes between the Knights of Labor and the AFL reflected a profound transformation of working-class consciousness, the replacement of an idealistic vision of solidarity by a hard-headed practical business union-ism. Though the unions may have proclaimed adherence to working-class solidarity, according to this interpretation, in practice they ignored un-skilled workers, avoided the independent political action that had been a hallmark of the Knights, and rejected radical dreams of overturning the wage system. See Norman J. Ware, *The Labor Movement in the United States, 1860–1890* (New York, 1929), pp. xii–xiii; Commons, *History of Labor*, 2:471–95, 514–20; Philip S. Foner, *History of the Labor Movement in the United States* (New York, 1947), 2:157–88, 279–87; and Grob, *Workers and Utopia*, pp. 119–86. As this chapter will show, the notion of prac-tical trade unionists eclipsing reformist visionaries does not constitute a satisfactory interpretation of the trajectory of the labor movement in these years.

5. CBLS, *First Biennial Report, 1887–88*, pp. 100–101; Stephen J. Leonard, "The Denver Chamber of Commerce and Board of Trade from 1884 to 1900" (M.A. thesis, University of Wyoming, 1966), p. 74.

6. Guide to the Local Assemblies, p. 29; *JUL*, 10 Apr. 1885; CBLS, *Third Biennial Report, 1891–92*, p. 51; *LE*, 24 Dec. 1887; George G. Kirstein, *Stores and Unions: A Study of the Growth of Unionism in Dry Goods and*

Department Stores (New York, 1950), pp. 4–12. Six of Denver's thirteen local assemblies had been "mixed" ones in 1886. For good discussions of the question of "mixed" assemblies, see Garlock, "A Structural Analysis of the Knights of Labor," pp. 54–56, and William C. Birdsall, "The Problem of Structure in the Knights of Labor," *Industrial and Labor Relations Review* 6 (July 1953): 532–46.

7. Garlock, "A Structural Analysis of the Knights of Labor," p. 255; *LE,* 19 Feb. 1887; John Laslett, *Labor and the Left: A Study of Socialist and Radical Influences in the American Labor Movement, 1881–1924* (New York, 1970), pp. 10–11, 19; Stromquist, *Generation of Boomers,* pp. 66–69.

8. *JUL,* 27 Oct. 1887, 25 July 1889; *LE,* 19, 26 Feb., 5 Mar. 1887; Grob, *Workers and Utopia,* p. 103. L.A. 3897, in Highlands, which lasted through 1887, though listed as mixed, was in reality a "brewers assembly," functioning as a trade union.

9. CBLS, *Third Biennial Report, 1891–92,* p. 53; Garlock, "A Structural Analysis of the Knights of Labor," p. 255.

10. *JUL,* 22 Nov. 1888, 7 Aug. 1890; *JKL,* 20, 27 Nov. 1890; *RMN,* 12 Nov. 1890. For a persuasive critique of the view that the Knights collapsed during 1887–88, see Garlock, "A Structural Analysis of the Knights of Labor," pp. 9–15, who argues that "although membership declined drastically after the feverish growth of 1886, organizational toeholds gained in 1886 were extended in 1887 and not significantly relinquished even as members continued to withdraw." He also notes that 3,000 new local assemblies were organized between 1888 and 1896. This organization was far from dead in the late 1880s. See also Richard Oestreicher, "A Note on Knights of Labor Membership Statistics," *LH* 25 (Winter 1984): 102–8.

11. KOL, *Proceedings of the Fourteenth General Assembly, 1890,* pp. 11–12; *Proceedings of the Fifteenth General Assembly, 1891,* pp. 2, 75; *UPEM,* May 1886, p. 109; *JUL,* 15 Aug. 1889.

12. *RMN,* 30 Nov. 1887; *LE,* 12 Feb. 1887; *UPEM,* Jan. 1887, p. 30, Apr. 1887, p. 91; *The New Nation,* 12 Dec. 1891, p. 735; Timberlake, *Prohibition,* p. 90; Jameson, *Building Colorado,* p. 18.

13. *JKL,* 27 Nov. 1990; Minutes of UBCJA Local No. 460, 16 Jan. 1891, WHC. The AFL endorsed woman's suffrage at its 1891 convention.

14. *UPEM,* June 1889, p. 160, Feb. 1890, p. 23; Charles Jacob Stowell, *The Journeymen Tailors Union of America* (Urbana, Ill., 1918), pp. 67–69. See also Levine, *Labor's True Woman,* pp. 149–53.

15. CBLS, *First Biennial Report, 1887–88,* p. 134; *UPEM,* May 1887, p. 127; Leonard, "Denver's Foreign Born," p. 151; *RMN,* 5 May 1890; *Gompers Papers,* 2:288, 410, 457. Menche, who lived in Denver from 1890 to 1896, was an organizer for the AFL and the Denver Trades Assembly's delegate to several AFL conventions.

16. Patricia A. Cooper, *Once a Cigar Maker: Men, Women, and Work*

Culture in American Cigar Factories, 1900–1919 (Urbana, Ill., 1987), pp. 24–25, 42–43, 64; Denver Chamber of Commerce, *Fourth Annual Report, 1886*, p. 29; Andrew A. Hensley, *Denver: Pencil Sketches and Graver Strokes* (Denver, 1886), p. 81; *DR*, 24 Aug. 1892; *African Advocate*, 15 Nov. 1890.

17. Garman quoted in Carl Wilburn McGuire, "History of the Colorado State Federation of Labor, 1896–1905" (M.A. thesis, University of Colorado, 1938), p. 28. For a full discussion of the founding of the State Federation, see chapter 5 in this volume.

18. Minutes of DTU No. 49, 6 Dec. 1891; Philip Taft, *The A.F. of L. in the Time of Gompers* (New York, 1957), pp. 85–94. Peace talks between the two organizations failed on this occasion, as they had in 1889.

19. For detailed accounts of these events, see Ware, *The Labor Movement in the United States*, pp. 258–79; Commons, *History of Labor*, 2:396–413; and Philip Foner, *History of the Labor Movement*, 2:78–80, 132–44.

20. See *Gompers Papers*, 2:17–19.

21. CBLS, *First Biennial Report, 1887–88*, p. 81; "Report of Joseph R. Buchanan, Delegate to the 10th General Assembly, K. of L., to Members of D.A. 89," KOL Records, Bancroft Library.

22. *JSP*, 16 Jan. 1887; *UPEM*, Jan. 1887, p. 17; *JUL*, 4, 25 June, 27 Oct. 1887.

23. *JSP*, 16 Jan. 1887; *Gompers Papers*, 2:19–23; *LE*, 19, 26 Feb., 26 Mar. 1887; Samuel Gompers, *Seventy Years of Life and Labor: An Autobiography* (New York, 1925), 1:275.

24. *JUL*, 29 Jan. 1887; Thomas Neasham to Terence V. Powderly, 10 Jan., 28 Feb., 29 Mar., 24 Apr. 1887, Powderly Papers; *LE*, 7, 14 May 1887; *JSP*, 22 May 1887; KOL, *Proceedings of the Eleventh General Assembly, 1887*, pp. 1505–11; Browne, *The Catholic Church*, pp. 276–79; Letter of commendation to Burnette G. Haskell from the Social League of Denver, 18 Sept. 1887, IWA Records. Powderly's supporters among the UP shop workers, on the other hand, felt that he had "nobly defended the order against the malicious attack of the Anarchist element in the city" and that "the line has been clearly drawn between legitimate labor and demagogism, between Knights of Laborism and ultra Socialism." Resolutions supporting Powderly were also passed by L.A. 1424, Denver's pioneer mixed assembly, and L.A. 3714, the leather workers assembly. See *UPEM*, June 1887, pp. 154–55, July 1887, pp. 202–3.

25. KOL, *Proceedings of the Eleventh General Assembly, 1887*, pp. 1280, 1505–11, 1632–33, 1636–37; Buchanan, *Labor Agitator*, pp. 323–29; Philip Foner, *History of the Labor Movement*, 2:162–66; Paul Avrich, *The Haymarket Tragedy* (Princeton, N.J., 1984), pp. 348–50; *LE*, 29 Oct. 1887.

26. *Gompers Papers*, 2:81–88; Gompers, *Seventy Years*, 1:302–3; Abbott, "Boom State and Boom City," pp. 218–19; King, *History of the Government of Denver*, pp. 98–101; *UPEM*, July 1887, p. 160, Nov. 1887, p. 319.

27. Minutes of UBCJA Local No. 460, 26 Dec. 1890, 2 June, 21 July 1891.

28. U. S. Circuit Court, Nebraska District, Oliver Ames, II, et al. v. Union Pacific Railway Company, et al., *Record in the Matter of the Petition of the Receivers in Reference to Wage Schedules of Employees* (Omaha, 1894), pp. 533–34; Stromquist, *Generation of Boomers*, pp. 66–69; Klein, *Union Pacific*, pp. 623–24.

29. *UPEM*, Apr. 1887, p. 71, July 1887, p. 185, Aug. 1887, pp. 194–95, 209–10, Mar. 1888, pp. 35–36, May 1893, pp. 101–2; Montgomery, *Fall of the House of Labor*, p. 209; U. S. Circuit Court, *Ames v. Union Pacific, Record*, pp. 354–58.

30. CBLS, *First Biennial Report, 1887–88*, pp. 118–32; David Montgomery, "Strikes in Nineteenth-Century America," *Social Science History* 4 (Feb. 1980): 89–93.

31. U. S. Commissioner of Labor, *Tenth Annual Report, 1894*, 1:78–88; Montgomery, "Strikes," pp. 91–93; Montgomery, *Workers' Control*, pp. 18–24. See also Stromquist, *Generation of Boomers*, pp. 21–47, and Jon Amsden and Stephen Brier, "Coal Miners on Strike: The Transformation of Strike Demands and the Formation of a National Union," *Journal of Interdisciplinary History* 7 (Spring 1977): 583–616.

32. U. S. Commissioner of Labor, *Tenth Annual Report, 1894*, 1:78–88; *UPEM*, July 1888, p. 191, Nov. 1890, p. 319; CBLS, *Third Biennial Report, 1891–92*, p. 174; *RMN*, 21, 22, 23 Dec. 1888, 1 Jan. 1890; Klein, *Union Pacific*, pp. 623–24; John Swinton, *Striking for Life: Labor's Side of the Labor Question* (Philadelphia, 1894), p. 78. The support that these control struggles generated among other Denver's trade unionists is demonstrated by Carpenters Local No. 460's decision to appropriate $10 for the support of the 1890 switchmen's strike. See Minutes of UBCJA Local No. 460, 17 Dec. 1890.

33. CBLS, *Third Biennial Report, 1891–92*, pp. 189–91.

34. Ibid., pp. 192–200; *RMN*, 16 Oct. 1892; U. S. Commissioner of Labor, *Tenth Annual Report, 1894*, 1:82–85.

35. CBLS, *First Biennial Report, 1887–88*, pp. 72–73; *Third Biennial Report, 1891–92*, pp. 174–75; *LE*, 21 May 1887; Clarence E. Bonnett, *History of Employers' Associations in the United States* (New York, 1956), p. 340; Minutes of UBCJA Local No. 460, 26 May 1891; *JKL*, 25 June 1891.

36. *RMN*, 2 May 1889; Bonnett, *History of Employers' Associations*, p. 322; CBLS, *Third Biennial Report, 1891–92*, pp. 181–89; U. S. Commissioner of Labor, *Tenth Annual Report, 1894*, 1:83–84; Stowell, *Studies in Trade Unionism*, p. 123.

37. *LE*, 29 Jan., 12, 19 Feb. 1887; *RMN*, 22, 25 Feb. 1887.

38. Commons, *History of Labor*, 2:463–5.

39. Wright, *Politics of Populism*, pp. 109–10; *DTR*, 29 Aug. 1888. The

reform orientation of the party is also illustrated by its nomination of a woman, Mrs. Alvina R. Washburne of Larimer County, for the state office of Superintendent of Public Instruction.

40. Wright, *Politics of Populism*, pp. 104–9; Welty, "The Greenback Party in Colorado," pp. 301–11; West, "Dry Crusade," pp. 108–13; Bird, "The History of Third Parties," pp. 30–39.

41. Bird, "The History of Third Parties," p. 40; *JSP*, 1 May 1887; *RMN*, 6 Apr. 1887, 16 Sept., 2 Nov. 1888; *DR*, 8 Apr. 1887, 29 Aug., 11, 16, 17 Sept. 1888; Wright, *Politics of Populism* pp. 109, 130.

42. *LE*, 5 Mar. 1887; Commons, *History of Labor*, 2:446.

43. *LE*, 15 Jan., 5 Mar. 1887. On Lennon's earlier alliance with the Democrats, see chapter 3 of this book.

44. *RMN*, 9 Nov. 1888; Jon C. Teaford, *The Unheralded Triumph: City Government in America, 1870–1900* (Baltimore, 1984), pp. 21, 92–93; King, *History of the Government of Denver*, pp. 124–25; Platt Rogers, "Municipal Condition of Denver," *Proceedings of the Second National Conference for Good City Government* (Philadelphia, 1985), pp. 426; Rider, "The Denver Police Department," pp. 352–55; Fink, *Workingmen's Democracy*, pp. 225–26.

45. *LE*, 14 May 1887; *JSP*, 29 May 1887. The action also reflected the continuing influence of the Irish Land League and its tactic of the "rent refusal."

46. *LE*, 1 Jan., 26 Feb., 5 Mar. 1887; Wright, *Politics of Populism*, p. 116, notes that while Colorado Union Labor party leaders demanded greater governmental power, "they also voiced suspicion of the structures of government as they then existed." For the labor movement's outlook on political action and the state generally, see Montgomery, "Labor and the Republic," pp. 201–15; and Fink, *Workingmen's Democracy*, pp. 18–37. For Lum, see Avrich, *Haymarket Tragedy*, pp. 317–21.

47. *JSP*, 4 May 1884; *LE*, 20 Feb. 1886.

48. Wright, *Politics of Populism*, pp. 109–10, 129–30; Commons, *History of Labor*, 2:468–70; *DR*, 23 July 1888.

49. *UPEM*, Jan. 1887, p. 30.

50. CBLS, *Third Biennial Report, 1891–92*, pp. 203, 207–9, 214.

51. CBLS, *Third Biennial Report, 1891–92*, pp. 205, 215–27; *UPEM*, Mar. 1887, p. 34; *Trade and Labor*, 1 Jan. 1892.

52. Buchanan, *Labor Agitator*, pp. 59–64; *Portrait and Biographical Record of Denver and Vicinity, Colorado* (Chicago, 1898), pp. 552, 568–69, 711–12.

53. Wright, *Politics of Populism*, p. 54–55; King, *History of the Government of Denver*, pp. 105–6.

54. Wright, *Politics of Populism*, p. 55; Buchanan, *Labor Agitator*,

p. 263; *LE*, 29 Oct. 1887; *UPEM*, Aug. 1887, p. 222, May 1888, p. 127, Apr. 1891, p. 93.

55. *JKL*, 20 Nov. 1890.

56. *DR*, 14 Nov. 1890; *RMN*, 9 Nov. 1890.

57. *JKL*, 25 June 1891; *Aspen Union Era*, 17 Sept. 1891; *UPEM*, Dec. 1892, pp. 348–49, Apr. 1893, pp. 93–94.

58. George M. McConaughy to Davis H. Waite, 10 Nov. 1892, Davis H. Waite Papers, CSA; *DCD, 1892, 1893*; G. Michael McCarthy, "Colorado's Populist Leadership," *CM* 48 (Winter 1971): 35–36. A proposal that "that the organized labor element of the cities should be represented" on the state central committee of the party was defeated at the 1891 convention. See *Aspen Union Era*, 17 Sept. 1891.

59. Wright, *Politics of Populism*, p. 156; *UPEM*, June 1893, pp. 144–45. Such views were so widespread in Denver, that the pro-Populist editor of the *Union Pacific Employees Magazine* felt compelled to try to refute them at great length.

60. For the SLP's relationship to the labor movement in these years, see Philip Foner, *History of the Labor Movement*, 2:296–99; David Herreshoff, *American Disciples of Marx: From the Age of Jackson to the Progressive Era* (Detroit, 1967), pp. 121–29; L. Glenn Seretan, *Daniel DeLeon: The Odyssey of an American Marxist* (Cambridge, Mass., 1979), pp. 145, 149–50, 159–62; and Mark Erlich, "Peter J. McGuire's Trade Unionism: Socialism of a Trades Union Kind," *LH* 24 (Spring 1983): 165–97.

61. Marlatt, "Buchanan," pp. 175, 181; SLP materials, Benjam M. Hurwitz Papers, DPL; Bird, "The History of Third Parties," pp. 61, 64–66.

62. For other efforts to trace the origins of syndicalism back into the nineteenth century and to connect it with the practice of trade unionism, see Will Herberg, "American Marxist Political Theory," in *Socialism and American Life*, ed. Donald Drew Egbert and Stow Persons (Princeton, 1952), 2:491–92, 496–97; William M. Dick, *Labor and Socialism in America: The Gompers Era* (Port Washington, N.Y., 1972); and, most importantly, David Montgomery, "Trade Union Practice and the Origins of Syndicalist Theory in the United States" (Paper, n.d.). Montgomery suggests a line of influence extending directly from Haskell's IWA to the Industrial Workers of the World.

63. Marlatt, "Buchanan," p. 181; Minutes of UBCJA Local No. 460, 16 Jan., 29 Sept. 1891; Jameson, *Building Colorado*, p. 18.

64. *LE*, 1 May 1886.

65. Minutes of the San Francisco Central Committee, IWA, 24 June 1884, 24 Feb. 1885, IWA Records, Bancroft Library; Richard T. Ely, *The Labor Movement in America* (1886; reprint ed., New York, 1905), pp. 251–53.

66. Buchanan, *Labor Agitator*, pp. 254–73.

67. Boyd, *A History*, p. 409; *JSP*, 25 July 1886.

68. *LE*, 5, 12 Feb., 5, 26 Mar., 28 May 1887; Ray Reynolds, *Cat's Paw Utopia* (El Cajon, Calif., 1972) pp. 51–52; Robert S. Fogarty, *All Things New: American Communes and Utopian Movements, 1860–1914* (Chicago, 1990), pp. 124–28. Trade union practices and protosyndicalist ideas had an equally great impact on the Kaweah cooperative colony in California, in which Haskell was involved, for this grew directly out of the San Francisco labor movement and was based on the trade union-oriented ideas of Laurence Gronlund. See Robert V. Hine, *California's Utopian Colonies* (1953; reprint ed., New Haven, Conn., 1966).

69. *LE*, 26 June 1886, 5 Mar., 28 May 1887. For the radical democratic strain in syndicalism, see James Joll, *The Anarchists* (1964; reprint ed., Cambridge, Mass., 1979), pp. 193–98. For the characterization of communal experiments like Topolobampo as backward-looking, see Quint, *Forging of American Socialism*, pp. 280–318. For a more recent assessment that disputes this view, and also provides evidence for Topolobampo's widespread influence, see Fogarty, *All Things New*.

70. Buchanan, *Labor Agitator*, p. 266; letter of commendation to Haskell from Social League of Denver, 18 Sept. 1887, IWA Records. For more recent assessments of Haskell, see Saxton, *The Indispensable Enemy*, pp. 193–98, and Bernard K. and Lillian Johnpoll, *The Impossible Dream: The Rise and Demise of the American Left* (Westport, Conn., 1981), pp. 180–204.

71. On the structure of the league, see letter of commendation cited above, marginal note (probably by Haskell).

72. Morris Hillquit, *History of Socialism in the United States* (New York, 1903), pp. 231–32; Johnpoll and Johnpoll, *The Impossible Dream*, pp. 191–92; *LE*, 20 Aug. 1887. The Rocky Mountain Social League also demanded that the SLP finance the publication of the *Labor Enquirer*.

73. Hillquit, *History of Socialism*, p. 232; SLP, *Proceedings of the National Convention, 1887*, pp. 6–7, 12–13. My interpretation of Gronlund is indebted to the suggestions in Montgomery, "Trade Union Practice," which makes a strong case for his protosyndicalism. Ironically, Gronlund was a member of the SLP committee that rejected the Rocky Mountain Social League's unity proposal.

74. Though his importance as the first American Marxist theorist is well established, there are no full-length studies of Gronlund. For some background, see Stow Persons, "Introduction" to Laurence Gronlund, *The Cooperative Commonwealth* (1884; reprint ed., Cambridge, Mass., 1965), pp. vii–xxvi; Quint, *Forging of American Socialism*, pp. 28–30; and Solomon Gemorah, "Laurence Gronlund—Utopian or Reformer?" *Science and Society* 33 (Fall-Winter 1969): 446–58.

75. Persons, "Introduction," pp. xxi–xxii; Quint, *Forging of American Socialism*, pp. 46–48, 224.

76. Gronlund, *Cooperative Commonwealth*, pp. 152, 244; Montgomery, "Trade Union Practice," pp. 24–25.

77. Elliott Shore, *Talkin' Socialism: J. A. Wayland and the Role of the Press in American Radicalism, 1890–1912* (Lawrence, Kans., 1988), pp. 23–24.

78. *The New Nation*, 24 Dec. 1892, p. 755; Quint, *Forging of American Socialism*, pp. 179–80; Shore, *Talkin' Socialism*, pp. 25–27. Copies of the paper are no longer extant.

79. Richard Hofstadter, *Social Darwinism in American Thought* (1944; reprint ed., Boston, 1955), pp. 114–16; Thomas, *Alternative America*, p. 269.

80. *Gompers Papers*, 2:287–88.

Chapter 5: Depression, Populists, and Industrial Unionism, 1893–98

1. Vernon H. Jensen, *Heritage of Conflict: Labor Relations in the Nonferrous Metals Industry up to 1930* (Ithaca, N.Y., 1950), p. 66.

2. William D. Haywood, *Bill Haywood's Book: The Autobiography of William D. Haywood* (New York, 1929), p. 237. See also Joseph Robert Conlin, *Bread and Roses Too: Studies of the Wobblies* (Westport, Conn., 1969), pp. 8–16.

3. *UPEM*, Aug. 1887, p. 209, Mar. 1888, p. 64. According to a Denver Knight, car repairmen made only $1.65 a day in the late 1880s and one nineteen-year-old helper in the boiler shop made only 65 cents a day.

4. U.S. Circuit Court, Ames v. Union Pacific, *Record*, p. 408; James H. Ducker, *Men of the Steel Rails: Workers on the Atchison, Topeka & Santa Fe Railroad, 1869–1900* (Lincoln, Neb., 1983), pp. 4–5, 106.

5. "Report of Joseph R. Buchanan, Delegate to the 10th General Assembly, K. of L., to Members of D.A. 89," KOL Records, Bancroft Library.

6. Laslett, *Labor and the Left*, p. 13; CBLS, *First Biennial Report, 1887–88*, pp. 71–72.

7. Ray Ginger, *Eugene V. Debs: A Biography* (1949; reprint ed., New York, 1962), pp. 60–61; *UPEM*, Apr. 1888, p. 73, Nov. 1889, pp. 296–97, Dec. 1889, pp. 324–26. For a thorough discussion of the Supreme Council and its critics, see Stromquist, *Generation of Boomers*, pp. 73–79.

8. *UPEM*, July 1890, p. 184; Stromquist, *Generation of Boomers*, p. 76.

9. *UPEM*, June 1893, pp. 142–44, Oct. 1893, p. 282, Nov. 1893, pp. 316, 319; Stromquist, *Generation of Boomers*, p. 84.

10. Athearn, *Union Pacific Country*, pp. 355–69; Gerald G. Eggert,

Railroad Labor Disputes: The Beginnings of Federal Strike Policy (Ann Arbor, Mich., 1967), pp. 85–87, 120, 128–29; U.S. Circuit Court, Ames v. Union Pacific, Record, pp. 289–92. Notoriously antiunion, Dundy had employed a loose interpretation of the Interstate Commerce Act to enjoin a boycott during the 1888 Burlington strike. For the Denver and Rio Grande Railroad strike, see chapter 3 in this volume.

11. U.S. Circuit Court, Ames v. Union Pacific, Record, pp. 772–78; Eggert, Railroad Disputes, pp. 122–23, 129.

12. William E. Forbath, Law and the Shaping of the American Labor Movement (Cambridge, Mass., 1991), pp. 59–79; Eggert, Railroad Labor Disputes, pp. 130, 232–35; Ginger, Debs, pp. 115–16; Nick Salvatore, Eugene V. Debs: Citizen and Socialist (Urbana, Ill., 1982), pp. 118–19.

13. Wright, Politics of Populism, pp. 166–67; Forest Lowell White, "The Panic of 1893 in Colorado" (M.A. thesis, University of Colorado, 1932), pp. 6–8.

14. Carlos C. Closson, Jr., "The Unemployed in American Cities," Quarterly Journal of Economics 8 (Jan. 1894): 207–8; William Alexander Platt, "The Destitute in Denver," Harper's Weekly, 19 Aug. 1893, p. 787; White, "Panic of 1893," pp. 23–25, 49–50, 57–60, 107–8.

15. McGuire, "Colorado State Federation of Labor," p. 8; White, "Panic of 1893," pp. 63–64; CBLS, Fourth Biennial Report, 1893–94, pp. 21–22, 245; DR, 6 Feb. 1893; RMN, 6 Feb. 1893.

16. White, "Panic of 1893," pp. 59–60; RMN, 2, 30 July 1893; Closson, "Unemployed in American Cities," p. 208; UPEM, Aug. 1893, p. 223.

17. White, "Panic of 1893," pp. 64–66; RMN, 12, 19, 20, 26 July 1893; DR, 24 July 1893.

18. Closson, "Unemployed in American Cities," pp. 209–10; Montgomery, Workers' Control, p. 144; White, "Panic of 1893," pp. 72–76.

19. Platt, "Destitute in Denver," p. 787. For a similar argument, see H. Roger Grant, Self-Help in the 1890s Depression (Ames, Iowa, 1983), pp. vii–viii, who maintains that "the togetherness spawned by efforts of the down-and-out to improve their immediate lot created bonds that were vital to subsequent political activities that saw the fusion of classes, 'the people,' against the business elite." What Grant calls "togetherness," I argue in this chapter, could lead to industrial unionism as well as to political action.

20. McGuire, "Colorado State Federation of Labor," pp. 37–40.

21. McGuire, "Colorado State Federation of Labor," p. 42; UPEM, Aug. 1893, pp. 205–6; RMN, 18 July 1893.

22. CBLS, Fourth Biennial Report, 1893–94, pp. 21–22; Wright, Politics of Populism, pp. 171–72.

23. CBLS, Fourth Biennial Report, 1893–94, pp. 245–46; Leon Webber Fuller, "The Populist Regime in Colorado" (Ph.D. diss., University

of Wisconsin, 1933), pp. 273–76; *RMN*, 2 July 1894; McGuire, "Colorado State Federation of Labor," p. 49.

24. David H. Bennett, *The Party of Fear: From Nativist Movements to the New Right in American History* (Chapel Hill, N.C., 1988), pp. 171–79; John Higham, *Strangers in the Land: Patterns of American Nativism, 1860–1925* (1955; reprint ed., New York, 1971), pp. 77–87; Leonard, "Denver's Foreign Born," pp. 205–6. The only full study of the APA is Donald L. Kinzer, *An Episode in Anti-Catholicism: The American Protective Association* (Seattle, Wash., 1964).

25. Edward Keating, *Gentleman from Colorado: A Memoir* (Denver, 1964), pp. 59–60; Samuel Wallace Johnson, *Autobiography of Samuel Wallace Johnson*, (Denver, 1960), pp. 91–92; Kinzer, *Episode in Anti-Catholicism*, p. 102; *DCD, 1893; UPEM*, Nov. 1893, pp. 320, 340; Wright, *Politics of Populism*, p. 193. McGuire, "Colorado State Federation of Labor," p. 48, argues that the APA "was used to split the workers' organizations during conflicts with capital," though he provides no evidence to back up the claim.

26. Leonard, "Denver's Foreign Born," pp. 207–8; Wright, *Politics of Populism*, pp. 191–3.

27. Keating, *Gentleman from Colorado*, p. 60; Leonard, "Denver's Foreign Born," pp. 214; *RMN*, 26 Nov. 1893.

28. Gompers, *Seventy Years*, 1:403–6, 414; Philip Foner, *History of the Labor Movement*, 2:274–75, 361–64; Salvatore, *Debs*, pp. 105–8, 135–37; Higham, *Strangers in the Land*, pp. 71–72; A. T. Lane, *Solidarity or Survival: American Labor and European Immigrants, 1830–1924* (New York, 1987), pp. 75–116.

29. CSFL, *Proceedings of the Second Annual Convention, 1897*, pp. 38–39; McGuire, "Colorado State Federation of Labor," pp. 87–88; *Appeal to Reason*, 2 May 1896. The Colorado State Federation of Labor did not affiliate with the AFL until 1905.

30. CSFL, *Proceedings of the First Annual Convention, 1896*, pp. 9, 12, 15; U.S. Industrial Commission, *Report, 1901*, 12:244–46.

31. Jensen, *Heritage of Conflict*, pp. 54–59; Dubofsky, *We Shall Be All*, pp. 19–39; McGuire, "Colorado State Federation of Labor," pp. 85–89; Laslett, *Labor and the Left*, pp. 242–50; Michael Neuschatz, *The Golden Sword: The Coming of Capitalism to the Colorado Mining Frontier* (New York, 1986), pp. 25–42.

32. Laslett, *Labor and the Left*, pp. 10–15; Ginger, *Debs*, pp. 197–99.

33. Colorado General Assembly, *Official Roster, 1901;* IWW, *Proceedings of the First Convention, 1905*, p. 3.

34. Biographical material and scrapbook in Roady Kenehan Collection, WHC; *Colorado Catholic*, 30 July 1892; *Horseshoers' Magazine*, Nov. 1905, pp. 88–89.

35. Commons, *History of Labor*, 2:509–14; Philip Foner, *History of the Labor Movement*, 2:287–92. For the fullest study of the debate over the political program, see J. F. Finn, "AF of L Leaders and the Question of Politics in the early 1890s," *Journal of American Studies* 7 (Dec. 1973): 243–65.

36. *Gompers Papers*, 3:596; Gompers, *Seventy Years*, 1:355.

37. AFL, *A Verbatum Report of the Discussion on the Political Programme, at the Denver Convention of the American Federation of Labor, December 14, 15, 1894* (New York, 1895), pp. 8, 43, 60–61. J.F. Finn, who stresses Lennon's influence at the convention, argues that the AFL treasurer was motivated by his erroneous belief that Morgan's program was an attempt by the SLP to control the trade union movement. See Finn, "AF of L Leaders," pp. 254–55.

38. AFL, *Verbatum Report*, pp. 3, 22, 29, 30–31, 36–37, 61; *LE*, 16 July, 20 Aug. 1887. For the role of philosophical anarchism in the debate, see Finn, "AF of L Leaders."

39. AFL, *Verbatum Report*, pp. 26, 62; AFL, *Proceedings of the Fourteenth Annual Convention, 1894*, pp. 9, 37–39; *RMN*, 18 Dec. 1894; *MM*, Feb. 1900, p. 2, Apr. 1900, pp. 10–11, June 1900, pp. 1–2.

40. CSFL, *Proceedings of the First Annual Convention, 1896*, pp. 22, 24–25; McGuire, "Colorado State Federation of Labor," p. 81; *Appeal to Reason*, 23 May 1896. In his opening address to the Federation in 1897, Thum called not only for throwing resources into "forming unions where they are needed," but also for "political action by the State Federation, with a view of obtaining possession of the legislative branch of the city, county and state governments." The convention supported him on his first point, but not on his second. CSFL, *Proceedings of the Second Annual Convention, 1897*, p. 30.

41. For recent work emphasizing the role of skilled craftsmen in the upheavals of the 1930s, see Ronald W. Schatz, *The Electrical Workers: A History of Labor at General Electric and Westinghouse, 1923–60* (Urbana, Ill., 1983) and Peter Friedlander, *The Emergence of a UAW Local, 1936–1939: A Study in Class and Culture* (Pittsburgh, 1975). For reviews of the literature, see David Brody, "The CIO after 50 Years," *Dissent*, Fall 1985, pp. 457–72; and Robert H. Zieger, "Toward a History of the CIO: A Bibliographical Report," *LH* 26 (Fall 1985): 487–516.

42. CBLS, *Fourth Biennial Report, 1893–94*, pp. 240–41, 245; U.S. Commissioner of Labor, *Tenth Annual Report, 1894*, pp. 82–89; White, "Panic of 1893," p. 63; Fuller, "The Populist Regime in Colorado," pp. 248, 276–77.

43. CBLS, *Fourth Biennial Report, 1893–94*, pp. 241–45; Wright, *Politics of Populism*, pp. 179–80. According to the *Colorado Catholic*, 30 June

1894, deputies were recruited from among APA members, and they erected a sign saying "To Hell with the Pope" at their encampment in Cripple Creek. The role of the APA in labor disputes in is an important topic that calls for further research.

44. CBLS, *Fourth Biennial Report, 1893–94*, p. 240; U.S. Commissioner of Labor, *Tenth Annual Report, 1894*, pp. 82–85.

45. CBLS, *Fourth Biennial Report, 1893–94*, pp. 240–41; U.S. Commissioner of Labor, *Tenth Annual Report, 1894*, pp. 82–85; White, "Panic of 1893," pp. 63, 68–71; *RMN*, 22, 29 Aug., 10 Dec. 1893; *DR*, 22, 23 Nov. 1893.

46. CSFL, *Proceedings of the First Annual Convention, 1896*, pp. 7, 21; McGuire, "Colorado State Federation of Labor," p. 70. On Britain's new unionism, see E. J. Hobsbawm, *Labouring Men: Studies in the History of Labour* (London, 1964), pp. 158–230; and A. E. P Duffy, "New Unionism in Britain, 1889–1890: A Reappraisal," *Economic History Review*, 2nd ser., 14 (Dec. 1961): 306–19.

47. Hobsbawm, *Labouring Men*, pp. 144–45, 181–82, suggests that for the unskilled workers who stood at the center of the British labor explosion of 1889–92, a political consciousness preceded a trade union consciousness. See also H. A. Clegg, Alan Fox and A. F. Thompson, *A History of British Trade Unions Since 1889* (London, 1964–85), 1:89–91.

48. The parallel with the 1930s here is striking. While Roosevelt and the Democratic victories of 1932 and 1934 helped politicize factory workers, who then organized industrially (sometimes employing the slogan, "the President wants you to join a union"), the established AFL leadership (with the exception of John L. Lewis and his allies) remained aloof.

49. Keating, *Gentleman from Colorado*, pp. 55–59; Colorado State Board of Canvassers, "Abstract of Votes, Arapahoe County, 1892," Ward E, Precinct 9, CSA.

50. Wright, *Politics of Populism*, p. 192; *UPEM*, June 1890, p. 160; Aaron I. Abell, *American Catholicism and Social Action: A Search for Social Justice, 1865–1950* (Garden City, N.Y., 1960), pp. 82–83. For a more detailed discussion of Malone, see David Brundage, "Irish Workers and Western Populism: A Catholic Newspaper in the 1890s," in *The Press of Labor Migrants in Europe and North America, 1880s to 1930s*, ed. Christane Harzig and Dirk Hoerder (Bremen, West Germany, 1985), pp. 369–84.

51. F. Lehman, president of the Denver Pattern Makers Union, to Davis H. Waite, 12 Jan. 1893, Waite Papers, CSA; Wright, *Politics of Populism*, pp. 172–77.

52. Fuller, "The Populist Regime," pp. 276–77.

53. S. H. H. Clark and other UP Receivers to Waite, 18 Apr. 1894, Waite Papers; Fuller, "The Populist Regime," pp. 277–79; White, "Panic

of 1893," pp. 67–68; *RMN*, 23 July 1894; Carlos A. Schwantes, *Coxey's Army: An American Odyssey* (Lincoln, Neb., 1985), pp. 209–12.

54. Fuller, "The Populist Regime," pp. 279–80; Schwantes, *Coxey's Army*, p. 108.

55. Waite to Moses Hallet, 19 Apr. 1894, Waite Papers; Wright, *Politics of Populism*, pp. 180–81; CBLS, *Fourth Biennial Report, 1893–94*, p. 247.

56. Wright, *Politics of Populism*, p. 170; *UPEM*, Aug. 1893, p. 204.

57. Waite to Moses Hallet, 5 July 1894, Waite Papers; Wright, *Politics of Populism*, pp. 170–71.

58. Resolutions of Aspen Trades Assembly, 10 Aug. 1893, Waite Papers; Wright, *Politics of Populism*, pp. 170–71; *UPEM*, Aug. 1893, p. 204.

59. This is James E. Wright's interpretation. See Colorado State Board of Canvassers, "Abstract of Votes, Arapahoe County, 1894," Ward E, Precinct 9; Wright, *Politics of Populism*, pp. 201, 283. As Wright notes, the lack of reliable social and economic data for Denver's wards and precincts makes it "next to impossible" to assess the voting of the city's industrial workers and laborers.

60. Ralph Field to Waite, 7 Nov. 1894, Waite Papers.

61. CBLS, *Fifth Biennial Report, 1895–96*, p. 23.

62. CBLS, *First Biennial Report, 1887–88*, pp. 120–21; *JSP*, 17 Aug. 1884.

63. *UPEM*, May 1888, p. 127, June 1888, p. 157, Sept. 1888, pp. 287–88; Yvonne Johnson, "Globeville: Denver's Melting Pot" (Paper, 1974), p. 4, WHC; U.S. Immigration Commission, *Immigrants in Industry*, pt. 25, vol. 3, p. 163; Leonard, "Denver's Foreign Born," p. 149.

64. U.S. Industrial Commission, *Report, 1901*, 12:312, 317.

65. CBLS, *Fifth Biennial Report, 1895–96*, p. 23; *Denver Times*, 17 June 1900.

66. *Industrial Advocate*, 7 May, 2, 9 July 1897; *Denver Times*, 17 June 1900; CSFL, *Proceedings of the Third Annual Convention, 1898*, pp. 20–21, 23–24.

67. *Industrial Advocate*, 7, 14, 28 May, 24 Sept., 1897.

68. Ibid., 11 Mar., 15 Apr., 1898.

69. CSFL, *Proceedings of the Third Annual Convention, 1898*, pp. 28–29; McGuire, "Colorado State Federation of Labor," pp. 87–88; *Industrial Advocate*, 15 Apr. 1898.

Chapter 6: The Emergence of Western Working-Class Radicalism, 1899–1905

1. IWW, *Proceedings of the First Convention, 1905*, p. 7.

2. IWW, *Proceedings of the First Convention, 1905*, p. 6. On the Colorado labor wars, see Dubofsky, *We Shall Be All*, pp. 36–56; George G.

Suggs, Jr., *Colorado's War on Militant Unionism: James H. Peabody and the Western Federation of Miners* (Detroit, 1972); and Neuschatz, *The Golden Sword.*

3. For IWW attitudes, see IWW, *Proceedings of the First Convention, 1905,* pp. 3–8. For the contours of the merger movement, see Alfred D. Chandler, Jr., *The Visible Hand: The Managerial Revolution in American Business* (Cambridge, Mass., 1977), pp. 331–44, and Naomi R. Lamoreaux, *The Great Merger Movement in American Business, 1895–1904* (New York, 1985).

4. Fell, *Ores to Metals,* pp. 220–25.

5. Ibid., p. 227; *MM,* May 1900, p. 20.

6. Fell, *Ores to Metals,* p. 227; Wiberg, *Rediscovering Northwest Denver,* p. 163; Alan Derickson, *Workers' Health, Workers' Democracy: The Western Miners' Struggle, 1891–1925* (Ithaca, N.Y., 1988), pp. 53–55; *MM,* May 1900, p. 20; *ALUJ,* 9 July 1903.

7. *MM,* Apr. 1900, p. 9; U.S. Industrial Commission, *Report, 1901,* 12:317; Haywood, *Bill Haywood's Book,* p. 95.

8. Fell, *Ores to Metals,* p. 226; David L. Lonsdale, "The Fight for an Eight-Hour Day," *CM* 43 (Autumn 1966): 39–40.

9. Fell, *Ores to Metals,* pp. 226–27.

10. Ibid., p. 227; *MM,* Apr. 1900, p. 9.

11. Fell, *Ores to Metals,* pp. 228–30; *MM,* Apr. 1900, p. 10.

12. Fell, *Ores to Metals,* pp. 227–29.

13. Ibid., p. 230.

14. *MM,* Apr. 1900, p. 11, May 1900, pp. 17–20.

15. Lonsdale, "Fight for an Eight-Hour Day," pp. 246–47.

16. *MM,* Apr. 1900, p 9; Haywood, *Bill Haywood's Book,* pp. 94–95; Joseph R. Conlin, *Big Bill Haywood and the Radical Union Movement* (Syracuse, N.Y., 1969), pp. 32–33.

17. Taft, *A.F. of L. In the Time of Gompers,* p. 155; Jensen, *Heritage of Conflict,* p. 68.

18. Minutes of UBCJA Local No. 55, 18 Nov. 1898; CBLS, *Ninth Biennial Report, 1903–4,* pp. 168–70.

19. Philip Foner, *History of the Labor Movement,* 3:416; *ALUJ,* 27 Nov. 1902.

20. CBLS, *Eighth Biennial Report, 1901–2,* pp. 326–27; *ALUJ,* 27 Nov. 1902, 15 Jan., 5 Feb. 1903.

21. McGuire, "Colorado State Federation of Labor," pp. 88–89, 92–94; CBLS, *Eighth Biennial Report, 1901–2,* pp. 326–29; *MM,* Dec. 1901, p. 4; Minutes of DTU No. 49, 6 Oct., 3 Nov. 190 1 .

22. McGuire, "Colorado State Federation of Labor," p. 93; Minutes of DTU No. 49, 6 Apr. 1902.

23. *MM*, Apr. 1902, pp. 2, 9, 12; Minutes of DTU No. 49, 6 Apr., 4 May 1902.

24. Minutes of DTU No. 49, 6 Apr. 1902.

25. McGuire, "Colorado State Federation of Labor," pp. 94–95; *ALUJ*, 11 Dec. 1902; Philip Foner, *History of the Labor Movement*, 3:423.

26. F. W. Ott, letter to *ISR*, Aug. 1902, p. 105.

27. Minutes of DTU No. 49, 5 Oct., 7 Dec. 1902; *ALUJ*, 19, 26 Feb., 19 Mar. 1903.

28. Commons, *History of Labor*, 4:133–37; Marguerite Green, *The National Civic Federation and the American Labor Movement, 1900–1925* (1956; reprint ed., Westport, Conn., 1973), pp. 101–3; Montgomery, *Fall of the House of Labor*, pp. 272–74.

29. U. S. Congress, Senate, *Report on Labor Disturbances in the State of Colorado from 1880 to 1904, Inclusive*, S. Doc. 122, 58th Cong., 3d sess., 1905, pp. 46–50; *ALUJ*, 21, 28 May 1903.

30. *ISR*, Sept. 1903, pp. 240–41; Suggs, *Colorado's War on Militant Unionism*, pp. 146–48.

31. Minutes of International Iron Molders Union No. 188, 19 May, 2 June 1903, WHC; Green, *National Civic Federation*, p. 11; Cebula, *Glory and Despair*, pp. 35–36. See Montgomery, *Fall of the House of Labor*, pp. 263–65, for a discussion of the centrality of the suppression of sympathy strikes to the National Civic Federation's conciliation strategy.

32. Minutes of DTU No. 49, 15, 17 May 1903.

33. *ALUJ*, 4 Feb. 1904.

34. Lonsdale, "Fight for an Eight-Hour Day," pp. 346–47.

35. Ibid., pp. 347–48; U.S., Senate, *Report on Labor Disturbances in Colorado*, pp. 64–65; Ray Stannard Baker, "The Reign of Lawlessness: Anarchy and Despotism in Colorado," *McClure's*, May 1904, p. 52.

36. U.S., Senate, *Report on Labor Disturbances in Colorado*, pp. 136–37; Haywood, *Bill Haywood's Book*, p. 99; Fell, *Ores to Metals*, pp. 241–42.

37. *ALUJ*, 16, 30 July 1903; Fell, *Ores to Metals*, p. 242.

38. Haywood, *Bill Haywood's Book*, p. 101.

39. Ibid., p. 95; Philip Foner, *History of the Labor Movement*, 3:435–36.

40. Philip Foner, *History of the Labor Movement*, 3:419–20.

41. *ALUJ*, 11 Dec. 1902.

42. For other examples of this new strength, see *ALUJ*, 22, 29 Jan. 1903.

43. *ALUJ*, 3 Sept. 1903; Louis Levine, "The Development of Syndicalism in America," *Political Science Quarterly* 28 (Sept. 1913): 461–62; Salerno, *Red November, Black November*, pp. 58–60.

44. *Voice of Labor*, June 1905, pp. 12–13.

45. Wright, *Politics of Populism*, pp. 210–19; McGuire, "Colorado State Federation of Labor," pp. 178–84.

46. Wright, *Politics of Populism*, p. 218; *MM*, Dec. 1900, pp. 3–4, Feb. 1901, p. 3–4.

47. Keating, *Gentleman from Colorado*, pp. 79–83; Leonard, "Denver's Foreign Born," pp. 159–60. See also John D. Buenker, *Urban Liberalism and Progressive Reform* (New York, 1973), pp. 32–41 .

48. *ALUJ*, 21 May, 16 July 1903; Keating, *Gentleman from Colorado*, pp. 159–61.

49. Wright, *Politics of Populism*, pp. 241–42; Suggs, *Colorado's War on Militant Unionism*, p. 186; McGuire, "Colorado State Federation of Labor," p. 194 .

50. IWW, *Proceedings of the First Convention, 1905*, p. 1.

51. John Robert Morris, "David Hanson Waite: The Ideology of a Western Populist" (Ph.D. diss., University of Colorado, 1965), p. 244; Rudolph, "The Chinese in Colorado," pp. 11–12, 105–6.

52. CBLS, *Fifth Biennial Report, 1895–96*, p. 16; U.S. Industrial Commission, *Report, 1901*, 12:313; *ALUJ*, 30 July 1903.

53. *ALUJ*, 30 July 1903.

54. Philip Foner, *History of the Labor Movement*, 3:427–28.

55. Ibid., 3:428; *ALUJ*, 30 July 1903.

56. See Robert Larson, "The White Caps of New Mexico: A Study of Ethnic Militancy in the Southwest," *PHR* 44 (May 1975): 171–86; Andrew Bancroft Schlesinger, "Las Gorras Blancas, 1889–1891," *Journal of Mexican American History* 1 (Spring 1971): 103–5; and Robert J. Rosenbaum, *Mexicano Resistance in the Southwest: "The Sacred Right of Self-Preservation"* (Austin, Tex., 1981), pp. 99–139.

57. See Juan Gómez-Quiñones, *Development of the Mexican Working Class North of the Rio Bravo: Work and Culture among Laborers and Artisans, 1600–1900* (Los Angeles, 1982), pp. 43–46, and his important article, "The First Steps: Chicano Labor Conflict and Organizing, 1900–1920," *Aztlán* 3 (1972): 13–49. See also Deutsch, *No Separate Refuge*, pp. 24–26.

58. *MM*, 31 Oct. 1907, p. 5; Ozawa, "Japanese in Colorado," pp. 34–41, 65–81.

59. *ALUJ*, 27 Nov. 1902, 12 Mar. 1903.

60. Ibid., 27 Nov. 1902, 1 Jan., 12 Mar. 1903.

61. On earlier employer associations in Denver, see Bonnett, *History of Employers' Associations*, pp. 340, 385, 439, and chapter 4 in this book. For the similar stance of the national Citizens Industrial Association, in which the Denver Citizens Alliance participated, see Green, *National Civic Federation*, pp. 118–20, 124. Although it had been organized in 1903 by the antiunion David M. Parry, president of the National Association

of Manufacturers, the Citizens Industrial Association claimed to be an organization of neither labor nor capital, but rather one founded "to control the two and make them behave."

62. *ISR*, May 1902, p. 822; George Kindel Collection, WHC.

63. See George G. Suggs, Jr., "Religion and Labor in the Rocky Mountain West: Bishop Nicholas C. Matz and the Western Federation of Miners," *LH* 11 (Spring 1970): 190–206.

64. Suggs, *Colorado's War on Militant Unionism*, p. 69; Suggs, "Religion and Labor," p. 206; Wright, *Politics of Populism*, p. 243.

65. *ALUJ*, 6 Aug. 1903; *Voice of Labor*, May 1905, p. 8.

Epilogue

1. *Voice of Labor*, May 1905, p. 14, June 1905, p. 13; IWW, *Proceedings of the First Convention, 1905*, pp. 11, 23–24, 28, 567.

2. For a good discussion, see Dubofsky, *We Shall Be All*, pp. 96–105.

3. Philip Foner, *History of the Labor Movement*, 4:208–9; Helen Marot, *American Labor Unions* (New York, 1914), p. 261.

4. Daniel T. Hobby, " 'We Have Got Results' ": A Document on the Organization of Domestics in the Progressive Era," *LH* 17 (Winter 1976): 103–8; Philip Foner, *Women and the American Labor Movement*, pp. 407–11.

5. Kirstein, *Stores and Unions*, pp. 205, 211; *ALUJ*, Nov. 1904.

6. Dorsett, *The Queen City*, pp. 137–47; J. Paul Mitchell, "Boss Speer and the City Functional: Boosters and Businessmen versus Commission Government in Denver," *Pacific Northwest Quarterly* 63 (Oct. 1972): 155–64; Fred Greenbaum, *Fighting Progressive: A Biography of Edward P. Costigan* (Washington, D.C., 1971), pp. 77–78.

7. Greenbaum, *Fighting Progressive*, pp. 16–54; E.K. MacColl, "John Franklin Shafroth, Reform Governor of Colorado, 1909–1913," *CM* 29 (Jan. 1952): 42–44; Kenehan Papers, WHC.

8. For Colorado's reputation in labor circles, see the discussion in Robert Hunter, *Labor in Politics* (Chicago, 1915), pp. 125–30.

9. On this last point, see Preston, "Shall This Be All?" p. 139. For two fine examples of the kind of research needed on hard rock miners and their communities, see Derickson, *Worker's Health, Workers' Democracy* and David M. Emmons, *The Butte Irish: Class and Ethnicity in an American Mining Town, 1875–1925* (Urbana, Ill., 1989).

Index

Solidarity and Fragmentation: Working People and Class
Consciousness in Detroit, 1875–1900
Richard Oestreicher

Counter Cultures: Saleswomen, Managers, and Customers
in American Department Stores, 1890–1940
Susan Porter Benson

The New England Working Class and the New Labor History
Edited by Herbert G. Gutman and Donald H. Bell

Labor Leaders in America
Edited by Melvyn Dubofsky and Warren Van Tine

Barons of Labor: The San Francisco Building Trades and
Union Power in the Progressive Era
Michael Kazin

Gender at Work: The Dynamics of Job Segregation by Sex
during World War II
Ruth Milkman

Once a Cigar Maker: Men, Women, and Work Culture in American
Cigar Factories, 1900–1919
Patricia A. Cooper

A Generation of Boomers: The Pattern of Railroad Labor Conflict in
Nineteenth-Century America
Shelton Stromquist

Work and Community in the Jungle: Chicago's Packinghouse
Workers, 1894–1922
James R. Barrett

Workers, Managers, and Welfare Capitalism: The Shoeworkers and
Tanners of Endicott Johnson, 1890–1950
Gerald Zahavi

Men, Women, and Work: Class, Gender, and Protest in the
New England Shoe Industry, 1780–1910
Mary Blewett

Workers on the Waterfront: Seamen, Longshoremen,
and Unionism in the 1930s
Bruce Nelson

German Workers in Chicago: A Documentary History of Working-Class
Culture from 1850 to World War I
Edited by Hartmut Keil and John B. Jentz

On the Line: Essays in the History of Auto Work
Edited by Nelson Lichtenstein and Stephen Meyer III

Upheaval in the Quiet Zone: A History of Hospital Workers'
Union, Local 1199
Leon Fink and Brian Greenberg

Labor's Flaming Youth: Telephone Operators and Worker Militancy,
1878–1923
Stephen H. Norwood

Another Civil War: Labor, Capital, and the State in the
Anthracite Regions of Pennsylvania, 1840–68
Grace Palladino

Coal, Class, and Color: Blacks in Southern West Virginia, 1915–32
Joe William Trotter, Jr.

For Democracy, Workers, and God: Labor Song-Poems and
Labor Protest, 1865–95
Clark D. Halker

Dishing It Out: Waitresses and Their Unions in the Twentieth Century
Dorothy Sue Cobble

The Spirit of 1848: German Immigrants, Labor Conflict, and the
Coming of the Civil War
Bruce Levine

Working Women of Collar City: Gender, Class, and Community
in Troy, New York, 1864–86
Carole Turbin

Southern Labor and Black Civil Rights: Organizing Memphis Workers
Michael K. Honey

Radicals of the Worst Sort: Laboring Women
in Lawrence, Massachusetts, 1860–1912
Ardis Cameron

Producers, Proletarians, and Politicians: Workers and Party Politics
in Evansville and New Albany, Indiana, 1850–87
Lawrence M. Lipin

The New Left and Labor in the 1960s
Peter B. Levy

The Making of Western Labor Radicalism:
Denver's Organized Workers, 1878–1905
David Brundage

DAVID BRUNDAGE is an associate professor of community studies at the University of California, Santa Cruz. He was born in San Francisco and received his B.A. from Reed College, an M.A. in comparative labour history from the University of Warwick, England, and a Ph.D. in history from the University of California, Los Angeles. He has published in *Labor History*, the *Journal of American Ethnic History*, and in other journals and anthologies. He is coauthor of *Who Built America? Working People and the Nation's Economy, Politics, Culture and Society* (1989–92).